IEE Control Engineering Series 24
Series Editors: Prof H. Nicholson
Prof B.H. Swanick

REAL-TIME COMPUTER CONTROL

REAL-TIME COMPUTER CONTROL

Edited by
S. Bennett
and D.A. Linkens

Keywords

1. *Computer control*
   dynamic
2. *Expert systems*
3. *Process control*

P

23.1.86

Peter Peregrinus Ltd
On behalf of the Institution of Electrical Engineers

Published by: Peter Peregrinus Ltd., London, UK.

© 1984: Peter Peregrinus Ltd.

ISBN 0 86341 018 9

Printed in England by Short Run Press Ltd., Exeter

Contents

List of contributors

Chapter 1
Dr. D.J. Sandoz
University of Manchester

Chapter 2
Dr. J.B. Knowles
UKAEA, Winfrith

Chapter 3
Dr. D.W. Clarke
University of Oxford

Chapter 4
Dr. A.S. Morris
University of Sheffield

Chapter 5
Dr. S. Bennett
University of Sheffield

Chapter 6
Dr. S.J. Young
UMIST

Chapter 7
Dr. A. Wilkins
Systime Ltd.

Chapter 8
Professor M.J.H. Sterling
University of Durham

Chapter 9
Dr. M.L. Bransby
Scientific Services Department
North East Region, CEGB

Chapter 10
Mr P.A.L. Ham
NEI Parsons Ltd.

Chapter 11
Mr J.B. Edwards
University of Sheffield

Chapter 12
Mr R. Merryweather
Pilkington Bros. Ltd.

Chapter 13
Dr. J. Billingsley
Portsmouth Polytechnic

Chapter 14
Dr. D.A. Linkens
University of Sheffield

Chapter 15
Mr R.W. Sutton
General Electric Company

Preface

Following a review of postgraduate training by the Science and Engineering Research Council Education and Training Panel for Control Engineering, a series of graduate vacation courses for research students was established in 1975. The scheme includes a series of one-week modules, organised by a Planning Panel and held at a major Control Centre in the UK.

This text contains the notes of the main lectures of the second vacation course on Computer Control held at the University of Sheffield in April 1984, and is the fifteenth course in the present SERC Control Series. The purpose of the course is to provide a survey of the current theory and practice of computer control for Control Engineering research students working in UK Universities and Polytechnics, and for other interested research workers, academic staff and industrialists.

The course included a relatively wide range of topics concerned with the requirements for real-time languages, techniques for digital controller design and expert systems, and applications of online computers including power station control, power system scheduling, mining, glass manufacture, flexible manufacturing systems, robotics and biomedicine.

Computer-based systems, particularly for data acquisition and signal processing, including filtering, parameter estimation and real-time control, are now finding widespread applications in many areas, and the present course material should prove particularly useful as a state-of-the-art guide to this very important area of study.

As Chairman of the Course Planning Panel, I would like to thank the panel members for their cooperation and contribution in developing the framework of the course, and particularly Dr. Stuart Bennett and Dr. Derek Linkens for acting as Course Directors and for their efforts in organising a successful course.

H. Nicholson
University of Sheffield
March 1984

Introduction

The use of automatic feedback control in the process industries began in the 1930's with the introduction of pneumatic and hydraulic two and three-term controllers. By 1960 a wide range of electronic, pneumatic and hydraulic controllers had become available, since then there has been a changeover to the use of computers for process control and in particular the impact of the microprocessor over the last ten years has been such that the use of the microprocessor has become the norm. In Chapter 1, Sandoz outlines the developments since 1960 and briefly describes the control requirements in the process industries.

The design of feedback controller algorithms can be approached either from noise-free deterministic considerations or noise-contaminated stochastic methods. Also, design may concentrate on a single loop structure or it may consider an interacting multi-loop environment. Each of these approaches can be found in the Chapters of this book which deal with the design of feedback regulator algorithms.

The most commonly employed feedback algorithm found in process control is that of the PID regulator. This is very widely used in single and multi-loop applications particularly where little is known about the process dynamics. The tuning of the PID coefficient is a common 'art' amongst process control engineers. In Chapter 1 direct digital control (DDC) using a difference equation equivalent to the classic analogue three-term controller is described. Integral control action is normally essential to remove offset from the set-point in the plant output and the problems due to 'integral-wind up' caused by actuator saturation are well known as are the techniques for integral desaturation. The use of PID control is so widespread that application languages for process control normally provide the algorithm as a standard function (Bransby Chapter 9).

Apart from on-line tuning of PID controller parameters a wealth of knowledge exists for the classical design of single-loop systems based on deterministic conditions. The extension of methods due to Nyquist, Bode etc., for continuous analogue systems to discrete digital systems presupposes some knowledge of z-transforms and there are now several books dealing with discrete control system design

(Franklin and Powell (1), Kuo (2), Katz (3)).

Knowles, in Chapter 2, discusses a number of simple techniques which facilitate the conversion of continuous control concepts to digital computer application. Choice of sampling frequency is fundamental, while limitations due to coefficient quantisation and arithmetic roundoff noise are clearly important. The design of digital compensators is mainly approached in the frequency domain using classical servomechanism techniques suitably adapted for discrete implementation. Brief consideration is also given to filter rejection of unwanted signals due to noise or resonances, and to the use of multi-rate sampling to reduce actuator wear and output ripple. There are now available a number of software packages for control system design for both continuous and discrete systems, and Morris in Chapter 4 describes the features of one such package used in the Department of Control Engineering at the University of Sheffield.

If Chapters 1 and 2 represent the intuitive and classical approaches to controller design, then Clarke in Chapter 3 represents the current interest in self-adaptive control for industrial processes. The widespread use of tuned PID regulators underlines the twin requirements of the process control industry - those of the ability to cope with unknown process dynamics and the need for 'robust' controller algorithms. The current interest in self-tuning control majors on these two concepts. The two schools of thought in self-tuning control are commonly referred to as 'implicit' and 'explicit' protagonists. In the implicit self-tuner the controller parameters are estimated directly without estimation of the process dynamics in contrast to the explicit approach which first estimates the plant dynamics and subsequently solves an identity for determination of the controller parameters. The origins of the implicit approach are found in optimal control theory and stochastic regulation, whereas the explicit method stems from classical deterministic servomechanism design methods. In Chapter 3 a wide-ranging review of many aspects of self-tuning is given, including a description of the basic principles and underlying identification strategies for self-tuning simple software modules. The important area of software protection (jacketting) is highlighted.

With the growth in automation the question of reliability has become of increasing importance and Ham in Chapter 10 describes briefly some of the concepts involved before considering the application of reliability techniques to the design of a highly reliable turbine governing system.

The weakest area in ensuring reliable operation of computer control schemes is that of software design and implementation. It has only recently been recognised that real-time programming is significantly more difficult than ordinary sequential programming. Computer control systems involve concurrency (i.e. several programs apparently running at the same time), they have to run continuously, actions have to be performed within specified times and access to special input/output facilities is required. The development of high level languages greatly eased the problem of program design and implementation for ordinary sequential programming, but these programs do not provide access to interrupts, do not provide the ability to define sections of program as processes to be run concurrently, and do not provide facilities to program exception activities (i.e. actions to be performed on detection of a run-time error). In the early process control applications access to such facilities was obtained by writing the software entirely in assembler language and some users still adopt this approach. Users of this approach, in order to provide reliability, restrict themselves in subsequent designs to re-using existing modules and limiting new coding to a minimum. The major disadvantage is that in a time of rapid hardware development, a user may become heavily dependent on obsolete and expensive hardware. By the mid-1960's some of the companies involved in process control realized that similar facilities were required in many applications and began to produce operating systems specifically for real-time operation. Bennett in Chapter 5 discusses problems and developments in this area and Bransby in Chapter 9 describes the approach taken by the CEGB in addressing these problems. In Chapter 6, Young outlines the requirements for languages for real-time applications and considers in particular the approach taken by the designers of Ada to the problem of synchronization.

Applications of computer control involving dynamic systems are extending beyond the traditional areas of process control into, for example, mining and medicine. In Chapter 11 Edwards describes how the difficult multipass problem which arises in the steering of an underground coal-cutter can be solved by the use of computer control. Linkens in Chapter 14 gives a survey of the use of computer control in numerous aspects of biomedicine including routine drug therapy, hospital intensive care units, and anaesthetic administration in operating theatres.

Computer control techniques are also important in the development of manufacturing systems - a well established area is now material handling and Merryweather in Chapter 12 describes the system used by Pilkington Bros for Float Glass production lines. Newer areas are in Flexible Manufacturing systems (Wilkins Chapter 7) and in robotic applications (Billingsley, Chapter 13).

The reduction in hardware costs for computer systems over the past ten years has made distributed control schemes economically viable. The use of such schemes in electricity supply is described by Sterling (Chapter 8) with respect to network scheduling, and by Bransby (Chapter 9) with respect to power generation.

REFERENCES

1. Franklin, G.F., Powell, J.D., 1980, Digital Control of Dynamic Systems, Addison Wesley, Reading, Mass.
2. Kuo, B.C., 1980, Digital Control Systems, Holt, Rinehart and Winston, New York.
3. Katz, P., 1981, Digital Control using Microprocessors, Prentice-Hall, Englewood Cliffs, NJ.

ACKNOWLEDGEMENTS

We wish to express our gratitude to all the contributors, to the members of the planning panel for their support and to the staff and students of the Department of Control Engineering, University of Sheffield, for their help and advice.

S. Bennett
D. A. Linkens
Sheffield
February 1984

Chapter 1

A survey of computer control

D.J. Sandoz

1.1 INTRODUCTION

The first use of computers to control industrial processes occurred in the early 1960's. There is, inevitably, a conflict of claims as to which country and company made the first application. In Britain, ICI led the way with an application on a chemical plant at Fleetwood in Lancashire. A Ferranti Argus 200 computer was used. This computer was programmed by physically inserting pegs into a plug board, each peg representing a bit in a computer memory word (it proved more reliable than its early successors because the destruction of memory contents required the dislodgement of pegs rather than the disruption of the magnetic status of ferrite cores). A British computer manufacturer in league with a British chemical company was amongst the first pioneers of the application of computers for process control.

The situation has changed. The technology of both hardware and software has progressed rapidly. The British computer industry has lost its early initiative and the greater part of progress today is motivated by developments from the United States. The biggest impact of all has come from the microprocessor. Computer control systems, once prohibitively expensive, can now be tailored to fit most industrial applications on a competitive economic basis. The use of microprocessors for process control is becoming the norm.

These advances have motivated many changes in the concepts of the operations of industrial processes. Video display terminals now provide the focus for operators to supervise plant. Large panels of instruments, knobs and switches are replaced by a few keyboards and screens. Control rooms are now much smaller and fewer people are required to supervise a plant.

Process computers now have the capability to implement sophisticated mathematical analysis to aid effective operation. Plant managers and engineers can be provided with comprehensive information concerning the status of plant operations. This motivates more effective overall management of process plant. Surprisingly, and in contrast, the concepts of basic feedback control implemented by the computers have changed little from the days when pneumatic instrumentation was the main means for implementation. Direct digital control is essentially a computer implementation of techniques that have long been established as standard for industrial process control.

This chapter reviews the main functions of a process control computer, including measurement and actuation, direct digital control, sequence control, supervisory control and operator communications. The hardware and software aspects of distributed and hierarchical computer control systems and the integrity and economics of computer operations are discussed. The intention is to provide a broad introductory overview of the significant features of computer control systems.

1.2   THE ELEMENTS OF A COMPUTER CONTROL SYSTEM

This section describes the main tasks that computer control systems perform.   Fig. 1.1 is a broad illustration of a computer control system. Signals are monitored from and are supplied to the computer process. Collected data are analysed at various levels to provide plant adjustments for automatic control or to provide information for managers, engineers and operators.

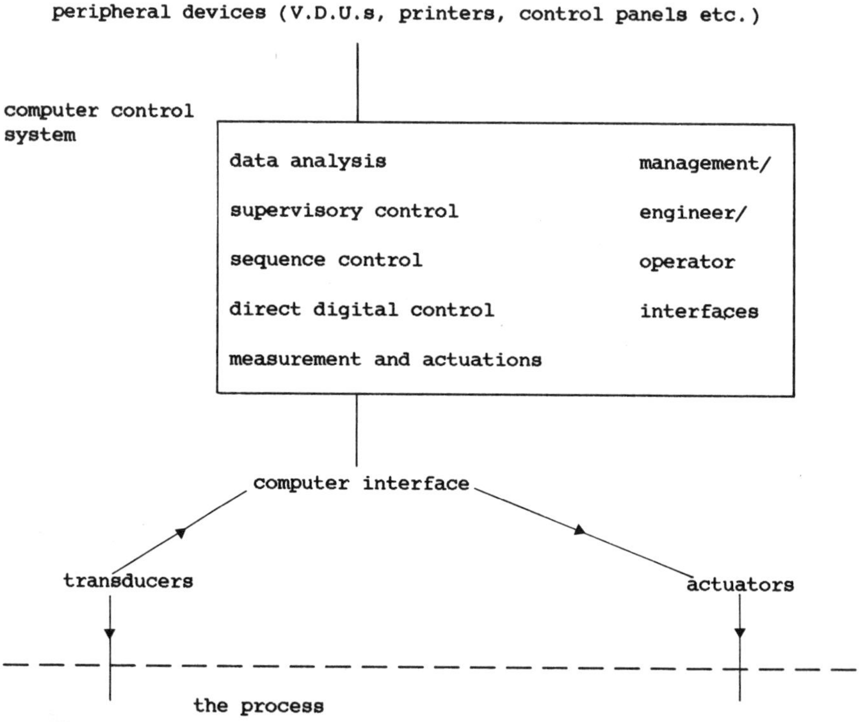

peripheral devices (V.D.U.s, printers, control panels etc.)

computer control
system

data analysis	management/
supervisory control	engineer/
sequence control	operator
direct digital control	interfaces
measurement and actuations	

computer interface

transducers   actuators

the process

Fig. 1.1   Schematic diagram of a computer control system

1.2.1 Measurement

The plant operation is monitored using transducers.   These are devices that generate an electrical signal that is proportional to a physical quantity on the plant that is to be measured (i.e., temperature, pressure, flow, concentration etc.).   The transducer signals are connected to the measurement interface of a computer system, which is usually standardised to accept signals of one particular kind.   A widely adopted standard is that the 0 to 100% range of any particular measurement converts to 4 to 20mA or 1 to 5V.   For example if a particular transducer monitors flow over the range 10 litres/hr to 50 litres/hr, then the transducer would be calibrated so that 10 litres/hr supplies 4mA and 50 litres/hr supplies 20mA to the computer interface.   A different standard may sometimes be adopted for temperature measurements taken via thermocouple or resistance thermometer transducers.

Another variety of measurement concerns the status of various aspects of the controlled process.   Is a valve open or closed?   Is a vessel full of liquid?   Is a pump switched on?   Such information would be supplied to the computer in digital form, perhaps by the opening and closing of relay switches or by the level of a TTL voltage.

The computer may also monitor digital data directly, via a serial or parallel data communications link.   Many transducers now utilise microprocessors, for example liquid concentration analysers.   Typically a microprocessor might apply statistical anlaysis to extract the required information from the monitored plant signal.   Given a numerical result it is then straightforward to effect the transfer to the control computer.

The control computer maintains a record of all of the measurements. Periodically this record is updated by scanning each of the signals connected to the interface.   Each measurement may be referenced, say, twice each second.   At these instances, the electrical signal is converted to a numerical equivalent by an analogue-to-digital converter (ADC).   If the ADC converts to a 10-bit binary number, which is commonly the case, then 4mA returns 0 and 20mA returns 1023 for the standard signal.   To be meaningful, the returned number must be scaled to engineering units.   For a transducer with a range of 10 to 50 litres/hr, 0 scales to 10 and 1023 to 50.   An intermediate value y ($0 < y < 1023$) scales to $(y/1023) \times 40 + 10$.   The incoming signal sometimes has to be linearised; certain flow transducers require the square root of a signal to be evaluated after measurement; thermocouples generate a voltage that relates to temperature via a polynomial formula which has to be evaluated after measurement.

If a measurement signal has a lot of noise superimposed upon it, digital filtering may be applied to smooth the signal.   In such a case, if a representative value is required every second, then the signal must be sampled and processed by the filter more frequently (say every 0.1 secs). The most commonly used filtering procedure employs the first order exponential algorithm.

$$yf_{k+1} = a.yf_k + (1-a)y_{k+1} \qquad k = 0, 1, 2 \ldots$$

where yf_k is the filtered value at instant k, y_{k+1} is the measurement at instant k+1 and $a = \exp(-T/\tau)$ with T = the interval k to k+1 (0.1 secs) and τ is the filter time constant.   The selection of the times T and τ depends upon the frequency at which the filtered measurement is wanted (1 second in this example) and the frequency and amplitude of the noise on the measurement.

Most measurements taken by the process control computer will also be checked to ascertain whether or not the plant is in a safe state of operation.   Two sets of limits usually relate to each measurement.   If the inner range is exceeded, a warning status is established.   If the outer range is exceeded then a 'red alert' condition applies. Automatic checking for such emergency conditions is a very important feature of the on-line computer.

Therefore, for on-line control, each measurement must be converted, possibly filtered, possibly linearised, scaled to engineering units and, finally, checked against alarm limits. The intervals between measurement samples may be quite long in some cases (many seconds) but in other cases many samples may have to be taken each second. If there are a lot of different measurements to be taken, and some installations require many hundreds, there is considerable data processing necessary to bring all of the measurements to a form meaningful for inspection by humans and for use in controllers. Careful choice of sampling intervals, e.g., by not monitoring signals more frequently than necessary, can reduce the computational burden. The selection of such intervals also requires care to ensure that problems such as signal aliasing do not arise.

<u>1.2.1.1 Actuation</u>. Control of plant is usually achieved by adjusting actuators such as valves, pumps and motors etc. The control computer may generate a series of pulses to drive the actuation device to its desired setting. In such a case, the drive signal would be generated as a relay contact closure or a change in voltage level. Alternatively, a voltage that is proportional to a desired setting may be produced by a digital-to-analogue converter (DAC). An actuation device will often supply a measurement back to the computer so that it is possible to check whether or not an actuation command has been implemented. The computation associated with actuation is usually small, however, some pulse driven actuators require frequent associated measurement to determine when the desired setting has been reached. In this case a more significant computational burden can be incurred.

<u>1.2.1.2 Direct digital control (DDC)</u>. Conventional analogue electronic control systems employ the standard three term algorithm

$$u = K_p \left(e + \frac{edt}{T_i} + T_d \cdot \frac{de}{dt} \right) \tag{1.1}$$

with $e = r - y$, y is the measurement, r is the reference or set point, e is the error, K_p is the controller gain ($1/K_p$ is the proportional band), T_i is the integral action time and T_d the derivative action time. There are variations on this form. Very few controllers actually use derivative action. If it is used de/dt is sometimes replaced by dy/dt to avoid differentiation of set point. Nearly all industrial control problems are solved by application of this algorithm or close variations to it.

Most DDC systems utilise a difference equation equivalent to the above algorithm. If the computer recalculates the actuation signal u every T seconds, then the most simple numerical approximation employs

$$\frac{de}{dt} \simeq \frac{e_k - e_{k-1}}{T} \quad \text{and} \quad e.dt = \Sigma\, e_k.T \quad k = 0, 1, 2, \ldots \tag{1.2}$$

with the interval k to $k+1$ equal to T seconds.

The control equation then results as

$$u_k = K_p \{ e_k + \frac{T \cdot s_k}{T_i} + \frac{T_d}{T} (e_k - e_{k-1}) \} \qquad\qquad (1.3)$$

with $s_k = s_{k-1} + e_k$ being the sum of errors.

The advent of cheap microprocessors has made it very simple to programme and implement this control equation. However, there are many traps into which the self-taught control engineer can fall. One of the most significant is associated with saturation of the actuation signal. This signal must be considered to lie within a defined range Umin/Umax. If the control signal saturates at either extreme careful consideration has to be given to the integral sum s_k at this stage. If the summation procedure were to continue unchecked s could take up a large and unrepresentive value which could lead to much degraded control system performance thereafter. Special procedures for integral desaturation have been developed to accompany the controller. These ensure that the actuation signal emerges from saturation at a timely moment so that an effective control system response is generated.

DDC may be implemented on a single loop basis by a single microprocessor controller or by a larger computer which could implement upwards of a hundred control loops. The total control system for an industrial process can become quite complex. DDC loops might be cascade connected, with the actuation signals of particular loops acting as set points for other loops. Signals might be added together (ratio loops) and conditional switches might alter signal connections. Fig. 1.2 is a diagram of a control system that has recently been implemented by a computer on an ICI plant. The pressure of steam produced by a boiler is to be controlled. This is achieved by regulating the supply of fuel oil to the burner. However, a particular mix of fuel and air is required to ensure efficient and non-polluting combustion. The purpose of this illustration is not to discuss how the control system achieves its objective, but rather to indicate some of the elements that are required for industrial process control. Such elements must be available as features of a process control computer.

Referring to Fig. 1.2 the steam pressure control system generates an actuation signal that is fed to an automatic/manual bias station. If the latter is selected to be in automatic mode, the actuation signal is transmitted through the device; if it is in the manual bias mode, the signal that is transmitted is one that has been manually defined (e.g., by typing in a value on a computer keyboard). The signal from the bias station is connected to two units, a high signal selector and a low signal selector. Each selector has two input signals and one output. The high selector transmits the higher of its two input signals and the low selector the lower of its two input signals. The signal from the low selector cascades a set point to the DDC loop that controls the flow of oil. The signal from the high selector cascades a set point to the DDC loop that controls the flow of air. Finally, a ratio unit is installed in the air flow measurement line. A signal that is generated from another controller is added to the air flow signal prior to its being fed to the air flow controller. This other controller is one that monitors the combustion flames directly, using an optical pyrometer for measurement, and thereby obtains a direct measure of combustion efficiency.

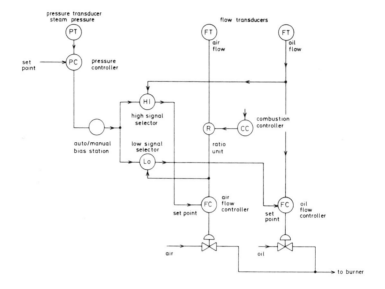

Fig. 1.2 Boiler pressure control system

Another controller that is of value but is not a feature of Fig. 1.2 is one based on the lead/lag transfer function. This can be used to provide feed-forward compensation so that the effect of disturbances upon the plant, for example because of an alteration in the environmental conditions, is minimised.

Hence there is much more to computer control than simple DDC. The boiler example is probably more complex than many industrial schemes although the use of additional signal processing over the above simple DDC is very common.

DDC is not restricted to the three-term algorithm described above, although the latter is almost universally used in the process industries. Algorithms based upon, for example z-transform design techniques can be equally effective and a lot more flexible than the three-term controller. However, the art of tuning three-term controllers is so well established amongst the control engineering fraternity that new techniques are slow to gain ground. The fact that three-term control copes perfectly adequately with 90% of all control problems is also a deterrent to general acceptance of new concepts for control system design.

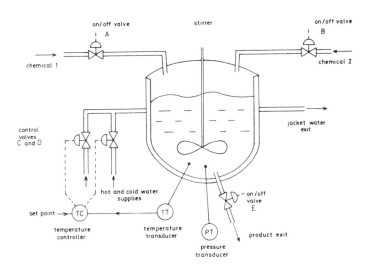

Fig. 1.3 A chemical reactor

<u>1.2.1.3 Sequence control</u>. Many industrial processes are required to be automatically sequenced through a number of stages during their manufacturing operations. For example, consider the manufacture of a chemical that is produced by reacting together two other chemicals at a particular temperature. Fig. 1.3 illustrates a typical plant arrangement for this purpose. The chemicals react in a sealed vessel (the reactor). The contents are temperature controlled by feeding hot or cold water to the water jacket that surrounds the vessel. This water flow is manipulated by adjusting the control valves C and D. On/off valves A, B and E in the chemical supply and vessel exit pipelines are used to regulate the flow of material into and out of the vessel. The temperature of the vessel contents and the pressure at the bottom of the vessel are monitored.

    The manufacturing procedure for this plant might involve the following stages of operation.

1) Open valve A to charge chemical 1 to the reacting vessel.
2) Check the level of chemical in the vessel (by monitoring the pressure vessel). When the required amount of chemical has been charged, close valve A.
3) Start the stirrer to mix the chemicals together.
4) Repeat stages 1 and 2, with valve B, in order to charge the second chemical to the reactor.
5) Switch on the three-term controller, and supply a set point so that the chemical mix is heated up to the required reaction temperature.

6) Monitor the reaction temperature. When it has reached set point, start a timer to time the duration of a reaction

7) When the timer indicates that the reaction is complete, switch off the controller and open valve C to cool down the reactor contents. Switch off the stirrer.

8) Monitor the temperature. When the contents have cooled, open valve E to remove the product from the reactor.

When implemented by a computer, all of the above decision-making and timing is based upon software. For large chemical plants, such sequences can become very lengthy and intricate, especially when a plant involves many reaction stages. For the most efficient plant operation, a number of sequences might be in use simultaneously (e.g., in the context of the above example a number of reactions might be controlled at the same time). Very large process control computers are often dedicated almost exclusively to supervising such complex sequence-control procedures.

1.2.1.4 Supervisory control systems. Supervisory control systems are used to specify or optimise the operation of the set of DDC (or conventional analogue control) systems that are controlling a plant. For example, the objective of a supervisory system might be to minimise the energy consumption of a plant or to maximise its production efficiency. A supervisory system might compute the set points against which the plant control systems are to operate or it might re-organise the control systems in some way.

A simple example of where a supervisory control scheme can be utilised is illustrated in Fig. 1.4. Two evaporators are connected to operate in parallel. Material in solution is fed to each evaporator. The purpose of the plant is to evaporate as much water from the solution as possible. Steam is supplied to a heat exchanger linked to the first evaporator. Steam for the second evaporator is supplied from vapours boiled off at the first evaporation stage. To achieve maximum evaporation the pressures in the evaporation chambers must be as high as safety considerations will allow. However, it is necessary to achieve a balance between the two evaporators. For example, if the first evaporator is driven flat out then this might generate so much steam that the safety thresholds for the second evaporator are exceeded. A supervisory control scheme for this example will have the task of balancing the performance of both evaporators so that, overall, the most effective rate of evaporation is achieved.

In most industrial applications supervisory control, if used at all, is very simple and is based upon knowledge of the steady-state characteristics of the plant to define the required plant operating status. In a few situations, very sophisticated supervisory control algorithms have proved beneficial to plant profitability. Optimisation technqiues using linear programming, gradient search methods (hill climbing), advanced statistics and simulation have been applied. In association with these techniques, complex non-linear models of plant dynamics and economics have been solved continuously in real time in parallel with plant operation, in order to determine and set up the most effective plant operating point. An example is the processing of crude oil by distillation. The most profitable balance of hydrocarbons can be produced under the direction of a complex supervisory control system.

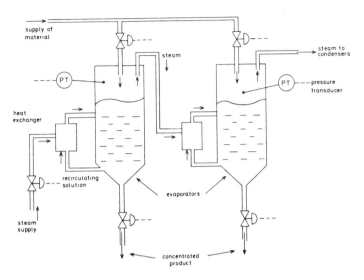

supply of
material

steam

steam to
condensers

PT

PT --- pressure
transducer

heat
exchanger

recirculating
solution

evaporators

steam
supply

concentrated
product

Fig. 1.4   An evaporation plant

1.2.1.5 The engineer and the process control computer.   The control
engineer has the task of specifying the various roles of the process-control
computer and of implementing the specification.   His duties may be itemised
as follows (presuming the decision has been made as to the most suitable
computer system for the job in hand):

1.   To define measurements and actuations and set up scaling and filter
     constants, alarm and actuation limits, sampling intervals etc.
2.   To define the DDC controllers, the interlinking/cascade connections
     between them and any other elements within the control system
     configuration.
3.   To tune the above control systems, i.e., select appropriate gains, so
     that they perform according to some desired specification.
4.   To define and programme the sequence control procedures necessary
     for the automation of plant operation.
5.   To determine and implement satisfactory supervisory control schemes.

     The control engineer may also have the job of determining how the
plant operator is to use the computer system in the day-to-day running of
the plant.

     Clearly, for a large application, all of these duties would be beyond
the scope of a single person and a team of people would be involved, one
of whom would most certainly be a computer programme.   The latter phase,
implementaion of supervisory control, could be a project of many months if
some of the more sophisticated techniques above mentioned are utilised.

The programming effort involved in establishing a complete working computer-control system could be considerable if the engineer had to start from scratch.   However, process control applications have many aspects in common and standard packages of computer software are now available with many computing systems, thus minimising the effort required to establish a working control system.   Facilities are available to permit the engineer to translate directly from specification charts and control system diagrams, such as that of Fig. 1.2, to a computer based implementation.   The engineer defines the data base but does not have to write the software for the DDC systems.   The standard software is usually sold with the computer system to form a complete process-control package.

There has been a very significant short-coming with such standard packages.   They have provided for the definition and structuring of control systems but, until recently, there has been nothing available on the market to provide the control engineer with an aid for tuning the control systems. The engineer has had to rely completely upon his own experience of tuning three-term controllers.   The quality of the tuning of industrial control systems has been generally poor (perhaps because in lots of situations it does not matter much anyway).   In the last 18 months, facilities for the automatic   tuning   of   controllers   have   been   launched   by   various manufacturers.   These are often packed within a standard microprocessor unit.   The techniques have had teething problems but these are slowly being ironed out and the facilities represent significant progress for the control engineer.

Software packages for sequence control and supervisory control must be a lot more flexible than those for DDC.   Sequencing the supervisory requirements   will   differ   greatly   from   plant   to   plant   whereas   DDC configurations utilise a very limited range of standard operations.   The standard packages therefore provide the engineer with a higher level language to programme the required sequence of commands.   A variety of such languages exist   The most common are very similar to BASIC, with additional features to facilitate the real-time aspects and communications with the plant interface.   If the language is interpretive (i.e., lines of programme are compiled at the time of execution), it is often possible to build up a sequence procedure while the computer is online to the plant. Supervisory control might require extensive calculations for which interpretive operation could be too slow and cumbersome.   In this case, a language such as Fortran or Pascal might be utilised and compilation would be necessarily offline.   For the simpler supervisory schemes, the BASIC type languages are perfectly adequate.   The U.S. Department of Defense has defined a language called Ada as the standard for real time aplications and this is likely to make an impact on control system packages in the future.

1.2.1.6 Facilities for plant operator and plant manager.   The plant operator must be provided with facilities that permit the straightforward operation of the plant on a day-to-day basis.   The operator requires to be presented with all information relevant to the current state of operation of the controlled process and its control systems.   In addition it is necessary for him to be able to interact with the plant, for example to change set points,   to manually adjust actuators, to acknowledge alarm conditions etc.

A specially designed operator's control panel is a feature of nearly all computer control systems.   Such a panel would typically consist of special keyboards, perhaps tailor-made for the particular plant that is controlled, and a number of display screens and printers.   The video displays permit the operator to inspect, at various levels of detail, all monitored areas of the plant. The standard software packages supplied with computer control systems normally provide a range of display formats that can be used for the presentation of information. Typically, these might be an alarm overview display presenting information relating to the alarm status of large groups of measurements; a number of area displays presenting summaries of details concerning the control systems associated with particular areas of the process; and a large number of loop displays, each giving comprehensive details relating to a particular control loop. The control engineer selects the parameters that are to be associated with the individual displays, as part of the procedure of defining the data base for the computer system. The display presentations might be in the form of ordinary print-outs, or trend graphs of measurements, or schematic diagrams (mimics) of plant areas, with numerical data superimposed at appropriate locations. Colour-graphic displays are now commonplace.

The above standard displays will not suit all requirements. For example, sequence control procedures might require special display presentation formats so that the operator can establish and interact with the current stage of process operation. Such displays would most likely be produced by programminug them specially using the BASIC type language referred to above.

The special operator keyboards are usually built to match the standard display structures (for example by specifying particular keys to be associated with the selection of displays for particular plant areas). It is thereby straightforward for the operator to quickly centre upon aspects of interest. Commonly, if a particular control loop is pinpointed on a display, perhaps by use of a cursor or a light pen, then this will permit the operator to make direction adjustments to that loop using special purpose keys on a keypad.

The plant manager requires to access different information from the process control computer than the operator. He will need hard copy print-outs that provide day-to-day measures of plant performance and a permanent record of the plant operating history. Statistical analysis might be applied to the plant data prior to presentation to the manager so that the information is more concise and decisions are therefore more straightforward to make. The manager will be interested in assessing performance against economic targets, given the technical limitations of the plant operation. He will determine where improvements in plant operation might be possible. He will be concerned, along with the control engineer, with the operation of the supervisory control systems and will set the objectives for these top-level control systems.

1.3   HARDWARE FOR THE COMPUTER CONTROL SYSTEMS

In this chapter it has been assumed so far that the process control computer is a single hardware unit, that is, one computer performing all of the tasks itemised in section 1.2.2. This was nearly always the case with early computer control systems. The recent rapid developments of solid state and digital technology led to a very different approach to the hardware configuration of computer control systems.

Fig. 1.5 illustrates a typical arrangement that might now apply with many modern systems. The tasks of measurement, DDC, operator communications sequence control etc., are distributed amongst a number of of one form or another. The microcomputers are linked together via a common serial communications highway and are configured in a hierarchical command structure.

Fig. 1.5 indicates 5 broad levels of division in the structure of the hierarchy of microcomputer units. These correspond in the main with functions described in section 1.1.2.

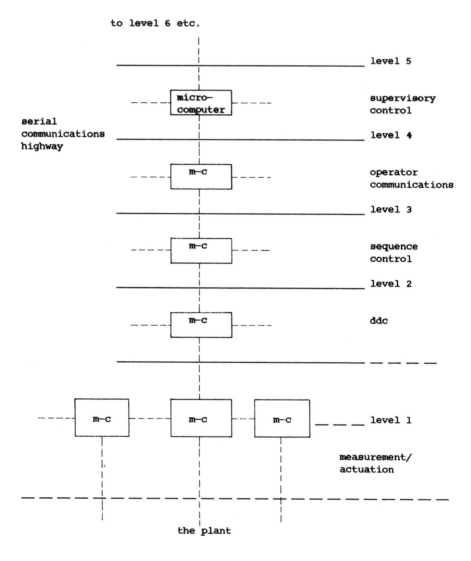

Fig. 1.5 A distributed and hierarchical microcomputer system

Level 1: – all components and plant interfacing associated with measurement and actuation. This level provides the measurement and actuation data base for the whole system.

Level 2: – all DDC calculations.

Level 3: – all sequence control calculations.

Level 4: – operator communications.

Level 5: – supervisory control.

Level 6: – communications with other computer systems.

The boundaries between the levels do not have to be rigid, for example a unit for DDC might also perform some sequence control or might interface directly to the plant. The units for operator communications will drive the operator control panels and the associated video displays. The levels within the system define a command structure. Thus the microcomputer for supervisory control may direct the sequence control computers which, in turn, provide set points for the DDC computers etc.

The major features and advantages of this distributed/hierarchical approach are:

i)   If the computational tasks are shared between processors, then system capability is greatly enhanced. The burden of computation for a single processor becomes very great if all of the described control features are included. For example, one of the main computing loads is that of measurement scanning, filtering and scaling. This is not because any one calculation is onerous but rather because of the large number of signals involved and the frequency at which calculations have to be repeated. Separation of this aspect from DDC, if only into two processors, greatly enhances the number of control loops that can be handled. The DDC computer will collect measurements already processed, via the communications link, at a much lower frequency than that at which the measurement computer operates.

ii)   The system is much more flexible than a single processor. If more control loops are required or an extra operator station is needed, then all that is necessary is to add more boxes to the communications link. Of course, the units already in the system must be updated to 'be aware' of the additional items.

iii)   If any unit should fail, the implications are not catastrophic, only one portion of the overall system will be out of commission, not the whole assembly.

iv)   It is much easier to make software changes to the distributed system. For example, if a supervisory control programme is to be altered, then only the associated microcomputer need be called off-line. The risks of causing total system failure because of computer programming faults are very much reduced.

v)   The units in the system can become standardised. This should lead to a much lower cost facility overall (some larger established manufacturers are still quoting prices that are of the same order as for older type computer control systems but smaller firms are beginning to dramatically undercut these prices). Thus, typically, a microprocessor for DDC might be standardised to cater for 16 loops. All of the necessary aspects such as gains, limits, set points, etc., would be communicated from elsewhere via the highway. An application requiring 80 control loops would therefore utilise 5 such DDC boxes. In fact, at the extreme low end of the computer control market there are microprocessor units that implement a single control loop. These, to all external appearances, apart from their data link facility, look very similar to conventional electronic three-term controllers.

vi)   The interlinking of the microcomputer units by a serial highway means that they can be dispersed over quite a wide area. The highway may easily stretch for a mile or even more if telecommunications devices are used. An advantage is that it makes it unnecessary to bring many cables carrying transducer signals to the control rooms. The measurement microprocessors can be sited close to the source of the signals (i.e., near the plant) and then only a serial link need be taken to the control room. Another advantage is that it is straightforward to set up multiple operator control terminals at different sites in the factory. Hierarchical distribution of process-control computers is not an innovation with microcomputers. Very large chemcial processes, or even complete factories, for which a large capital outlay for control systems can be justified, have employed the above principles. It is the reductions in cost and size of the computing facilities that have made the technology the most attractive for the majority of industrial control applications today.

1.4   INTEGRITY OF COMPUTER CONTROL SYSTEMS

One of the main barriers to the use of computer control systems, apart from expense, has been mistrust of the computer. A conventional instrumentation and control system uses many individual units and the failure of one or a few can be tolerated without having to shut down plant operations. If all of these units are replacd by a single computer then a break down of the computer can result in a complete loss of all control systems, with unfortunate consequences. The typical mean-time-between-failures for early computer control systems has been in the region of 3 to 6 months. Many applications have therefore only used a computer for aspects such as sequence and supervisory control for which certain degrees of failure can be tolerated. Continuous feedback control has, in these cases, continued to be implemented by electrical or pneumatic instrumentation.

The solution to the problem of computer failure has been to provide back-up systems to take over if a computer failure occurs. The backup system might be a bare minimum of analogue controllers that are switched in automatically. The difficulty with this approach is that if the computer does not fail for a long time the plant staff might forget how to operate the back-up system. Wise users occasionally switch off the computer deliberately. An alternative back-up mechanism is to duplicate the computer system so that if one fails, another takes over. Certain applications, e.g., in the nuclear industry, triplicate the control computers. The above options are expensive and it has proved difficult to establish change-over mechanisms that are guaranteed not to disrupt the plant in any circumstances.

The new microcomputer technology has alleviated many of the problems of integrity. Units, such as operator stations, may be duplicated on data highways at low cost. Units are now programmed to have a self-diagnosis capability so that they can automatically dectect and report the occurrence of faults. The most vulnerable aspect of the new approach is the communications links. If one is broken, then all means of access to units on the wrong side of the break are lost, and for this reason, the communications links are often duplicated. Change over between links is automatic if a fault if detected.   Some manufacturers' systems permit duplication to be extended to cover almost every unit within the distributed network.   Mean-time-between-failures that would result in a total loss of plant control, are quoted at between 50 and 100 years.   Needless to say, at such levels of duplication the systems cease to be cheap.

1.5   THE ECONOMICS OF COMPUTER CONTROL SYSTEMS

Before the advent of microprocessors, computer control systems were very expensive.   When a new industrial process was being designed and built, or an old one being re-instrumented, a strong case had to be presented to use a computer instèad of conventional instrumentation.

In some cases computers have been used because, otherwise, plants could not have been made to work profitably.   This is particularly the case with large industrial processes that require the application of complex sequencing procedures.   The computer system permits repeatability in quality that is essential, for example, with manufacturing plants in pharmaceutical industry.   Flexibility of the computer is also important in these circumstances.   Conventional instrumentation is difficult to modify if, for example, a sequencing procedure is to be altered to suit the manufacture of a different product.   Reprogramming using a sequence language is comparatively straightforward.

Many large continuous processes (oil refineries, evaporators etc.) are also computer controlled.   These processes stay in a steady state of operation for long periods and require little sequencing.   They do incorporate many control loops.   The usual justification for computer control in these circumstances has been that it will make plant operation more profitable.   Such statements are often based upon the argument that even a small increase in production (say 1 to 2%) will more than pay for the computer systems.   In the event, it has often been difficult to demonstrate that such improvement has resulted.   The author is aware of one major installation where production has declined following the introduction of computers.   The pro-computer lobby argue that it would have declined even more if the computer had not been there!   The major benefits with continuous processes should arise through a better understanding of the process that invariably follows the application of computer control, and through the implementation of appropriate supervisory control schemes that maintain the plant closer to desired thresholds of operation.

The scene relating to the justification for computer control systems has now changed dramatically.   The fall in cost and the improvement in reliability mean that for many industrial applications, both major and minor, it is automatic to install computer controls.   In any event, microprocessor units are now cheaper than many of the equivalent analogue instruments, which will become obsolete before too long.

1.6   FUTURE TRENDS

The advent of the microcomputer has probably had more impact upon the discipline of control engineering than any other.   Applications are now blossoming in all areas of industry on plants both large and small.   The hardware revolution is still taking place but future changes are not likely to be as dramatic as in recent years.   The question for the future is: 'Will there be an accompanying revolution in the control techniques that are implemented by the new hardware?'

An immense amount of effort has been devoted to academic control engineering research over the past two decades. Numerous novel control procedures have been postulated and proved effective, but only in numerical simulations. So many of the developed procedures could be summarised by the statement 'and here is yet another example of a controller for the linear plant described by the state of space equation $\underline{x} = \underline{A}\,\underline{x} + \underline{B}\,\underline{u}'$. There has been very little application of these novel techniques, particularly in the process industries. They have remained very much the domain of the expert in applied mathematics. In industry the three-term controller has continued to be the fundamental control unit and will remain so for a long time to come.

The emphasis in control systems research and development must, and will, change. Much greater emphasis will be given to applying the new techniques and making them work. Computers will be used not only for the implementation of controllers but also to assist with defining controller configurations and with tuning, so that the best controlled performance is achieved. Already, simple tuning facilities are available and these will become more sophisticated and effective in the very near future. Techniques such as computer-aided design, identification of plant dynamics and adaptive/self-tuning control will become features of standard software packages supplied by the manufacturers of the hardware. It is possible to conceive of a new kind of box appearing on the data highway of Fig. 1.5, one for the design of control systems, a facility to assist the control engineer.

The increased emphasis on applications in control engineering research will motivate more problem specific solutions. The preoccupation of recent years with general theory will fade (as it must do anyway since linear control theory must be almost played out by now and extension to non-linear situations almost always requires a special case consideration). Greater attention will be given to consideration of supervisory control methods. This is the area where real financial returns from control systems can be made, by improving the productivity and efficiency of plant operations.

1.7   CONCLUSIONS

This chapter provides an introduction to the current state of the area of computer control systems. Many manufacturers provide standard system packages that implement the described features. Well known names such as Honeywell, Foxboro, Taylor and Kent cater for the distributed and hierarchical approach decribed in section 3. (TDC 2000, FOXNET, MOD III and P4000 respectively). Firms such as Negretti and Zambra, and Bristol Automation are marketing attractive microprocessor based systems (MPC 80 and MICRO B) for the smaller applications of say 50 control loops plus sequencing. Even the microprocessor companies themselves, such as Texas Instruments and DEC, are beginning to produce their own variations of distributed process control systems. The market is lively and competitive and costs are falling in line with the general downward trend of the price of computing equipment. Computer control is becoming commonplace.

Applications of new concepts in control theory have lagged far behind the boom in hardware. It is anticipated that this will change and that the technology of process control will be refreshed, in its turn, in the next few years. Facilities will become available to assist the control engineer to obtain better performance from the controlled plant than is currently possible unless a great deal of design effort is applied. The use of more sophisticated procedures for improved process control will become more common.

BIBLIOGRAPHIC NOTES

1. A best appreciation of the current state of computer systems is obtained by reference to manufacturer's publicity literature. Honeywell have produced a number of pamphlets under the title "An Evolutionary Look at Process Control' in support of their TDC 2000 system. These provide a well presented overview of many of the aspects discussed in this paper. Taylor, Foxboro and Kent produce similar documentation relating to their new process control systems, but of rather less value educationally. Interesting contrasts between the various systems can be established by perusing this literature. A good sample of the capabilities of smaller systems can be established from the literature of Negretti and Zambra in support of their MPC 80 system.

2. For DDC:
   WILLIAMS, T. J.: 'Direct digital control and its implications for chemical process control', Dechema Monographien, 1965, v.53, No. 912-924, pp. 9-43.
   DAVIES, W. D.: 'Control algorithms for DDC', Instrument Practice for Process Control and Automation, 1967. v.21, pp. 70-77.

3. For supervisory control concepts:
   LEE, GAINS, ADAMS.: 'Computer process control: Modelling and Optimisation', (Wiley, 1968).

4. For discrete control systems
   FRANKLIN, G.F., POWELL, J.D.: 'Digital Control of Dynamic Systems', (Addison Wesley, Reading, Mass, 1980).
   CADZOW, J.A., MARTINS, H.R.: 'Discrete time and computer control systems' (Prentice Hall, Englewood Cliffs, 1970).

5. For self-tuning control systems
   HARRIS, C. J. and BILLINGS, S. A.: 'Self-tuning and adaptive control: theory and applications'. Peter Peregrinus 1981.

Chapter 2

Some DDC system design procedures

J.B. Knowles

2.1 INTRODUCTION

As a result of the enormous impact of microprocessors, electronic engineers, with sometimes only a cursory background in control theory, are being involved in direct digital control (DDC) system design. There is now a real need for an easily understood and simply implemented design technique for single-input DDC systems which is the object of this chapter. The proposed design procedure is shown as a flow chart in Fig. 2.1, and it contains appropriate references to sections of text that treat the more important issues in detail. It is hoped that this diagram will provide a systematic approach to DDC system design, as well as an appreciation for the organisation of the text. The experienced designer will notice the absence of such topics as:

(i)   'Bumpless transition' criteria during changes from automatic to manual control.
(ii)   Provision for timed sequential operations to cope with fault conditions.

These aspects have been deliberately omitted because they are considered to be separate programming issues once control in the normal operating regime has been achieved.
Digital realisations of conventional three-term controllers have the advantage of: wide applicability, theoretical simplicity and ease of on-line tuning. However, the resulting closed-loop performance is generally inferior to that obtainable with other algorithms of similar numerical complexity. The graphical compensation procedure (2) described in Section 2.3 copes with the design of digital three-term controllers and these high performance units with equal ease. Also the technique is readily exploited by virtue of its simple calculations (amenable even to slide-rule treatment). Furthermore, it is shown to result in an 'even-tempered' closed-loop response for all input signals; unlike DDC systems synthesised by time-domain procedures.
Compared to analogue controllers, digital controllers offer distinct advantages in terms of: data transmission, interconnection, auxiliary data processing capabilities, fault tolerance, tamper resistance etc. However, a digital

controller must evidently provide a control performance at least as good as that of the analogue controller it replaces. In this respect, it is suggested that sampling and word-length effects are designed to be normally negligible relative to the control accuracy specification. When this objective is frustrated by computer performance constraints these degenerate effects can be evaluated from formulae given in the text.

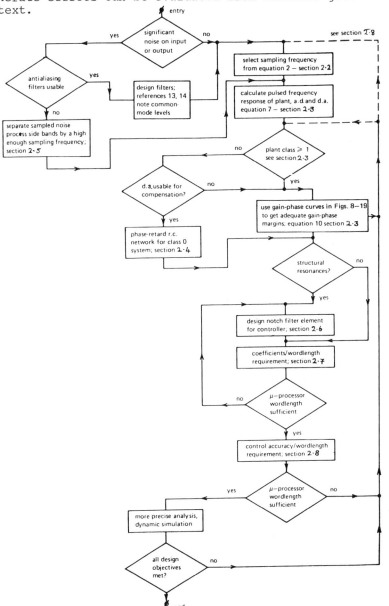

Fig. 2.1   DDC design scheme

2.2   CHOICE OF SAMPLING FREQUENCY

The first step in design of a DCC system of the form shown in Fig. 2.2 is the selection of an appropriate sampling rate (T). Distortion in the form of spectral side-bands centred on integral multiples of the sampling frequency (1/T) is inherently produced by the periodic sampling of information, and the perfect (impractical) recovery of the signal requires the complete elimination of these harmonics (3). A suitable practical choice of sampling frequency limits the distortion (or aliasing) by imposing a large enough frequency separation between the side-bands and the original unsampled signal spectrum for the low-pass plant elements to effect an adequate attenuation. Where comprehensive plant records for an existing analogue control scheme are available, the sampling period for a replacement DDC system is sometimes decided on the basis of requiring a 'small change' in the time dependent error or deviation signal during this interval. In the author's opinion, engineering judgements of this form are valuable only as confirmation of a fundamentally based and experimentally confirmed analysis.

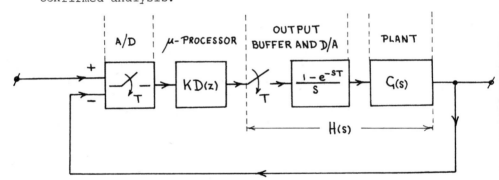

Fig. 2.2   Single input, unity feedback DDC system

For a sinusoidal input:

$$x(t) = A \sin(wt) \qquad (2.1)$$

Knowles and Edwards (4) show that the average power of the control error component due to imperfect side-band attenuation is bounded by:

$$\overline{\varepsilon^2}_R \leqslant A^2 g^2 w_s^{-(2R + 2)} M_p^2 w^2 \, |G(jw)|^{-2} \qquad (2.2)$$

where:

$$G(s) \simeq \left. \frac{g}{s^R} \right|_{s \to \infty} ; \quad M_p = \text{Closed-loop peak magnification}$$

$$w_s = 2\pi/T \qquad (2.3)$$

Equation (2.2) reveals that the high frequency components of the continuous input spectrum generate relatively the greatest distortion and loss of control accuracy. Thus a simple design criterion for selecting the sampling frequency is to ensure that the right-hand-side of equation (2.2) represents an admissible loss of control accuracy for the largest permissible amplitude sinusoid at the highest likely signal frequency. This calculation is not only easily performed, but it is independent of subsequent stabilisation calculations. However, if computer loading demands the lowest possible consistent sampling frequency, it is then necessary to follow an interactive procedure which involves the digitally compensated system and the formula (4):

$$\overline{\varepsilon^2}_R = \pi^{-3} g^2 w_s^{-2R} \int_{-\infty}^{\infty} |K^*(jw)/H^*(jw)|^2 \sin^2(wT/2) \emptyset_x(w) \, dw \tag{2.4}$$

where $K^*(jw)$ defines the overall pulsed frequency response of the stabilised closed-loop system, and $\emptyset_x(w)$ is the input signal power spectrum.

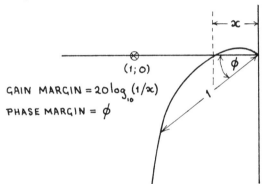

GAIN MARGIN = $20 \log_{10}(1/x)$

PHASE MARGIN = ϕ

Fig. 2.3 Nyquist diagram illustrating the gain/phase margin criterion

2.3 FREQUENCY DOMAIN COMPENSATION METHOD

For most practical applications, necessary and sufficient conditions for the DDC system in Fig. 2.2 to be stable are that the open-loop pulsed frequency response:

$$KD(z)H(z)\big|_{z = \exp(j2\pi fT)} \triangleq KD^*(jf)H^*(jf) \tag{2.5}$$

does not encircle the $(-1,j0)$ point. Furthermore, given that the polar diagram of $KD^*(jf)H^*(jf)$ is of the general form shown in Fig. 2.3, then an adequately damped time domain response is produced when the defined Gain and Phase Margins are greater than about 12dB and 50° respectively. It is evidently important to confirm that these stability margins are maintained over full-range of plant parameter variations or uncertainties. Denoting the Laplace transfer

function of the plant, ADC, DAC and data smoothing elements
by H(s) then the corresponding pulsed frequency response is
obtained (3, 5) as:

$$H^*(jf) = \frac{1}{T} \sum_{-\infty}^{\infty} H(j2\pi f - j2\pi nf_s) \qquad (2.6)$$

Data sampling frequencies selected according to the criterion
in Section 2.2 allow the above expression to be closely
approximated by:

$$H^*(jf) \simeq \frac{1}{T} H(s)\Big|_{s = j2\pi f} \qquad (2.7)$$

over the range of frequencies that determine closed-loop
system stability. If the data smoothing element consists of
a zero-order hold, and the combined gain of the ADC and DAC
converters is K_T, the required pulsed frequency response
$H^*(jf)$ is readily calculable from:

$$H^*(jf) = K_T \exp(-j\pi fT) \cdot \left[\frac{\sin(\pi fT)}{\pi fT}\right] \cdot G(s)\Big|_{s=j2\pi f} \qquad (2.8)$$

For ease of nomenclature in the following discussion, the
number of pure integrations in the plant transfer function
G(s) is termed the 'class' of the system. In general, it is
recommended that one stage of phase-lead compensation is
included for each pure integration in the plant. Thus for
a class 1 system, the discrete compensator takes the form:

$$KD(z) = K \left(\frac{z - a_1}{z - a_2}\right) \text{ with } 0 \leqslant a_2 < a_1 < 1 \qquad (2.9)$$

where the pole at $z = a_2$ is necessary for physical realis-
ability. Observe that digital realisations of PI and PD
controllers can be represented in the form of equation (2.9).
Typical graphs of the gain and phase of $(\exp(j2\pi fT) - a)$ to
normalised frequency (fT) are given in Figs. 2.4, 2.5,
2.6 and 2.7 for real and complex values of a, which
corresponds to a controller zero or pole location. As with
analogue networks, increasing amounts of phase-lead are seen
to be associated with increasingly severe rising gain-
frequency characteristics. If the maximum phase-lead per
stage is much above the recommended value of 55°, the rising
gain-frequency response of the discrete controller causes the
locus $KD^*(jf)H^*(jf)$ to bulge close to the (-1, j0) point
which aggravates transient oscillations.

Pursuing a maximum bandwidth control system design, the
measured or calculated values of $H^*(jf)$ are first used to
determine the frequency (f_B) for which:

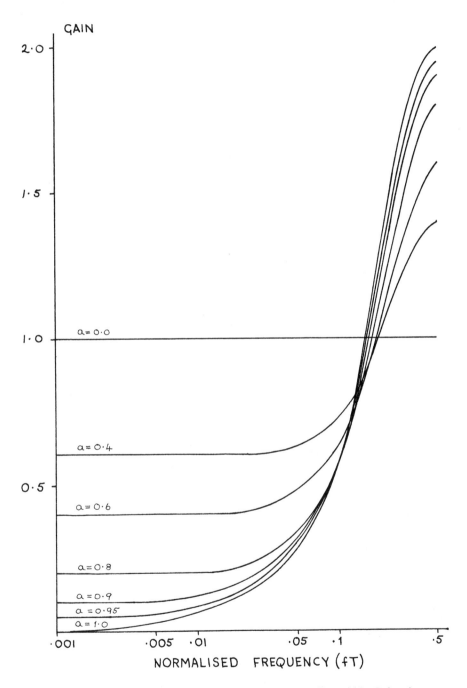

Fig. 2.4 Graph of the magnitude of $(\exp(j2\pi ft)-a)$
          to base fT

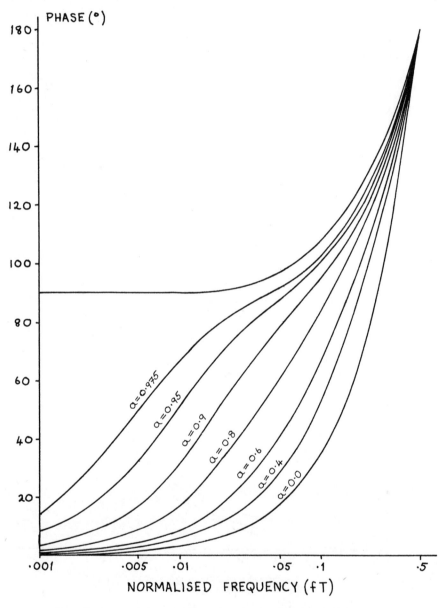

Fig. 2.5   Graph of the phase of (exp(j2πfT)-a) to
base fT

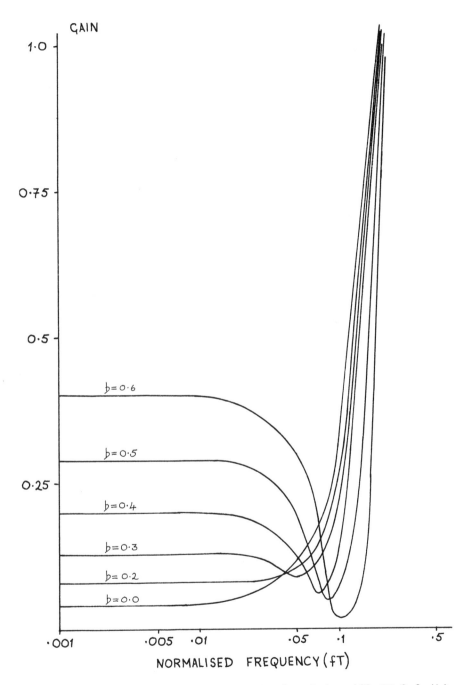

Fig. 2.6 Graph of the magnitude of (exp(j2πfT-0.8-jb).
exp(j2πfT-0.8+jb)) to base fT

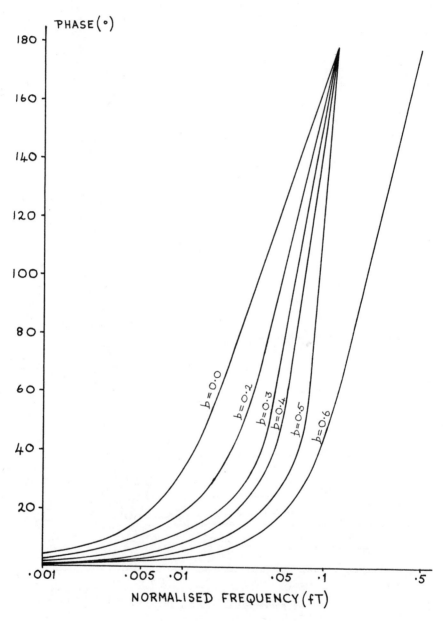

Fig. 2.7   Graph of the phase of (exp(j2πfT-0.8-jb).
exp(j2πfT)-0.8+jb)) to base fT

$$\underline{/\text{H}^*(jf_B)} + 55^\circ \times \text{Number of Phase-lead Stages} = -130^\circ$$

$$(2.10)$$

(a Bode or Nyquist diagram is helpful in this respect)

This procedure with an appropriate choice of the scalar gain constant (K) is clearly orientated towards establishing an adequate Phase Margin. By means of Fig. 2.5, which shows $\underline{/\exp(j2\pi fT)-a}$ to base of fT, real controller zero(s) are selected to give on average no more than 70° phase-lead per stage at f_BT. In the case of a class 1 system, the controller pole is chosen from the same graph to produce around 15-20° phase-lag at f_BT. For a class 2 system, complex controller poles have a definite advantage over their counterparts, because Fig. 2.7 for example shows that relatively less phase-lag is generated at a given frequency. Consequently, complex poles may be placed relatively closer to the (-1, j0) point thereby enhancing the zero-frequency gain of the discrete controller, and the load disturbance rejection capability of the control system. Finally, by means of a Bode or Nyquist diagram, the scalar gain factor (K) is set so as to achieve a closed-loop peak magnification of less than 1.3 and a Gain-Margin of about 12dB. Although this maximum bandwidth design procedure may not be ideal for all applications it is nevertheless adaptable. For example, the pulsed transfer function of a conventional PI controller may be written as:

$$KD(z) = (K_P + K_I) \left(\frac{z - a}{z - 1}\right) \; ; \; a = \frac{K_P}{K_P + K_I}$$

and the graphs in Figs. 2.4 and 2.5 may be applied to select suitable values for 'a' and K_P and K_I, which uniquely specify the controller. Again, the design curves may be used to match the frequency response function of a digital controller to that of an existing analogue controller for the range of frequencies affecting plant stabilisation.

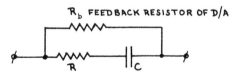

R_b FEEDBACK RESISTOR OF D/A

Fig. 2.8   Phase-retard compensation using DAC

2.4   THE COMPENSATION OF CLASS 0 (REGULATOR) SYSTEMS

The performance and stability of class 0 systems are generally improved by the inclusion of phase-lag compensators, whose analogue transfer function has the general form:

$$R(s) = K \left(\frac{1 + s\alpha\tau}{1 + s\tau} \right) \tag{2.11}$$

where the attenuation constant α is less than unity but
greater than 1/12 for practical applications. An ADC (6) is
frequently time-division multiplexed between several controllers, but each loop normally has exclusive use of its own
DAC which can serve useful dual roles. Fig. 2.8 shows a
series resistor and capacitor connected across the feedback
resistor (R_b) of a DAC, and this is proposed for the phase-
lag compensation of class 0 DDC systems. Apart from the
benefits accruing from savings in computing time, the use of
analogue networks in this instance is superior to digital
because experience shows that an appreciable phase-lag then
occurs over a markedly narrower range of frequencies for the
same attenuation constant. The importance of this fact will
become apparent after the following description of phase-lag
network design.

The first step in the compensation process is to
determine the frequency w_B rads/sec for which the phase of
the frequency response function $H^*(jw)$ is -130°. If the Gain
and Phase Margins of the uncompensated regulator are
satisfactory, but the problem is to reduce the zero-frequency
control error to ε_{DC}, then set

$$10/\alpha\tau = w_B \tag{2.12}$$

and

$$\alpha = \left(\frac{\varepsilon_{DC}}{1 - \varepsilon_{DC}} \right) H^*(0)$$
$$K = 1/\alpha \tag{2.13a}$$

With these parameters the gain and phase of R(s) for
frequencies above w_B are effectively unity and zero
respectively. Hence inclusion of the network increases the
zero-frequency gain of the open-loop response without altering the original satisfactory stability margins. Alternatively, if the zero-frequency control accuracy is acceptable,
but improvements in stability margins are desired, then select
parameters according to equation (2.12) and

$$K = 1$$
$$\alpha = 1/|H^*(jw_b)| \text{ for a } 50^\circ \text{ Phase Margin} \tag{2.13b}$$

With these values, the gain and phase of R(s) for frequencies
above w_b are α and zero respectively. Hence inclusion of the
network improves the Gain Margin by the factor $20 \log_{10}(1/\alpha)$,
without altering the original satisfactory open-loop zero-
frequency gain. Both the above design techniques for phase-
lag networks are based on sacrificing phase in a relatively
unimportant portion of the Nyquist diagram for gain in a
separate region that markedly influences control accuracy or
stability. As the frequency range over which the network
produces an appreciable phase-lag widens, this simple design

procedure becomes evidently complicated by the progressive
overlap of these regions of gain and phase changes.

2.5 NOISY INPUT OR OUTPUT SIGNALS

The operational amplifier associated with a DAC can also
be used for additional signal conditioning. Sometimes the
input or output signal of a control system is heavily con-
taminated by relatively wide-bandwidth noise. If it is
impractical to low-pass filter these signals to prevent
aliasing (13, 14), then an irrevocable loss of control
performance can only be prevented by employing a sampling
frequency which largely separates the side-bands of the
sampled noise process. Unnecessary actuator operations, and
therefore wear and tear, are sometimes avoided in this
situation by including an averaging calculation in the
digital compensator. In these circumstances, the side-band
attenuation achieved by the plant is rendered less effective
if the output sampling rate of the controller is reduced to
an integral sub-multiple of its input rate. As an alternative solution to this noisy signal problem, it is proposed
that a suitable capacitor is placed in parallel with the
feedback resistor of the DAC.

2.6 STRUCTURAL RESONANCES AND DIGITAL NOTCH NETWORKS

A servo-motor is coupled to its load by inherently
resilient steel drive shafts, and the combination possesses
very selective resonances because the normal dissipative
forces are engineered to be relatively small. In high power
equipment (radio telescopes, gun mountings, etc) the frequency
of such structural resonances can be less than three times
the required servo-bandwidth, and consequently their presence
markedly complicates the compensation procedure. Viewed on a
Nyquist diagram, the resonances cause the locus to loop-out
again from the origin to encircle the $(-1, j0)$ point.
Analogue controllers obtain system stability under these
conditions by processing the error or deviation signal with
tuned notch filters (eg Bridged-Tee) which block the excitation of each oscillatory mode. For a resonance peak at
w_0 rad/sec, the same effect is provided by the following
digital filter:

$$N(z) = K_N \frac{(z - z_0)(z - z_0{}^*)}{(z - r_0 z_0)(z - r_0 z_0{}^*)} \qquad (2.14)$$

where:

$$z_0 = \exp(jw_0 T) \; ; \; z_0{}^* = \exp(-jw_0 T) \; ; \; 0 \leqslant r_0 < 1 \quad (2.15)$$

and unity gain at zero-frequency is achieved by setting:

$$K_N = \left| \frac{1 - r_0 z_0}{1 - z_0} \right|^2 \qquad (2.16)$$

In order to null a mechanical resonance, its bandwidth and centre-frequency must both be matched by the digital filter. As may be appreciated from the pole-zero pattern of the filter, no larger notch bandwidth than necessary should be used in order to minimise the phase-lag incurred at sero-frequencies. It remains therefore to relate the notch band-width (B_{NO}) to the parameter r_O.

The gain-frequency response function of the proposed digital filter is given by:

$$|N^*(jw)| = K_N \left| \frac{(\exp(jwT) - z_O)(\exp(jwT) - z_O^*)}{(\exp(jwT) - r_O z_O)(\exp(jwT) - r_O z_O^*)} \right|$$

(2.17)

Defining the frequency deviation variable:

$$\delta = w - w_O$$

(2.18)

then a power series expansion of exponential function of δ yields the first order approximation:

$$|N^*(j\delta)| = \frac{K_{NO}}{\sqrt{1 + \left(\frac{1 - r_O}{T\delta}\right)^2}} \quad \text{for } \delta T \ll 1$$

(2.19)

where:

$$K_{NO} = K_N \left| \frac{1 - \exp(-j2w_O T)}{1 - r_O \exp(-j2w_O T)} \right|$$

(2.20)

Equation (2.19) evidently has complete similarity with the gain-frequency characterisitcs of an analogue notch filter in the vicinity of its anti-resonance. Accordingly, its band-width is defined as the frequency increment about w_O within which the attenuation is greater than 3dB:

$$B_{NO} = \pm \left(\frac{1 - r_O}{T}\right)$$

(2.21)

Calculated or measured plant frequency responses may there-fore be used in conjunction with equations (2.15) and (2.21) to specify suitable values for w_O and r_O in equation (2.14), and the resulting filter is incorporated as an algebraic factor in the pulse function of the discrete controller.

2.7   COEFFICIENT QUANTISATION IN A DISCRETE CONTROLLER

The coefficients in a pulse transfer function usually require rounding in order to be accommodated in the finite wordlength format of a microprocessor or minicomputer. Because generous stability margins are normally employed, coefficient rounding is normally unimportant as regards the practical realisation of phase-lead or phase-lag pulse transfer functions. However, it is well-known that increas-ingly severe digital filter specifications (cut-off rate, bandwidth, etc) accentuate computer wordlength requirements

(8, 9). Hence it is generally prudent to examine the word-length necessary to counter acute structural resonances by the proposed form of digital notch filter.
By writing the equation (2.14) as:

$$N(z) = K_N \frac{z^2 - az + 1}{z^2 - rbz + r^2} \qquad (2.22)$$

coefficient rounding on $\{a, rb, r^2\}$ is seen to modify both the centre-frequency and the bandwidth of a notch filter design. Ideally with no rounding the coefficients in equation (2.22) are specified by:

$$a = a_o; \quad (rb) = (r_o b_o); \quad a_o = b_o = 2 \cos (w_o T); \quad (r^2) = (r_o^2) \qquad (2.23)$$

and defining for the practical situation the variables

$$a = 2 \cos (w_1 T); \quad b = 2 \cos (w_2 T) \qquad (2.24)$$

$$\delta = w - w_1 \quad ; \quad \varepsilon = w_1 - w_2 \qquad (2.25)$$

one obtains the gain-frequency response function of the realisations as:

$$|N^*(jw)| = K_N \left| \frac{\exp(j\delta) - 1}{\exp(j\delta + j\varepsilon) - r} \right| \left| \frac{1 - \left[\exp -j(w + w_1)T\right]}{1 - r\exp\left[-j(w + w_2)T\right]} \right| \qquad (2.26)$$

Thus the centre-frequency of the filter is not at w_1, and the shift due to the finite wordlength is evaluated directly from equation (2.24) as:

$$\delta w_o = \frac{1}{T} \left[\cos^{-1}(a/2) - \cos^{-1}(a_o/2)\right] \text{ rad/sec} \qquad (2.27)$$

It is interesting to note that the change in centre-frequency cannot be obtained by differentiating equation (2.24) because a second-order approximation is required if the coefficient a_o approaches -2. In the vicinity of the anti-resonance and with fine quantisation:

$$\delta T \ll 1 \text{ and } \varepsilon T \ll 1 \qquad (2.28)$$

and under these conditions a power series expansion of the exponential terms in equation (2.26) yields:

$$|N^*(j\delta)| \simeq \frac{K_N'}{\sqrt{(1 + \varepsilon/\delta)^2 + ((1 - r)/\delta T)^2}} \qquad (2.29)$$

where:

$$K_N' = K_N \left| \frac{1 - \exp(-j2w_1 T)}{1 - r \exp(-j2w_2 T)} \right| \qquad (2.30)$$

Thus the bandwidth (B_N) of the realisation satisfies:

$$\left(1 + \frac{\varepsilon}{B_N}\right)^2 + \left(\frac{1 - r}{B_N T}\right)^2 = 2 \qquad (2.31)$$

or:

$$B_N^2 = 2\varepsilon B_N + \varepsilon^2 + \left(\frac{1 - r}{T}\right)^2 \qquad (2.32)$$

For small enough perturbations about the ideal situation defined in equation (2.23), it follows that:

$$\left|\delta B_{NO}\right| \leqslant \left.\left|\frac{\partial B_N}{\partial \varepsilon}\right|\right|_O \left|\delta \varepsilon\right| + \left.\left|\frac{\partial B_N}{\partial r}\right|\right|_O \left|\delta r\right| \qquad (2.33)$$

From equation (2.23), (2.25) and (2.32) one obtains:

$$\delta \varepsilon \leqslant 2\delta w_o \; ; \; \delta r \leqslant q/4r_o \qquad (2.34)$$

$$\left.\left|\frac{\partial B_N}{\partial \varepsilon}\right|\right|_O = 1; \quad \left.\left|\frac{\partial B_N}{\partial r}\right|\right|_O = 1/T$$

where the width of quantisation is defined by:

$$q = 2^{-(\text{wordlength} - 1)} \qquad (2.35)$$

Hence the change in the notch bandwidth of the filter due to coefficient rounding is bounded by:

$$\left|\delta B_{NO}\right| \leqslant 2\left|\delta w_o\right| + \frac{q}{4T \; (1 - B_{NO} \; T)} \qquad (2.36)$$

As a design example, consider the realisation of a notch filter with: centre frequency 12 rad/sec, bandwidth ±1 rad/sec and a sampling period of 0.1 sec. Equation (2.23) defines the ideal numerator coefficient as:

$$a_o = 0.724716 \qquad (2.37)$$

With an 8-bit machine format, the actual numerator coefficient realised is:

$$a = 0.718750 \qquad (0.1011100) \qquad (2.38)$$

so that from equation (2.27):

$$\delta w_o = 0.032 \text{ rad/sec} \qquad (2.39)$$

and the change in filter bandwidth evaluates from equation (2.36) as:

$$\delta B_{NO} \leqslant 0.087 \text{ rad/sec} \qquad (2.40)$$

Thus in practical terms, an 8-bit microprocessor is about sufficient for realising this particular filter specification.

2.8 ARITHMETIC ROUNDOFF-NOISE IN A DISCRETE CONTROLLER

Arithmetic multiplications implemented by a digital computer are subject to rounding errors due to its finite wordlength. As a result, random noise is generated within the closed-loop and the control accuracy is degenerated. In extreme cases, the control system can even become grossly unstable. It is therefore important to relate the loss of control accuracy to the wordlength of the discrete controller. The analysis in (10) provides an easily calculable upper-bound for the amplitude of the noise process present on the error signal due to arithmetic rounding in a discrete controller. With a directly programmed compensator for example, this upper-bound is given by:

$$|\varepsilon_Q| \leqslant \left(\frac{\text{Number of Significant Multiplications in KD(z)}}{2K|\Sigma \text{ Numerator Coefficients}|}\right) q \qquad (2.41)$$

where a 'significant' multiplication does not involve zero or a positive integral power of 2 including 2^0. During a normally iterative design procedure, equation (2.41) is valuable as a means of comparing the multiplicative rounding error generated by various possible controllers. In pre-liminary calculations, the pessimism of this upper-bound is of little consequence (the formula over-estimated by about 2-bits in the example considered in (10)). However, a more accurate estimate of performance degeneration due to multi-plicative rounding errors can be economically important for the finalised design when it is realised on a bit-conscious microprocessor. For this purpose, the analysis in (11) and (12) is recommended because one straight-forward calculation quantifies the loss of control accuracy as a function of controller wordlength.

As described earlier, the sampling frequency of a DDC system must be high enough to prevent an unacceptable loss of control accuracy or fatigue damage to plant actuators. However, strangely enough, it is possible in practical terms for the sampling frequency to be made too high. Reference to Figure 2.5 shows that by increasing the sampling frequency, the phase-lead required at a particular frequency can only be sustained by moving the compensator zero(s) closer to unity. (To preserve load disturbance rejection, the zero-frequency gain of the controller $(KD(z)|_{z=1})$ must be maintained by then moving the pole(s) also closer to unity.) As a result, the algebraic sum of the compensator's numerator coefficients is reduced, and multiplicative round-off noise on the error signal is increased according to Equation (2.41). Thus the choice of an unnecessarily high sampling frequency can entail unjustified expense in meeting long wordlength requirements.

2.9 MULTIRATE AND SUBRATE CONTROLLERS

A subrate digital controller has its output sampler operating an integral number of times slower than its input.

In a multi-rate controller, the output sampler operates an integral number of times faster than its input. Section 2.5 describes how subrate systems prejudice ripple spectrum attenuation, and in practice excessive actuator wear seems best prevented for noisy input signals by the use of a single rate controller and a smoothing capacitor across the DAC unit. It is now pertinent to question if multi-rate systems afford any advantages over their more easily designed single-rate counterparts.

As a result of the higher pulse rate exciting the plant, Kranc (15) contends that the ripple performance of a multi-rate system is superior to that of a single-rate system, even though both cases have the same input sampling rate. However, it should be noted that the input sampler of the multi-rate sampler still generates spectral side-bands centred on multiples of $\pm w_O$, and that these are not eliminated in further modulation by the faster output sampler. Hence it is by no means self-evident that increasing the output sampling rate alone in a digital compensator effects an improvement in ripple attenuation. To clarify this issue and other aspects of performance, a comparison of single and multi-rate unity feedback systems is implemented in (16) for the plant and DAC transfer function

$$G(s) = \frac{e^{-sT}(1 - e^{-sT})}{s^3(s + 1)} \qquad (2.42)$$

with computer sampling periods of:

$$
\begin{aligned}
T_{in} &= T_{out} = 0.1 \text{ sec} \quad \text{Single-rate system} \\
T_{in} &= 3T_{out} = 0.1 \text{ sec} \quad \text{Multi-rate system}
\end{aligned}
\qquad (2.43)
$$

Both closed-loop systems are compensated to have virtually identical frequency and transient response characteristics. For two typical input spectra, calculations show that the output ripple power for the multi-rate system is a least a decade greater than that for the single-rate system. An intuitive explanation of this result may be based on the fact that in both systems the compensator and zero-order hold are attempting to predict some function of the error over the input sampling period. As each prediction inevitably incurs error, a multi-rate system makes more errors per unit time and thus gives the larger ripple signal. It may be argued that multi-rate controllers give potentially the faster transient response. However, the conclusion reached in (16) is that improvement in transient response leads to a further degradation in ripple performance.

2.10   TIME DOMAIN SYNTHESIS WITH POLYNOMIAL INPUTS

After a finite number of sample periods, a dead-beat DDC system tracks a specified input test polynomial exactly with no intersample error. As the output of a zero-order hold remains constant during an intersample period, it follows that with this data smoothing unit a dead-beat system is obtained only if:

(i)   The number of integrations in G(s) is at least equal to the degree of the specified input polynomial;

(ii) the closed-loop pulse transfer function is constructed to be a finite polynomial in z^{-1} (ie, all poles of K(z) at the origin).

It follows from Figure 2.2 that the pulse transfer function for the computer output sequence is K(z)/H(z). Therefore condition (ii) for a dead-beat response is satisfied when $K(z^{-1})$ is set equal to any finite polynomial in z^{-1}, which includes all zeros and the transport delay of H(z). Note that extra coefficients may be included in $K(z^{-1})$ to meet other design requirements. Having thus devised a closed-loop pulse transfer function to achieve a dead-beat response and other design criteria, the digital compensator required is given by:

$$D(z) = \frac{1}{H(z)} \frac{K(z)}{1 - K(z)} \qquad (2.44)$$

As an example (3) of a dead-beat design, suppose a 1 second sampling period, a zero-order hold and the plant:

$$G(s) = \frac{10}{s (s + 1)^2} \qquad (2.45)$$

The z-transformation of the hold and plant is:

$$H(z) = \frac{z^{-1} (1 + 2.34 \ z^{-1}) (1 + 0.16 \ z^{-1})}{(1 - z^{-1}) (1 - 0.368 \ z^{-1})^2} \qquad (2.46)$$

so that condition (ii) implies that:

$$K(z^{-1}) = z^{-1}(1 + 2.34 \ z^{-1})(1 + 0.16 \ z^{-1})(a_0 + a_1 z^{-1} + a_2 z^{-2} + \ldots) \qquad (2.47)$$

or,

$$1 - K(z^{-1}) = 1 - a_0 z^{-1} - (a_1 + 2.5a_0)z^{-2} - (a_2 + 2.5a_1 + 0.3744a_0)z^{-3} -$$
$$(a_3 + 2.5a_2 + 0.3744a_0)z^{-4} + \text{etc} \qquad (2.48)$$

If the other design requirement is zero steady-state error for a ramp input, then as the control error sequence is:

$$E(z^{-1}) = \left[1 - K(z^{-1})\right] \frac{z^{-1}}{(1 - z^{-1})^2} \qquad (2.49)$$

it follows that $1 - K(z^{-1})$ must include $(1 - z^{-1})^2$ as a factor so that:

$$1 - K(z^{-1}) = (1 - z^{-1})^2 (b_0 + b_1 z^{-1} + b_2 z^{-2} + \ldots) \qquad (2.50)$$

After equating coefficients of z^{-1}, it evolves that $\{a_0 \; a_1\}$ and $\{b_0 \; b_1 \; b_2\}$ are the only consistent and linearly independent sets to satisfy simultaneously equations (2.48) and (2.50) with

$$a_0 = 0.73; \; a_1 = -0.47$$

Thus the synthesised dead-beat closed loop pulse transfer function is:

$$K(z^{-1}) = 0.73 \; z^{-1} + 1.35 \; z^{-2} - 0.9 \; z^{-3} - 0.18 \; z^{-4} \tag{2.51}$$

A minimum variance DDC system achieves zero steady-state control error at the sampling instants for a particular polynomial input, and it also minimises the sum of the squares of the control error sequence for the same or a different polynomial input. For example, if the design criterion is for zero steady-state control error for a ramp input, then equation (2.50) defines $1 - K(z^{-1})$ and the corresponding error sequence for step input is:

$$E(z^{-1}) = z^{-1}(1 - z^{-1})(1 + b_1 \; z^{-1} + b_2 \; z^{-2}) \tag{2.52}$$

and as,

$$\sum_{n=0}^{\infty} e_n^2 = \frac{1}{2\pi j} \int_{|z| = 1} E(z) \; E(z^{-1}) \; z^{-1} dz \tag{2.53}$$

then by Cauchy's Theorem:

$$\sum_{n=0}^{\infty} e_n^2 = 1 + (b_1 - 1)^2 + (b_2 - b_1)^2 + b_2^2 \tag{2.54}$$

Differentiating the above variance yields the condition for its minimum as:

$$b_1 = 2/3, \; b_2 = 1/3 \quad \text{with} \quad \sum_{n=0}^{\infty} e_n^2 = 4/3 \tag{2.55}$$

and,

$$K(z^{-1}) = 4/3 \; z^{-1} - 1/3 \; z^{-2} \tag{2.56}$$

Attention could now be directed at the constraints in the above domain synthesis techniques; such as that all poles and zeros of $H(z)$ outside the unit circle should be included as factors of $1 - K(z)$ and $K(z)$ respectively (see Chapter 7, of (3) for example). However, it is more relevant to compare these time domain synthesis methods with the frequency domain compensation procedure described earlier in Section 2.3.

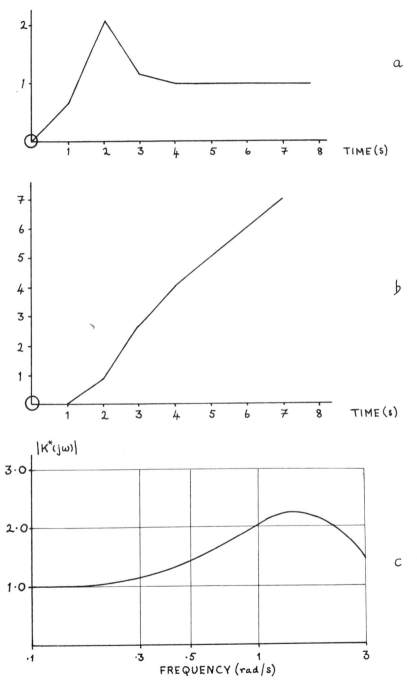

Fig. 2.9   Response characteristics of dead-beat system
(a) step response (b) ramp response (c) closed-loop frequency

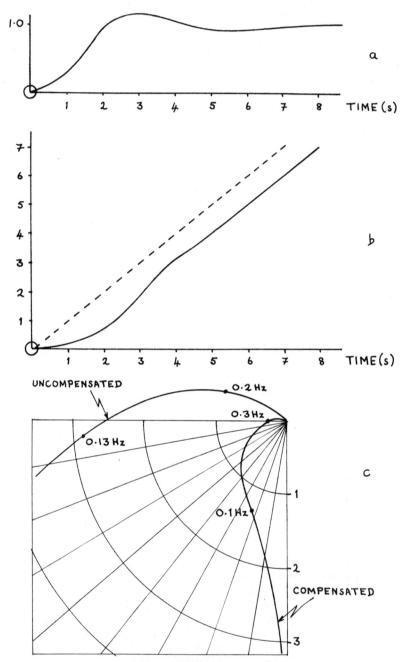

Fig. 2.10   Response characteristics of frequency domain
compensated system
(a) step response (b) ramp response (c) closed-loop response

2.11 COMPARISON OF TIME DOMAIN SYNTHESIS AND FREQUENCY DOMAIN COMPENSATION TECHNIQUES

A convenient starting point is Fig. 2.9 which shows that the step response of the time domain synthesised dead-beat system has a 100% overshoot, even though its ramp response is acceptable. Insight into this behaviour may be gained from the closed-loop frequency response K*(jw) of the system, which is also shown in Fig. 2.9. Noting that the spectrum X*(jw) of the input sequence $\{x_n\}$ always completely defines the sequence and vice-versa, then as:

$$Y*(jw) \quad = \quad K*(jw) \ X*(jw) \qquad (2.57)$$

it follows that minimal transmission distortion occurs when K*(jw) is unity over the range of significant spectral components. The overall frequency response in Fig. 2.9 displays a marked resonance at 1.6 rad/s, and the wider frequency spectrum of a step function compared to a ramp produces the relatively stronger excitation observed. For many purposes, the 100% overshoot in the step response would prove unacceptable.

With the proposed frequency domain compensation procedure, it is recalled that the Class 1 system in Equation (2.45) is compensated by the series element of the form:

$$D(z) \quad = \quad K\frac{(z - a)}{(z - b)} \qquad (2.58)$$

whose maximum phase-lead must not exceed about 55°. In order to achieve an adequate phase-margin ($\approx 50°$), the frequency (f_B) at which the phase lag of H*(jw) is 180° indicates the maximum bandwidth likely to be achieved. It is readily seen from Equation (2.45) that in this case:

$$f_B \ T \quad \approx \quad 0.16 \qquad (2.59)$$

However, Fig. 2.5 shows that the phase difference between the numerator and denominator of a discrete compensator is then well below the maximum, which occurs around:

$$fT \quad = \quad 0.03 \qquad (2.60)$$

More effective compensation can therefore be realised by decreasing the sampling period to 0.25 seconds (note the rms ripple error at 1 rad/s even with a sampling period of 1s is satisfactory; Equation (2.2) evaluates as 1.3×10^{-3}). The pulse frequency response of the open-loop uncompensated system is given in Fig. 2.10, and calculations based on Equation (2.8) differ in gain and phase by less than 0.01% from those computed using the z-transformation. As f_B T now equals 0.035, a digital compensator which provides 55° lead at this frequency is selected by means of Fig. 2.5 as:

$$D(z) \quad = \quad K\frac{(z - 0.9)}{(z - 0.4)} \qquad (2.61)$$

and a gain constant (K) of 0.4 realises a gain-margin of approximately 10 dB. The step and ramp responses of this frequency domain compensated system are also shown in Fig. 2.10, and the additional control error due to multiplicative rounding errors is derived from Equation (2.41) as:

$$|\varepsilon_Q| \;\geqslant\; 37.5 \; q \qquad\qquad (2.62)$$

which indicates that double precision arithmetic would be necessary on an 8 bit μ-processor. Observe that the proposed design technique has produced:

(i)   a control system which is reasonably damped by both step and ramp inputs;

(ii)   a conclusion that the rms ripple error is negligible;

(iii) a simpler, and therefore more easily 'tuned', digital compensator;

(iv)   quantification of the stability margins which are available to cope with plant parameter variations or uncertainties;

(v)   a conclusion that double precision arithmetic is necessary if the compensator is to be realised on an 8 bit micro-computer.

Finally, it should be noted that a control system's response must be judged in general terms of achieving a small enough error with actual plant inputs. Frequently, step or ramp inputs cannot be considered as representative of the real situation. Under such conditions, these simple test inputs form only a rapid method of discovering resonances in the closed-loop frequency response, which would cause distortion in the transmission of actual input signals.

3.12 CONCLUSIONS

A complete design scheme for single-input direct digital control systems has been presented. This includes a simple calculation for ensuring that the sampling rate is consistent with a system's accuracy specification or the fatigue-life of its actuators. The design of a suitable pulse transfer function for a plant controller is based on two simple rules and a few standard frequency response curves, which are easily computed once and for all time. Structural resonances are eliminated by digital notch filters, whose pole-zero locations are directly related to the frequency bandwidth of an oscillatory mode; exactly as with analogue networks (eg Bridged-Tee). In addition, a computationally simple formula provides an upper-bound on the amplitude of the control error component due to multiplicative rounding effects in the digital computer. The calculation enables the selection of the microprocessor wordlength necessary to meet the control system accuracy specification. A distinct advantage of the proposed comprehensive design technique is its numerical simplicity which eliminates the need for a complex computer-aided design facility.

Time domain synthesis of DDC systems to give dead-beat and minimum control error variance designs are also described in this chapter. An example of a dead-beat system is shown to have a poor step function response, though its ramp response is quite satisfactory. Examination of the corresponding closed-loop frequency response reveals the cause as a resonance which is excited more strongly by the relatively wider frequency spectrum of the step function. The proposed frequency domain technique applied to the same example yields a system with acceptable responses to both step and ramp inputs, and in addition it serves to demonstrate the inter-relationship between the sampling freuqency and the achievable closed-loop bandwidth.

2.13 REFERENCES

1. IEE Colloquium: Design of Discrete Controlers, London, December 1977.

2. Knowles J B. 'A Contribution to Direct Digital Control', Ph D Thesis, University of Manchester, 1962.

3. Raggazzini J R, Franklin G. 'Sampled Data Control Systems', (McGraw Hill, 1958).

4. Knowles J B, Edwards R. 'Ripple Performance and Choice of Sampling Frequency for a Direct Digital Control System', Proc IEE, 1966, v.133, p.1885.

5. Jury E I. 'Sampled-Data Control Systems', (John Wiley, 1958).

6. Mattera L. 'Data Coverters Latch onto Microprocessor', Electronics, September 1977, p.81.

7. Knowles J B, Edwards R. 'Aspects of Subrate Digital Control Systems', Proc IEE, 1966, v.133, p.1893.

8. Agarwal R C, Burrus C S. 'New Recursive Digital Filter Structures have a Very Low Sensitivity and Roundoff Error Noise', IEE Trans on Circuits and Systems, 1975, v.22, p.921.

9. Weinstein C J. 'Quantisation Effects in Digital Filters' Lincoln Laboratory MIT Rept 468, November 1969.

10. Knowles J B, Edwards R. 'Computational Error Effects in a Direct Digital Control System', Automatica, 1966, v.4, p.7.

11. Knowles J B, Edwards R. 'Effect of a Finite Wordlength Computer in a Sampled-Data Feedback System', Proc IEE, 1965, v.112, p.1197.

12. Knowles J B, Edwards R. 'Finite Wordlength Effects in Multirate Direct Digital Control Systems', Proc IEE, 1965, v.112, p.2377.

13. Wong Y T, Ott W E (of Burr-Brown Inc). 'Function Circuits - Design and Applications', (McGraw Hill, 1976).

14. Stewart R M. 'Statistical Design and Evaluation of Filters for Restoration of Sampled Data', Proc IEE, 1956, v.44, p.253.

15. Kranc G M. 'Compensation of an Error-Sampled System by a Multi-Rate Controller', Trans AIEE, 1957, v.76, p.149.

16. Knowles J B, Edwards R. 'Critical Comparison of Multi-Rate and Single-Rate DDC System Performance', JACC Computational Methods Session II, 1969.

APPENDIX 2.1   LIST OF SYMBOLS

f — Real frequency variable (Hz)

w — Real angular frequency (rad/s)

T — Sampling period

f_s — Sampling frequency applied to continous data (Hz) and $f_s \triangleq 1/T$

w_s — Angular sampling frequency applied to continuous data (rad/s)

M_p — Peak magnification of the closed-loop real frequency response of a DDC system

s — Complex frequency variable of Laplace Transformation

G(s) — Transfer function of plant

H*(jw) — Pulse real frequency response function of DAC, data hold, and plant

K*(jw) — Overall pulse real frequency response of closed-loop DDC system

ε_R — Error signal component due to imperfect attenuation of side-bands generated by sampling continuous input data to a DDC system

D(z) — Pulse transfer function of a digital compensator

K — Scalar gain constant associated with a digital compensator

K_P, K_I — Proportional and Integral gain terms in a PI controller

α — Attenuation constant in an analogue phase-lag compensator, whose transfer function is R(s)

f_B, w_B — Real frequency, angular frequency, at which the phase lag of open loop system is $-130°$

w_o — Centre frequency (rad/s) of a digital notch filter with pulse transfer function N(z)

B_{NO} — Bandwidth of digital notch filter N(z)

q   Width of data quantisation ($= 2^{-(\text{wordlength} -1)}$)

g   Asymptotic gain of plant G(s) - see Equation (2.3)

R   Rank of plant G(s) - see Equation (2.3)

Other variables are defined in the text.

Chapter 3

Self-tuning controller design and implementation

D.W. Clarke

3.1 INTRODUCTION

Servomechanism design which forms the basis for much current control theory depends on the availability of reasonably accurate plant models in either the time or the frequency domain. In process control these models are not generally known, so recourse is made to PID (three-term) regulators which can give satisfactory performance provided the corresponding coefficients have been properly tuned. However the objective of maintaining the measured variable at some specified set-point can be hard to achieve because of the following problems:

o   The plant may have complex dynamics with a great deal of phase lag. For example there may be several 'capacities' in cascade, or the transit time for the flow of material such as in paper-making may lead to a large dead-time.

o   Nonlinearities in the plant or the actuator may make the gain of the plant vary according to the set-point. For example in pH control the incremental gain can change by many decades, and in chemical or biochemical reactions the rate is exponentially dependent on temperature. Actuators such as valves generally exhibit dead-bands, hysteresis and saturation.

o   The dynamics may also vary with time, such as with the decay of a catalyst or the fouling of a heat-exchanger.

o   Interactions between loops are often such that they cannot be tightly tuned independently, and many plant are currently designed to minimise this effect at the cost of higher capital charges.

o   The material input into a process may vary in quality or there may be environmental disturbances (e.g. a change in cooling water temperature). These effects show themselves as 'load-disturbances' which generally have a non-stationary nature. This feature of disturbances acting on physical processes is the principal reason for the need to add integral action to a process control law.

The output measurement can also be corrupted by noise and quantization errors which restrict the maximum allowable phase advance of the controller.

Some of the above problems can be solved using PID regulators, and it is probably true to say that the three-term algorithm is more robust than most simple alternatives. However, although systematic manual tuning rules such as those proposed by Ziegler and Nichols (56) are available, the problem of finding the 'best' set of PID coefficients can be difficult and time consuming. It can be shown under quite general requirements, such as with quadratic costing or prespecified closed-loop dynamics, that the PID form is optimal for second-order plant subjected to load-disturbances of a Brownian motion type. On the other hand this implies that for more complex plant, such as those with dead-time, the PID algorithm is too simple and would have to be detuned (e.g. reduced gain). In these cases the automated tuning of PID regulators, such as proposed by Astrom (4), would not work well. The self-tuning designs described below, which are based on more advanced control laws, offer a successful alternative.

A self-tuning controller consists of a recursive parameter estimator (plant identifier) coupled with an analytical control design procedure, such that the currently estimated parameters (if adjudged to be valid) are used to provide feedback controller coefficients. The user's input is no longer the values of the PID 'knobs' K, Ti and Td, but rather the closed-loop performance objective which is required by the analytical design procedure. The important feature of self-tuning is that even if the plant model is not known the adaptation mechanism attains the desired closed-loop performance by automatically adjusting the controller parameters. For many plant the number of parameters that might be involved would be greater than the three of the PID form, and so could not practicably be manually tuned. On the other hand proofs of convergence (Ljung (39),(40)) of self-tuners to the 'true' controllers depend on assumptions about the process (linearity, stationarity, model-order,...) which in general cannot be justified. As with other 'intelligent' algorithms, the viability of a self-tuner in practice depends as much on the robustness of the basic design procedure and on appropriate 'jacketing' software as on theoretical convergence considerations.

Although a self-tuner can be derived by combining any reasonable controller design procedure with a recursive parameter estimator, this chapter will concentrate on two particular algorithms. The first is based on predictive control theory (Clarke and Gawthrop (14,15), Clarke (11)) as it can provide a wide class of useful performance objectives. The second is the pole-placement method (Wellstead et al (51), Clarke (12)) which can be effective for plant with variable dead-time. Both these methods have been widely used in practice, having been applied to industrial plant and made available commercially.

The chapter is organised as follows. The discretization of the continuous-time plant is briefly described, particularly with respect to the locations of the discrete-time zeros of the transfer-function and to possible models of typical load-disturbances. The general theory of predictive control is then shown to have interpretations as Smith predictive, 'detunable' model-reference and generalised minimum-variance laws. Extensions to include feedforward compensation for known disturbances are provided. The pole-placement method is derived to cover both the servo and the regulator problem, and in the latter case it is shown that a simple estimation algorithm (RLS) is sufficient. General recursive estimation methods based on minimising the prediction error are then discussed with particular emphasis on numerically stable versions of the Recursive Least Squares (RLS) method. A simple self-tuner is then provided as a combination of an estimator and a basic control law, and the outline of the corresponding program given. Applications of self-tuning are summarized together with a discussion of the important 'jacketing' software which is used to make the theory work reliably.

3.2   THE ASSUMED PLANT MODEL

To apply a self-tuner the structure (though not the parameters) of the process model must be assumed, and a principal requirement is that it is capable of at least approximating the behaviour of a broad class of processes. As in the main the set-point of a process control loop is constant over long periods, a locally-linearized model is often adequate:

$$y(t) = \frac{B_1(s)}{A_1(s)} u(t-T) + x(t) \qquad \ldots (3.1)$$

where $u(t)$, $y(t)$ are the plant input and output and T is the dead-time or transport-delay. A and B are polynomials in the differential operator $s = d./dt$ for which:

$$\text{degree } A_1(s) = n_1 > \text{degree } B_1(s) = m_1 \qquad \ldots (3.2)$$

In practice values of n_1 and m_1 in the range 1 to 3 are generally acceptable.

The signal $x(t)$ is a general disturbance term, though it would also include the effect of modelling errors on the output, and components of $x(t)$ could be:

1. a constant x_1 as processes do not generally have signals with zero mean, and the incremental gain $\partial y/\partial u$ does not equal the static gain y/u

2. a load-disturbance $x_2(t)$ which might slowly vary or consist of random steps at random times

3. a measured auxiliary signal $x_3(t)$ suitable for feedforward compensation

4. a stationary stochastic process $x_4(t)$ given by:

$$x_4(t) = \frac{C_2(s)}{A_2(s)} \xi(t) \qquad \qquad \ldots (3.3)$$

where A_2 and C_2 are further polynomials in s of degree n_2 and m_2, and $\xi(t)$ is a white-noise process. Most self-tuning theory concentrates on $x_4(t)$ whereas in practice $x_2(t)$ is more common though harder to analyse.

In computer control the plant is preceded by a zero-order-hold which provides a 'staircase' input (Franklin and Powell (24), Isermann (33)). If G(s) is the transfer-function relating y(s) to u(s), the discrete-time model is given by:

$$G(z^{-1}) = (1-z^{-1}) \ Z\{G(s)/s\}$$

and the Z-transform of G(s)/s is obtained by using partial-fraction expansion of G(s)/s and then transforming term by term. If now t is defined to be the discrete-time sample instant and z to be the forward shift operator, the discrete-time model corresponding to eqn.1 where x(t) is given by eqn.3 becomes the ARMAX (AutoRegressive Moving-Average eXtended) representation:

$$A(z^{-1})y(t) = B(z^{-1})u(t-k) + C(z^{-1})e(t) \qquad \ldots (3.4)$$

Here the dead-time is reflected in the k samples between a control action and the corresponding effect on the output; if h is the sample interval then $k = \text{INT}(T_d/h) + 1$. The polynomials A, B and C are all of degree $n = n_1+n_2$ in the backward shift operator z^{-1}, so the corresponding difference equation is:

$$y(t) + a_1 y(t-1) + \ldots + a_n y(t-n) = b_0 u(t-k) + \ldots + b_n u(t-k-n)$$

$$+ e(t) + c_1 e(t-1) + \ldots + c_n e(t-n)$$

The sequence $\{e(t)\}$ is serially uncorrelated with a common variance σ^2. As such model 4 is the one generally assumed in the self-tuning literature in which a linear dynamic process with dead-time is subjected to stationary disturbances with rational spectral density.

Many related models can be deduced depending on the assumed nature of x(t). Early work (Clarke and Gawthrop (14)) added a constant d to model $x_1(t)$ giving:

$$A(z^{-1})y(t) = B(z^{-1})u(t-k) + d + C(z^{-1})e(t) \qquad \ldots (3.5)$$

The value of d can be estimated along with the other plant parameters. However a Brownian motion model is more appropriate in practice (as well as leading naturally to integral action in the control law), in which case:

$$A(z^{-1})y(t) = B(z^{-1})u(t-k) + C(z^{-1})e(t)/\Delta \qquad \ldots (3.6)$$

where $\Delta = 1-z^{-1}$ is a differencing operator (Clarke et al (17)). In the following the general model:

$$A(z^{-1})y(t) = B(z^{-1})u(t-k) + x(t) \qquad \ldots (3.7)$$

is assumed, where the general disturbance $x(t)$ is interpreted according to context.

The ARMAX model is not the only one usable in deriving adaptive controllers. For example, eqn.4 can be divided by the polynomial A to give:

$$y(t) = A^{-1}B\, u(t-k) + A^{-1}C\, e(t)$$

in which long-division yields the <u>weighting-sequence</u> model:

$$y(t) = H_1(z^{-1})\, u(t) + H_2(z^{-1})\, e(t) \qquad \ldots (3.8)$$

where the polynomials H are in principle of infinite degree, though if A is stable and therefore has roots within the unit circle the expansion of 1/A converges and the polynomials H can be truncated after a finite number of terms. This is the approach of Richalet et al (46) in deriving their IDCOM controller; they make the further less appropriate assumption that $H_2 = 1$ implying that the disturbance is purely white noise.

3.2.1 <u>Discrete-time Zeros</u>.

Some self-tuners (e.g. model-reference type) are based on <u>cancellation</u> controller designs, in which the plant dynamics are first cancelled by terms in the controller whilst further terms provide the desired closed-loop performance. If the plant has zeros (root of B) outside the unit circle the corresponding controller poles induce instability as cancellation is inevitably inexact. Hence for these designs it is important to know when such zeros exist - in the literature they are somewhat loosely termed as nonminimum-phase. Now whereas there is a one-to-one relationship between continuous-time and discrete-time <u>poles</u> (given by the mapping z = exp(sh)), there is no such correspondence between the <u>zeros</u>. Indeed a continuous-time plant with no zero is discretized to give a B polynomial with n zeros in general (n-1 if the dead-time is an integral multiple of h). The following simple rules in which n is the order of the continuous-time plant cover some of the cases:

1. If the continous-time plant has n-1 or n zeros, the above mapping applies for small h. Hence a minimum-phase plant has a minimum-phase discrete-time model. This is one basis of Gawthrop's hybrid method (26).

2. If G(s) has j more poles than zeros, then for small h the discrete-time model is proportional to that of a j-integrator plant. In particular if j > 2 at least one zero lies outside the unit circle.

3. If G(s) is strictly proper (less than n zeros) then for <u>large</u> h the discrete-time model tends to G(0)/z, which has no zero.

4. Let δ be the <u>fractional</u> dead-time kh-T. Then if G(s) is proper and δ tends to h at least one zero of the discrete model becomes nonminimum-phase. A well-known example is the plant exp(-sT)/s whose discrete-time model has a zero outside the unit disc if h/2 < δ < h.

In practice plant engineers wish to sample as rapidly as possible (as they are used to PID regulators). The above rules imply that there is a strong possibility of a nonminimum-phase plant model; slower sampling to 'cure' the problem is at the cost of inferior control performance. What is required is a controller design which is relatively insensitive to the positions of the zeros.

3.3 PREDICTIVE MODELS

Predictive control theory has its roots in the work of Smith (49) in which a model with no dead-time is used to predict the output of a plant with dead-time. This allows the PID controller to be more tightly tuned as the term exp(-sT) is found to be eliminated from the characteristic equation. A Smith predictor, however, depends on a good plant model and does not predict the effects of the disturbance on the future output. More general predictors which form the basis of many self-tuning methods overcome these deficiencies. Let T be a <u>design</u> polynomial:

$$T(z^{-1}) = 1 + t_1 z^{-1} + \ldots + t_n z^{-n}$$

and consider the <u>identity</u> (or Diophantine equation):

$$T(z^{-1}) = E(z^{-1})A(z^{-1}) + z^{-k}F(z^{-1}) \qquad \ldots (3.9)$$

This equation can be used to obtain coefficients of the E and F polynomials given T, A and the dead-time k. Multiplying eqn.7 by E, replacing EA using eqn.9, and considering time t+k gives:

$$[T - z^{-k}F] \, y(t+k) = EB \, u(t) + E \, x(t+k)$$

or: $$T \, y(t+k) = F \, y(t) + G \, u(t) + E \, x(t+k) \qquad \ldots (3.10)$$

where the polynomial $G(z^{-1})$ = EB. Define <u>filtered</u> signals
u'(t) and y'(t) to be the known data u(t) and y(t) passed
through the (all-pole) filter 1/T, giving u'(t) = u(t)/T and
y'(t) = y(t)/T. Then a model which gives a prediction p(t)
of the future output y(t+k) from currently available data u'
and y' is:

$$p(t) = F(z^{-1}) y'(t) + G(z^{-1}) u'(t) \qquad \dots (3.11a)$$

and:

$$y(t+k) = p(t) + E(z^{-1}) x(t+k)/T(z^{-1}) \qquad \dots (3.11b)$$

In the purely deterministic case x(t+k) = 0 and thus the
prediction is exact if the polynomials F and G are known. In
the general case the quality of the predictor depends on the
choice of the polynomial T. Often the 'best' predictor is
required, and it is seen that if x = Ce and T = C the
prediction error in eqn.11b becomes simply Ee(t+k). Now
eqn.9 shows that the degree of E is k-1, so Ee(t+k) is a
moving-average of order k whose last term contains e(t+1) and
is therefore independent of u'(t) and y'(t). This is the
predictor which has minimal variance, and for this case p(t)
is often written as y*(t+k|t), i.e. the optimal prediction of
y(t+k) given data up to and including time t. However, x(t)
is not always describable by the simple form Ce(t), and
eqn.11 is merely considered to be a 'good' predictor.

3.3.1 <u>An Example</u>.

Consider the plant model:

$$(1 - 0.8z^{-1}) y(t) = 0.2 u(t-2) + (1 + 0.7z^{-1}) e(t)$$

where k=2, and the optimal prediction is when T = C in eqn.9:

$$(1 + 0.7z^{-1}) = (1 + e_1 z^{-1})(1 - 0.8z^{-1}) + z^{-2} f_0$$

Comparing powers of z^{-1} gives e_1 = 1.5, f_0 = 1.2 and so:

$$(1 + 0.7z^{-1}) y*(t+2|t) = 1.2 y(t) + (0.2 + 0.3z^{-1}) u(t)$$

$$\tilde{y}(t+2|t) = e(t+2) + 1.5 e(t+1)$$

The prediction variance is that of the remnant $\tilde{y}$, i.e.
$\sigma^2(1+1.5^2) = 3.25\sigma^2$. If k = 1 instead of 2 the prediction
variance is simply σ^2; this confirms the intuition that the
more distant the prediction horizon the less the expected
accuracy. This reduction of accuracy leads to a loss of
performance in a closed-loop control system in which output
fluctuations can become large if the dead-time is
significant; only feedforward can then improve matters.

3.3.2   General Predictive Models.

In general prediction (Yaglom (54), Clarke and Gawthrop (15)) we are concerned with an auxiliary plant output $\psi(t)$ produced by passing $y(t)$ through a prescribed transfer-function P:

$$\psi(t) = P(z^{-1}) \, y(t) = Pn(z^{-1})/Pd(z^{-1}) \, y(t) \qquad \ldots (3.12)$$

The identity 9 then becomes:

$$T(z^{-1})Pn(z^{-1}) = E(z^{-1})A(z^{-1}) + z^{-k}F(z^{-1}) \qquad \ldots (3.13)$$

Proceeding with the same development as before gives:

$$\psi(t+k) = F(z^{-1})y''(t) + G(z^{-1})u'(t) + Ex(t+k)/T \qquad \ldots (3.14)$$

where $y''(t) = y(t)/PdT$ and $u'(t) = u(t)/T$ are filtered signals. Hence:

$$p(t) = F(z^{-1}) \, y''(t) + G(z^{-1}) \, u'(t) \qquad \ldots (3.15a)$$

and:
$$\tilde{\psi}(t+k|t) = E(z^{-1}) \, x(t+k) \, /T(z^{-1}) \qquad \ldots (3.15b)$$

The argument for predicting an auxiliary output ψ is that the augmented plant G.P is 'easier' to control than the original plant.

Multi-step predictors can be derived for which the prediction horizon exceeds k, and hence some assumption must be made about future control actions (De Keyser and van Cauwenberghe (19)). Such predictors can be used with quadratic cost functions defined over a 'receding horizon'. Alternatively the predicted plant response could simply be displayed to the process operator, who could adjust the control actions accordingly (De Keyser and van Cauwenberghe (18)).

3.3.3   Incremental Predictors

Consider the plant model 6 with C = 1 and k = 1:

$$A(z^{-1}) \, y(t) = B(z^{-1}) \, u(t-1) + e(t)/\Delta, \text{ or:}$$

$$A(z^{-1}) \, \Delta y(t+1) = B(z^{-1}) \, \Delta u(t) + e(t+1)$$

Defining $A(z^{-1}) = 1 - z^{-1}A_1(z^{-1})$ the model becomes:

$$y(t+1) = y(t) + A_1(z^{-1}) \, \Delta y(t) + B(z^{-1}) \, u(t) + e(t+1).$$

This model predicts changes in the output y in terms of known changes in the current data Δy and Δu. This is important in applications as dc levels on the data do not affect the prediction performance. Moreover, when used in self-tuning the data-vectors have zero mean and hence give significantly better estimation properties.

3.4   PREDICTIVE CONTROL

Having derived predictors for both y(t+k) and ψ(t+k)   we
are now in a position to develop a range of control laws with
useful properties depending   on   the   choice   of   P   and   T.
Practical   features   of   the   controlled plant indicate which
choices are appropriate.   In the following the   set-point   is
denoted   as w(t);   in many cases w(t) remains constant but it
may undergo step changes at infrequent intervals.   Note   that
the   prediction involves the <u>current</u> control u(t) which is to
be chosen on   the   basis   of   its   effect   on   the   predicted
variable.

A simple policy is to choose u(t) such that p(t) becomes
equal to w(t):

i.e.   p(t) = w(t)   ... (3.16)

So that, using eqn.11a, the algorithm leads to:

$$F(z^{-1})\ y'(t) + G(z^{-1})\ u'(t) = w(t).$$

Hence, recalling that u'(t) = u(t)/T, this implies a control:

$$u(t) = \frac{T}{G} \{ w(t) - \frac{F}{T} y(t) \}$$

Solving to get the closed-loop equations, we have:

$$y(t) = w(t-k) + E\ x(t)/T \qquad\qquad ... (3.17a)$$

$$u(t) = \frac{A}{B} w(t) - \frac{F}{BT} x(t) \qquad\qquad ... (3.17b)$$

Eqn.17 shows that   this   control   law   produces   a   dead-beat
response to set-point changes (y(t+k) = w(t)).   The effect of
the   disturbances   x(t)   is   'tailored'   by   the   user-chosen
polynomial   T, so that the control signal amplitude following
a step change in x can be damped   by   choosing   a   'sluggish'
characteristic in T.   Note that the effect of the disturbance
on the controlled loop is simply that   of   the   error   of   the
prediction   model   of eqn.11b,   so a good prediction implies
good closed-loop performance.   For example, if T = C and   the
process   admits the stochastic model of eqn.4, the prediction
and   hence   the   control   is   minimum-variance, and   output
fluctuations   are   as   small   as possible.   This is useful in
quality control, such as when applied to a paper-making plant
in   which   the   thickness   of   the   sheet is to be maintained
within close limits.

Although the control policy is 'ideal', it achieves   its
objective   by   cancelling   the   plant dynamics, which as seen
before can cause instability when there are   nonminimum-phase

zeros. Even if there are no zeros outside the unit circle, their positions might lead to badly damped control signals.

3.4.1 Model-following Control.

In practice an engineer knows that dead-beat performance leads to excessive control signals, and he has an intuitive idea of the ultimate achievable speed of the closed-loop (e.g. by knowing the open-loop response). Hence a more appropriate objective is to make the closed-loop respond at a rate determined by a prescribed model M, such that if $x(t) = 0$:

$$y(t) = M(z^{-1}) \, w(t-k) \qquad \qquad \ldots (3.18)$$

If M = 1 dead-beat control is specified, but if M is equipped with dynamics the closed-loop would respond to steps (and to load-disturbances) with the corresponding speed. One obvious requirement is that the closed-loop gain is unity, so that $M(1) = 1$. One way to arrive at eqn.18 is to prefilter the set-point to give a new signal $w'(t) = Mw(t)$, and then to use dead-beat control with a set-point of $w'(t)$, though this would not affect the response to loads. It is therefore better in practice to embed the model within the closed-loop, as it can be shown (Lim (38)) that the resulting controller is more robust. This is done by using the auxiliary output described above.

If in the generation of ψ = Py the transfer-function P is chosen to be the inverse model P = 1/M, and eqn.16 uses the prediction of $\psi(t)$ instead of $y(t)$, then if x = 0 the closed-loop will satisfy $\psi(t+k) = w(t)$. Hence $y(t+k) = \psi(t+k)/P = w(t)/P = Mw(t)$, as required. In the general case where $x(t)$ is non-zero, the closed-loop equations become:

$$y(t) = M(z^{-1}) \left\{ w(t-k) + \frac{E}{T} x(t) \right\} \qquad \ldots (3.19a)$$

$$u(t) = M(z^{-1}) \left\{ \frac{A}{B} w(t) - \frac{F/Pd}{BT} x(t) \right\} \qquad \ldots (3.19b)$$

Note that the model M affects both the set-point and the disturbance responses. Hence P and T can be chosen in accordance with the expected variations in $w(t)$ and $x(t)$ and the loop then behaves as desired. However, eqn.19b shows that there are still cancellations in the forward path and the algorithm is therefore unsuitable for nonminimum-phase plant; this is a defect shared by 'model-reference adaptive controller' (MRAC) designs.

3.4.2   Control Weighting.

The Smith predictive approach inserts a controller L (generally PID) into the forward path which is fed by the prediction error rather than the conventional error $w(t) - y(t)$, and hence eliminates the dead-time from the characteristic equation. In the same way, the general predictive control is given by:

$$u(t) = \{ w(t) - p(t) \} / Q(z^{-1}) \qquad \qquad \ldots (3.20)$$

where $p(t)$ is given by eqn.11a for a 'generalised Smith' controller or eqn.15a for a 'detunable model-following' controller. The user-chosen transfer-function Q is typically such that $1/Q$ is of PI form, and in the non-adaptive case its parameters could be selected as with the Smith method (e.g. hand tuned). The original Smith algorithm is seen to be a subset of the above for the case where $P = T = 1$ and $x(t)$ is assumed to be constant.

Substituting for $p(t)$ from eqn.15a gives:

$$Q(z^{-1}) \, u(t) = w(t) - \{ F(z^{-1}) \, y''(t) + G(z^{-1}) \, u'(t) \}$$

and solving for the current control $u(t)$ gives:

$$u(t) = [Q + G/T]^{-1} \{ w(t) - F \, y(t)/TPd \}$$

The closed-loop equations are now:

$$y(t) = \frac{B}{PB + QA} \, w(t-k) + \frac{EB + QT}{PB + QA} \frac{x(t)}{T} \qquad \ldots (3.21a)$$

$$u(t) = \frac{A}{PB + QA} \, w(t) - \frac{F/Pd}{PB + QA} \frac{x(t)}{T} \qquad \ldots (3.21b)$$

The crucial point here is that this is no longer a cancellation law; the characteristic equation is instead $PB + QA = 0$. Often the transfer-function Q is written in the form λQ_1, and this gives the closed-loop poles to be the roots of $PB + \lambda Q_1 A = 0$. Hence λ is a root-locus parameter which moves the poles from B (small λ), which could be unstable, toward A (large λ). If the plant is open-loop stable this means that the plant will be closed-loop stable for large enough λ, even if it is nonminimum-phase. It is seen, though, that increasing λ 'detunes' the performance, as the closed-loop model is no longer specified by $1/P$ alone. In practice this has not been found to be significant. Note that the dead-time k has been eliminated from the loop, which is desirable for achieving tight control.

The predictive control method was developed following the seminal work of Astrom and Wittenmark (6), who invoked a minimum variance objective and thus produced a cancellation controller. The objective of Clarke and Gawthrop (14) was a generalisation of this, as it was shown that for $P = 1$, $T = C$ and $Q = \lambda$ the controller minimises a cost-function:

$$J = E \{ (y(t+k) - w(t))^2 + \lambda g_0 u^2(t) \mid t \}$$

where the expectation is conditioned on data acquired up to time t. In the general case, the controller of eqn.20 can be shown to minimise:

$$J_1 = E \{ (\psi(t+k) - w(t))^2 + g_0/q_0 (Qu(t))^2 \mid t \}$$

The effect of 'detuning' is seen both in the cost-functions and in the fact that the control u(t) can be written as:

$$u(t) = u*(t) / (1 + Q/g_0)$$

where u*(t) is the control required to attain exact model-following performance. For example, if Q is simply λg_0 with λ chosen to be 1, exactly half the model-following control is exerted. In general λ is use to 'trade' control variance against output variance, so that large control signals are not produced. In practice the effect of λ is good, in that a significant reduction in control effort is accompanied by only a small increase in output fluctuations, though counter-examples can be found.

3.4.3 Feedforward.

One nice feature of predictive control is that measurable load-disturbances can easily be included in the algorithm. Suppose one component of x(t) is a known signal v(t), giving a system model (c.f. eqn.4):

$$A(z^{-1}) y(t+k) = B(z^{-1}) u(t) + D(z^{-1}) v(t+k) + x_1(t+k)$$

where the variance of $x_1(t)$ is clearly less than that of x(t). This equation shows that the current control can be chosen to eliminate components of v(t) which are known at time t, but not future components. Hence complete elimination of v(t) is only possible if the delay in v is the same as or greater than the delay in u; one example is in metal rolling where the incoming guage can be measured. The control signal might still be large (see Allidina and Hughes (1)) and constraints might preclude complete removal of the effect of v(t).

Following the development of eqns.9 to 15, and defining polynomials E_1 and F_1 from the identity:

$$ED = E_1 + z^{-k} F_1,$$

Then:

$$\psi(t+k) = Fy''(t) + Gu'(t) + F_1 v'(t) + \{E_1 v(t+k) + Ex_1(t+k)\}/T$$

This gives a prediction signal:

$$p(t) = F y''(t) + G u'(t) + F_1 v'(t).$$

which can be used in the control law of eqn.20. If
$Q = 0 = E_1$ then no component of v remains in the output under
control: 'ideal' feedforward compensation.

Clearly as many feedforward signals as required can be
included in the predictor. One interesting use is to reduce
interactions between coupled loops by considering the input
and output of loop A, for example, to be feedforward signals
for other loops (Morris et al (42)). A single-loop
self-tuner can therefore be easily extended to the
multivariable case.

The predictive control method is very versatile: it can
cope with dead-time, provide a model-following loop, and
eliminate measurable disturbances. A parameter λ allows the
user to 'tune' the performance on-line to balance control
effort against output regulation. Moreover it is readily
included in a self-tuning controller.

3.5   POLE-PLACEMENT CONTROL

In a series of papers (e.g. (51)) Wellstead and his
coworkers developed the idea of using pole-placement as the
underlying design algorithm in a self-tuner. The
relationship between this approach and pure model following
was explored by Clarke (12). The idea is that the offending
zeros of the plant should not be cancelled by the controller,
which instead should place only the poles of the closed-loop
in desired locations (such as in 'minimum ripple' designs of
classical discrete-time theory).

Let $T(z^{-1})$ be the filter (observer) polynomial defined
before, and u'(t) and y'(t) be the corresponding filtered
signals u/T and y/T. Model 7 then becomes:

$$A(z^{-1}) \ y'(t) = B(z^{-1}) \ u'(t-k) + x(t) \ / \ T(z^{-1})$$

Let w(t) be the set-point and consider a general control:

$$G(z^{-1}) \ u(t) = H(z^{-1}) \ w(t) - F(z^{-1}) \ y(t)$$

Eliminating u(t) from these equations gives:

$$(AG + z^{-k}BF) \ y'(t) = BH \ w'(t-k) + x(t)/T$$

The left-hand side term $(AG + z^{-k}BF)$ is the closed-loop
characteristic polynomial, whose roots are the poles.
Suppose $Am(z^{-1})$ is a user-specified polynomial which has
roots in the desired pole locations. Then let polynomials F
and G be computed from the Diophantine equation:

$$A(z^{-1})G(z^{-1}) + z^{-k}B(z^{-1})F(z^{-1}) = T(z^{-1})Am(z^{-1})$$

The closed-loop equation then becomes:

$$Am(z^{-1}) \; y(t) = [B(z^{-1})H(z^{-1}) \; w(t-k) + x(t)] \; / \; T(z^{-1})$$

Now let the design polynomial H be given by $T(z^{-1})H_1(z^{-1})$,

giving: $y(t) = [BH_1 \; / \; Am] \; w(t-k) + x(t) \; /[AmT]$.

In this way Am determines the modes of the set-point response and AmT the modes of the disturbance response. To get zero steady-state error the gain between w and y should be unity; this is achieved by choosing the gain of H to give $B(1)H_1(1) = Am(1)$. It would appear that the roles of T and Am are interchangable, and that T is not really necessary. The discussion below shows that T is indeed useful in the self-tuning application of the pole-placement approach.

Suppose F_0 and G_0 are polynomials given by a related Diophantine equation:

$$A(z^{-1})G_0(z^{-1}) + z^{-k}B(z^{-1})F_0(z^{-1}) = C(z^{-1})Am(z^{-1})$$

where the disturbance x(t) is given by the stochastic model $C(z^{-1})e(t)$. When the polynomials F_0 and G_0 are used in a regulator - that is when w(t)=0, the output and the control signals are given by:

$$y(t) = G_0(z^{-1})/Am(z^{-1})e(t); \qquad u(t) = -F_0(z^{-1})/Am(z^{-1})e(t)$$

Now let $A_1(z^{-1})$ and $B_1(z^{-1})$ be polynomials which satisfy:

$$A_1(z^{-1})G_0 + z^{-k}B_1(z^{-1})F_0 = T(z^{-1})Am(z^{-1}) \qquad \dots (3.22)$$

where Am and T are the design polynomials described above. Consider now the sequence $A_1 y'(t) - B_1 u'(t-k)$:

$$A_1 y'(t) - B_1 u'(t-k) = [A_1 G_0 + z^{-k}B_1 F_0]/TAm \; e(t),$$

using the properties of u(t) and y(t) given above. But the term within the brackets [] is simply TAm, by the second Diophantine equation (22). Hence in closed-loop the input-output model is:

$$A_1(z^{-1}) \; y'(t) = B_1(z^{-1}) \; u'(t-k) + e(t) \qquad \dots (3.23)$$

The crucial point is that for arbitrary stable T and C the error term on the RHS of eqn.23 is simply e(t), and the unknown polynomial C need not be accounted for in the design. Hence a self-tuner would consist of the following:

1.   At each sample instant use filtered data u'(t-k) and y'(t) to estimate the parameters of the polynomials A_1 and B_1, using RLS as described below.

2.   Use $\hat{A}_1$, $\hat{B}_1$ and the design polynomials T and Am in eqn.22 to obtain controller parameters $\hat{F}_0$ and $\hat{G}_0$ (this can be quite time-consuming, involving the solution of a set of linear equations).

3.   Use $\hat{F}_0$ and $\hat{G}_0$ in the controller: $u(t) = -\hat{F}_0/\hat{G}_0 y(t)$.

4.   Return to 1.

T does not appear in the closed-loop performance, but its role now is to improve the behaviour of the parameter estimator, as it can be shown that if $T = C$ there is the fastest rate of convergence. Alternatively one could consider a T to act as a low-pass filter which removes high frequency noise from the data used in the estimation, giving greater reliability. Note that the above discussion relates to the use of pole-placement as a pure regulator; in the more general case with varying w(t) a full estimation of A,B <u>and</u> C is required. Even so, T still has a role to play in the estimation.

3.6   <u>RECURSIVE PARAMETER ESTIMATION</u>

The closed-loop model of eqn.23 and the predictor models of eqn.11a and eqn.15a contain parameters which depend on the unknown plant. The job of a parameter estimator is to provide these parameters for the control design algorithm based on available plant input/output data. Define $\theta = \{\theta_1, \theta_2, \ldots, \theta_n\}$ to be a vector of n unknown plant parameters and $\hat{\theta}(t)$ to be a vector of corresponding estimates available at time t. Let $s(t) = \{s_1, s_2, \ldots, s_n\}$ be a vector of available data, which is assumed to be <u>exactly</u> known at time t. A <u>predictor model</u> generates a prediction $\hat{y}(t)$ (or $\hat{\psi}$) depending on $\hat{\theta}(t-1)$ and $s(t)$:

$$\hat{y}(t) = f\{ \hat{\theta}(t-1); s(t) \}$$

and the scalar <u>prediction error</u> is defined to be:

$$\epsilon(t) = y(t) - \hat{y}(t) = y(t) - f\{ \hat{\theta}(t-1); s(t) \}$$

where y(t) is the new output measurement provided at time t. In what follows we restrict analysis to predictive models which are <u>linear in the parameters</u>, in which the prediction $\hat{y}$ is given by:

$$\hat{y}(t) = \sum_1^n \hat{\theta}_i(t-1) s_i(t) \qquad \ldots (3.24)$$

The plant is assumed to satisfy the linear equation:

$$y(t) = \sum_1^n \theta_i s_i(t) + e(t),$$

in which e(t) is a disturbance term. (This need not correspond to a linear dynamic plant model as, for example, s_i could be $u^2(t-i)$.) The above equations can be written concisely as:

$$\hat{y}(t) = \hat{\theta}'(t-1) s(t), \quad \text{and} \quad y(t) = \theta' s(t) + e(t),$$

so that if the parameter error $\tilde{\theta}(t)$ is defined to be $\theta - \hat{\theta}(t)$

then:

$$\epsilon(t) = \tilde{\theta}'(t-1)s(t) + e(t) = s'(t)\tilde{\theta}(t-1) + e(t)$$

This useful result shows that the prediction _error of the model depends on both the modelling error θ and the noise $e(t)$. Recall that the prediction is directly required in predictive control, so that this equation shows how a bad model can affect adaptive control performance.

A recursive prediction-error algorithm provides a new estimate $\hat{\theta}(t)$ using an equation of the form:

$$\hat{\theta}(t) = \hat{\theta}(t-1) + a(t)M(t)s(t)\epsilon(t) \qquad \ldots (3.25)$$

where $a(t)$ is a scalar 'gain-factor' giving the step length and $M(t)$ is a matrix which modifies the parameter update direction. In general we want the algorithm to have the following properties:

1. When little is known about the plant, for example when the self-tuner starts up, the parameter estimates are allowed to move rapidly, hopefully to the 'true' values θ. Here $\epsilon(t)$ is interpreted as a modelling error and we are considering the tuning phase.

2. During steady-state operation the movements of the estimates should be small as then $\epsilon(t)$ is mostly noise.

3. The allowable rate of movement in the steady-state should depend on the expected speed at which the true parameters might change. This is the adaptive phase.

4. The computational burden per sample instant should not change with time, nor should the data vectors be allowed to expand indefinitely.

5. If n is large a simplified approach might be required for computational reasons; otherwise the 'best' method should be used.

Note that eqn.25 can be written as:

$$\hat{\theta}(t) = [I - a(t)M(t)s(t)s'(t)]\tilde{\theta}(t-1) - a(t)M(t)s(t)e(t)$$

so that a value of $a(t)$, say, which rapidly reduces the error also increases the effect of $e(t)$ on the parameters.

3.6.1 Simple Algorithms.

Consider the 'cost-function' $J = \epsilon^2 = (\tilde{\theta}'s+e)^2$. The gradient ∇J of J has components $\partial J/\partial\theta_i$ which equal $-2\epsilon(t)s_i u(t)$. To minimise J using the method of steepest descent, we choose to change the parameter estimates in the direction of $-\nabla J$. The simplest such method, known as the LMS algorithm, puts a(t) = μ and M(t) = I, giving:

$$\hat{\theta}(t) = \hat{\theta}(t-1) + \mu\, s(t)\, \epsilon(t)$$

This involves very little computation (one multiplication and addition per parameter), and is used when n is large, such as with weighting-sequence models. Typical applications are to adaptive equalizers in communications. However, the adaptive gain μ has to be chosen with care: divergence is obtained if μ is too large, and the critical value of μ depends on the autocorrelation matrix of the input data, which is not generally known. For adaptive control better methods are required.

A 'recursive learning' method is used by Richalet (46) and was developed from purely deterministic considerations in which the noise e(t) is ignored and the objective is to adapt as rapidly as possible:

$$\hat{\theta}(t) = \hat{\theta}(t-1) + \lambda/[s'(t)s(t)]\, s(t)\, \epsilon(t)$$

This can be shown to converge if $0 < \lambda < 2$ and 'optimally' for $\lambda = 1$. It scales the adaptive gain using known data, and can be thought of as an optimal LMS design. The computational requirements are approximately doubled but it produces much better performance. Table 1 gives an outline Fortran routine for implementing the method. SCAPRO is a function which computes the scalar product of two arrays. The vectors S and THETA are of dimension N, the number of parameters. SMALL is a constant which prevents overflow if the data vector s(t) is null (quiescent conditions).

TABLE 3.1 The recursive learning method

```
        SUBROUTINE LEARN(Y,S,THETA,N,RLAMDA)
C

        PERR = Y - SCAPRO(THETA,S,N)       !prediction error ε
        UNDER = SCAPRO (S,S,N)             !denominator
        IF (UNDER .LT. SMALL) GOTO 999     !little data?
        GAIN = RLAMDA*PERR / UNDER         !adaptive gain
C

        DO 1 I = 1,N                       !N parameters
1       THETA(I) = THETA(I) + GAIN*S(I)
```

Under special circumstances where the components of s(t) are uncorrelated with variance s^2, and the variance of e(t) is σ^2, it can be shown that the variance of parameter estimate i converges for large t to:

$$\text{Var } \{\bar{\theta}_i\} \to \lambda\, \sigma^2 / [n(2-\lambda)s^2]$$

This result shows that a large signal/noise ratio s/σ and a small value of λ is required to get an accurate model. Hence to get good adaptive speed initially and a good model eventually a <u>variable</u> λ should be used.

3.6.2 Recursive Least Squares (RLS).

If the identification problem is treated in a classical statistical framework of finding the best estimates of θ given data $\{s(t),y(t); \; t=1..N\}$, the method of least-squares is optimal. A function

$$S(\hat{\theta}) = \sum_{1}^{N} \epsilon^{2}(t,\hat{\theta})$$

is defined and minimised with respect to $\hat{\theta}$. The formulation however leads to a set of n equations in the n unknown parameters in which the vectors and matrices involved expand with N, the experiment's duration; this is unsuitable for on-line use. Moreover, the estimate $\hat{\theta}(N)$ tends to a constant vector as N increases (i.e. the variance of $\hat{\theta}$ tends to 0). This is acceptable if it is known that the plant is constant, but in general we want to track (slowly) varying parameters. To solve these problems we use a recursive method and modify S to weight 'old' data using a FADING MEMORY:

$$S_{1}(\hat{\theta}) = \sum_{1}^{N} \beta^{N-t} \epsilon^{2}(t,\hat{\theta})$$

Here β (which is a number slightly less than 1) is called the FORGETTING FACTOR, as the contribution of data j samples in the past is weighted by β^{j}. A useful measure here is the 'asymptotic sample length' or 'data window': $\alpha = 1/(1-\beta)$, which is the approximate number of samples which are significant for the current estimate $\hat{\theta}(t)$.

It can be shown (see Clarke (11) that the recursive least squares (RLS) method which is an exact equivalent of the nonrecursive version and which minimises S_1 is:

$$\hat{\theta}(t) = \hat{\theta}(t-1) + K(t) \; \epsilon(t) \qquad \qquad \ldots (3.26a)$$

$$K(t) = P(t-1) \; s(t) \; / \; [\beta + s'(t)P(t-1)s(t)] \qquad \ldots (3.26b)$$

$$P(t) = [I - K(t)s'(t)] \; P(t-1) \; / \; \beta \qquad \qquad \ldots (3.26c)$$

where $K(t)$ is the 'Kalman-gain' vector and $P(t)$ is an $n{\times}n$ symmetric matrix.

Algorithm 26 operates as follows. Initially $P(0)$ is chosen, typically as γI where γ is 0.1-100, say. At each time t, $\epsilon(t)$ is computed using the the new data and eqn.24; then eqn.26b is used to update $K(t)$, then eqn.26c to update $P(t)$ and finally eqn.26a to obtain the new parameter estimates $\hat{\theta}(t)$. Note that the data storage ($\hat{\theta}$, s, P and K) and computational requirements stay constant with time.

One advantage of the RLS method is that the matrix $P(t)$ is proportional to the covariance of the parameter estimates, so that a near-singular P indicates that there are badly estimated directions in parameter space. This could indicate, for example, that the number of parameters is too large or that the data is bad.

In practice there can be numerical problems with the updating, particularly with eqn.26c. $P(t)$ should be symmetrical and positive definite, but round-off errors may induce P to lose symmetry or definiteness. In this case the algorithm will go unstable and the estimates 'explode'. This (by Sod's Law) does not usually happen until about 5000 iterations, so that it would not be detected in simulations but would inevitably occur in a real plant controller. The cure, which is essential is practice, is to update a factor of $P(t)$. As P is positive, it can always be written as UDU', where U is an upper-triangular matrix with units down the diagonal and where D is a diagonal matrix. The updating is now that of U and D, and P reconstructed (if desired) from UDU'. General ideas are in Bierman (8), and Fortran coding is in Clarke (10),(11); Peterka (44) describes a related 'square-root' method.

3.6.2.1 **Properties Of RLS**. - If $P(0) = \gamma I_n$, where γ is large and the plant is noise-free and if the $s(t)$-vector is 'persistently exciting' (e.g. with an injected test signal) and if the plant is accurately modelled by a constant parameter vector θ, then:

$$\hat{\theta}(t) \rightarrow \theta \; \underline{exactly} \; \text{in n steps.}$$

This is the fastest possible rate of convergence. For example, if the self-tuner has 5 parameters then 5 samples (after the data vectors have been filled) are sufficient to get good estimates. With this quality of estimation there is plenty of leeway to deal with drifting plant and with noise.

3.7 EXPECTED ACCURACY OF THE ESTIMATES

The accuracy of the estimated model is a function of several aspects of the design and of the practical aspects of the plant:

1. The signal/noise ratio: if this is small then either slow convergence (small adaptive gain) or a poor model (large adaptive gain) is obtained. If the method is to be used as part of a self-tuner (which requires suitable precautions) a small value of λ or a value of β near to 1 is needed.

2. The particular method used. Simple methods can be 'tuned' to give either reasonably fast convergence or good noise-rejection. The RLS/UDU is better as its gain is chosen optimally from the data. For example if $P(t)$ is large, which implies poor estimates, then $K(t)$ would be large and thus allow the estimates to move quickly.

3. The number of parameters estimated. In general the fewer
    the number of parameters the better the model is as a
    predictor, provided that it is adequate.   If too many
    parameters are involved there will be poorly estimated
    directions; this is more relevent to methods such as
    pole-placement than to predictive controllers.

4. The inadequacy of the model structure.   e.g.:
    o choosing n too small
    o rapid fluctuations in θ
    o nonlinearities in the plant and/or actuators
    o stiction in the actuator which stops the control
       signal affecting the plant
    o quantization noise in the output transducer
    o unmeasured load-disturbances not modellable as 'white
       noise'.

3.7.1   Bias And Extended Least Squares.

     Consider the difference equation corresponding to the
stochastic model 4, which can be written in the form:

$$y(t) = -a_1 y(t-1) - \dots + b_0 u(t-k) + \dots + \epsilon(t)$$

where: $\epsilon(t) = e(t) + \dots + c_n e(t-n)$ is NOT a white-noise
signal.

The above difference equation appears to satisfy eqn.24 with
$\theta = \{a_1,..,b_n\}$ and $s(t) = \{-y(t-1),..,u(t-k-n)\}$, but it fails
to satisfy a crucial assumption of prediction error theory:
that the data vector s(t) should be independent of the
disturbance. For example $E\{y(t-1)\epsilon(t)\} = c_1\sigma^2$.   This means
that the identification algorithms described above will lead
to biased estimates, which is clearly bad for adaptive
control.   This bias is however zero if ϵ is white or if it is
small.   Hence for deterministic control problems (which are
rare in process control) RLS is sufficient. A rough test is
that if the signal:noise ratio is less than 10:1 the problem
cannot be treated by the simpler deterministic approach.

     Sometimes the bias cannot be ignored, and moreover it
may be necessary to estimate the C parameters (for example
with pole-placement control where the set-point w(t) varies).
One way to get accurate estimates is to use extended least
squares which works as follows:

     If the error terms e(t-i) were known as well as u(t-i)
and y(t-i), we can use a prediction error method with
parameters $\theta = \{a_1,..,b_0,..,c_1..\}$ and   with   data
$\{-y(t-1),..,u(t-k),..,e(t-1)\}$. The corresponding error here
would be simply e(t), which is white, so RLS (etc.) would
give unbiased estimates.   As the noise term e(t-i) is not
known we proxy it by estimates $\hat{e}(t-i)$ given by the model:

$$\hat{e}(t) = y(t) + \hat{a}_1 y(t-1) + .. - \hat{b}_0 u(t-k) - .. - \hat{c}_1 \hat{e}(t-1) - ..$$

This estimated error is then used in the next iteration to proxy $e(t-1)$, etc., and it can be shown under certain circumstances that both the parameters and the proxied error converge to the true values. ELS is however less robust than RLS and should be used with care: there are certain C polynomials which do not allow convergence, though in practice good results have been reported.

Note here that there are two important special cases. In a pure regulator, a pole-placement method satisfies eqn.23 in which the error term is just $e(t)$, so simple RLS can be used. The predictive models of eqn.11a and eqn.15a for T = C have an error $Ee(t+k)$ which is in fact independent of the data $u(t)$ and $y(t)$. Hence RLS can again be used. In practice it has been found that if there are a reasonable number of set-point changes to keep up the signal/noise ratio that RLS is also effective even in cases where the above discussion would indicate bias.

3.8   SELF-TUNING

A self-tuner connects the estimator to a control design algorithm. To show how this is done the minimum variance self-tuner of Astrom and Wittenmark (6) will be described in which model 4 is assumed and where the predictor model 11 with T = C can be written:

$$C(z^{-1})p(t) = F(z^{-1})y(t) + G(z^{-1})u(t) \qquad \ldots (3.27a)$$

$$y(t+k) = p(t) + E(z^{-1})e(t+k) \qquad \ldots (3.27b)$$

The corresponding control law for $w(t) = 0$ is from eqn.16:

$$F(z^{-1})y(t) + G(z^{-1})u(t) = 0 \qquad \ldots (3.27c)$$

Now if $H(z^{-1}) = z[1-C(z^{-1})]$ the prediction at $t-k$ becomes:

$$p(t-k) = F(z^{-1})u(t-k) + G(z^{-1})u(t-k) + H(z^{-1})p(t-k-1)$$

But control 27c has set $p(t-k-1)$, $p(t-k-2)$ .. to 0, so:

$$y(t) = F(z^{-1})u(t-k) + G(z^{-1})u(t-k) + E(z^{-1})e(t)$$

i.e. $$y(t) = f_0 y(t-k) + .. + g_0 u(t-k) + .. + \epsilon(t) \qquad \ldots (3.28)$$

We can consider this model to predict the present outcome $y(t)$ based on previous data $y(t-k)$, $u(t-k)$. As $\epsilon(t)$ is simply a moving average of order k, it contains no term which is correlated with the data. Hence RLS (or any other estimation algorithm) can be used to obtain estimates of the unknown parameters $\{f_i, g_i\}$. The certainty-equivalent self-tuner simply accepts these estimates as if they were exact and exerts a control:

$$\hat{f}_0 y(t) + \hat{f}_1 y(t-1) + \ldots + \hat{g}_0 u(t) + \hat{g}_1 u(t-1) + \ldots = 0$$

Note that the control $u(t)$ is unaffected if an arbitrary factor α multiplies the above equation, implying that the estimates will not be unique. To avoid 'wandering' of the parameters, a value of any parameter can be assumed (this problem does not arise in the general case where $w(t)$ is nonzero). Typically a value $\bar{g}$ is assumed for g_0, and provided $0.5b < \bar{g} < \infty$ the algorithm will still converge to give the correct control action. The control is then:

$$u(t) = - [\hat{f}_0 y(t) + \ldots + \hat{g}_1 u(t-1) + \ldots] / \bar{g} \qquad \ldots (3.29)$$

and the corresponding model used in RLS estimation is:

$$y(t) - \bar{g}u(t-k) = f_0 y(t-k) + .+ g_1 u(t-k-1) + .+ \epsilon(t) \qquad \ldots (3.30)$$

The operation of the self tuner is as follows. At each sample instant t:

1. From the current output $y(t)$ form $y(t) - \bar{g}u(t-k)$ and update the parameters $\hat{f}$ and $\hat{g}$ using equations 26.

2. Given the parameter estimates, generate the control $u(t)$ from eqn. 29.

3. Shift all arrays along one place ready for the next sample.

4. Go to 1.

This self-tuner is called IMPLICIT as the estimated parameters are those of the feedback controller; an EXPLICIT self-tuner estimates the 'ordinary' plant model of eqn. 4 and then performs a design calculation (e.g. solves a Diophantine equation). Predictive controllers lead naturally to implicit self-tuners; explicit self-tuners (such as pole-placement) require more calculations and are possibly more sensitive to parameter errors. In MRAC designs (Narendra and Monopoli (43)) the terms are DIRECT and INDIRECT.

Suppose two routines SAVE and MOVE are available, in which SAVE moves old data one place along an array and slots in the new data, whilst MOVE transfers data from one array to another. Then the basic implementation of the above self-tuner is shown in Table 2.

TABLE 3.2 A self-tuner for minimising $E\{y^2(t)\}$

```
<acquire data y(t) into Y>
YBAR = Y - GBAR*USAVE(K)                  !ḡ fixed
CALL MOVE (YSAVE(K),S,NY)                 !old y into s(t)
CALL MOVE (USAVE(K+1),S(NY+1),NU)
CALL RLS (YBAR,S,THETA,NY+NU,FORGET)
U = -(SCAPRO(THETA,YSAVE,NY) +
+          SCAPRO(THETA(NY+1),USAVE,NU))/GBAR
IF (U .GT. UMAX) U = UMAX                 !clip u(t)
IF (U .LT. UMIN) U = UMIN
CALL SAVE (U,USAVE,NU+K)                  !save u(t)
CALL SAVE (Y,YSAVE,NY+K)                  !and y(t)
```

Note that the estimation requires data in the USAVE and YSAVE vectors as far as NU+K and NY+K in the past. Hence the self-tuning algorithm should be sequenced to allow the data vectors to be filled with good data before estimation is allowed to start. The clipping of u(t) in the above coding is to cover the practical case where there are physical limits on the control action. Suppose the desired value of U is 200, but the actuator saturates at 100. Then if the above clipping is not done, the data in the USAVE array would not correspond to that sent to the plant, and the estimated parameters would deviate from the true values.

3.8.1 Operating The Self-tuner.

There are several choices to be made to set-up a self-tuner for best performance. Mostly these are easy to make and the closed-loop control is relatively insensitive to the values chosen. Considering the simple algorithm described above, the relevant parameters are:

1. The sample-time h. This is generally the most critical parameter. Typically 1/10 of the dominant plant time constant is taken, but if there is a significant dead-time h should be such that k is 2-3. If the control is bad, possibly due to nonminimum-phase zeros, h should be increased or a different law such as pole-placement or general predictive control used instead.

2. The model order n. A good choice here is 3. The F polynomial has degree n-1 and the G polynomial has degree n+k-1, so about 2+4 = 6 (or 7) parameters would need to be estimated. If a control weighting Q is used fewer parameters can be effective.

3. The initial parameters $\hat{\theta}(0)$. A good choice is to make the start-up control a simple low-gain proportional law, or first to identify the plant in open-loop to obtain reasonable estimates.

4. The forgetting factor β. A data-window $\alpha = 1/(1-\beta)$ of 50 implies a 'rapidly' varying plant; if $\alpha = 1000$ the plant is taken to be reasonably steady. A <u>variable</u> forgetting factor can be used (Fortescue et al (23)), but the 'best' such algorithm is not clear. Generally P(0) is taken to be a large diagonal matrix, except when the initial parameters are well known (as in batch applications).

5. The fixed parameter $\bar{g}$. This can be done by making the corresponding element in P(0) zero; if the data is scaled properly (e.g. 0-100%) the value is quite easy to choose as it corresponds to the first nonzero value on the step response.

When the self-tuner has been set-up its operation can be sequenced: first the data vectors should be filled (about n+2k samples), then the parameters should be estimated (about a further 2n samples), then closed-loop control asserted. During the start-up phase a test-signal could be used. It may be possible to close the loop immediately (in simulations anyway), though quite large control signals could result which naturally would give good parameter estimates. By various choices of $\hat{\theta}(0)$, P(0) and constraints UMAX,UMIN a whole range of initial control actions are possible. For noncritical plant there is freedom to allow large controls, with correspondingly rapid tuning.

The simple minimum-variance control law is not recommended for practical applications as it cannot cope with nonminimum-phase plant or with variable dead-time. Either the detuned model-following or the pole-placement algorithms are preferable; there is then a rather more complex initialisation but again there is no difficulty in finding good values provided some plant knowledge is used (such as the open-loop response time).

3.9 <u>JACKETING</u>

In practice the parameter estimator is the critical part of a self-tuner: it should be switched on only if the data-vector is providing information which could improve the model. In many cases full adaptation during normal operating conditions would lead to a steady deterioration of the model as nonlinearities, quantization noise and load disturbances would predominate. 'Jacketing' software describes the process by which the estimator is monitored to allow or to inhibit estimation on the judgement of likely performance. At one extreme it could simply consist of a switch under the control of the operator, but in general the recursive estimator becomes:

$$\hat{\theta}(t) = \hat{\theta}(t-1) + j(t)\ a(t)\ M(t)\ s(t)\ \epsilon(t)$$

where j(t) is either 1 (enabled) or 0 (inhibited). The switch j(t) would be set to 0 depending on estimation 'dead-bands' Dx:

1. If $|\Delta u(t)|$ < Du the change of control might not affect
    the process (e.g. a valve with stiction).

2. If $|\Delta y(t)|$ < Dy the change in output might be due to
    measurement or to quantization noise. For example a real
    change less than one transducer quantum would not be
    detected, and a naive estimator would deduce a process
    gain of zero.

3. If $|y(t)-w(t)|$ < De the controlled plant could be in a
    quiescent state in which the data in unlikely to be
    exciting.

4. If $|\epsilon(t)|$ > Dϵ the prediction error could be due to a
    load-disturbance.

Note that even if j(t) is set to 0 by any of the above
conditions being true, the data vector s(t) should still be
updated in case estimation resumes later.

    Although self-tuning is derived assuming that the
currently estimated model is used in the controller, this
need not be the case. In practice <u>several</u> models can be
used:

1. θ_a = 'currently estimated model', updated when j=1.

2. θ_b = 'best model' used in the control design.

3. θ_c = 'initial model', etc.

A possible 'jacket' could consist of:

1. <u>if</u> good-data <u>then</u> ‹update θ_a›

2. <u>if</u> θ_a predicts better than θ_b for a while <u>then</u> ‹transfer
    θ_a to θ_b and update the controller parameters›

Another possibility is to monitor the predictions of all the
models to detect a significant plant change, and if so to
start self-tuning again from its initial conditions. Limits
on individual parameters or on the controller gain can be
included.

3.9.1 <u>Offsets</u>.

    An offset arises when the average value of y(t) does not
equal the set-point w(t), which is assumed to be constant.
Some self-tuning methods can lead to offsets if precautions
are not taken: a discussion is in Clarke et al (17).
Inspection of eqn.21 shows that with a general predictive
controller both Q(1) and E(1) should be 0, and P(1) should be
1. This implies that Q must contain a <u>differencing</u> element

and hence the associated cost-function J_1 weights <u>changes</u> in control $u(t)-u(t-1)$.

One way to avoid offsets is to augment the plant with an integrator and to ensure that the gain associated with $w(t)$ equals that of the gain of the feedback path. It is better, however, to use an incremental predictor as this also ensures that the data in $s(t)$ has zero mean - a precondition for good estimation performance. With simple assumptions about the plant (such as a Brownian motion disturbance $x(t)$) it is found that self-tuning PID control laws arise naturally (Gawthrop (27), Proudfoot et al (45)).

3.10 <u>APPLICATIONS</u>

A self-tuning controller is simple enough to be mounted on an 8-bit microcomputer (Clarke and Gawthrop (16)), even though floating-point arithmetic is required for the estimation as the parameters have a potentially wide dynamic range. Hence there are several implementation options:

o   as a stand-alone controller for critical single-loop applications (45); Andreiev(2); see also ASEA's NOVATUNE

o   as part of a DDC package with a more powerful CPU in which several loops are tuned simultaneously (Fjeld and Wilhelm (22))

o   as part of a distributed control system (Halme et al (30))

o   as a self-tuned predictor in which the operator closes the loop.

Practical experience with self-tuning has been growing rapidly over the last few years - more so than with any other control idea. This is because that the methods are not difficult to implement (though care with jacketing is required) and appear to meet a real industrial need. There are many cases in which self-tuning has been in routine operation on an industrial plant, and surveys appear in (5) (7) (9) (20) (21) (22) (32) (34) (41) (42) (43) (50) etc. These cover a wide range of processes from paper-making and ship-steering to batch-reactor and distillation column regulation. Simple self-tuners are being considered for applications such as heating and air-conditioning systems and diesel engine control. With the appearance of commercial self-tuners it is possible that adaptive control will become routinely applied in industry.

Self-tuners do not remove the need for the control engineer's skill, but now he has to consider the real control objective of the plant so that an appropriate design method can be chosen. Moreover the intelligence built into a self-tuner will enable automatic plant diagnosis to be included in a DDC package. Self-tuning theory itself is being extended to consider important questions of robustness (Gawthrop and Lim (28)) and new algorithms such as LQG (Lam (36)). The problems of convergence and of good jacketing (Schumann et al (48)) are also of central importance, particularly for processes with rapidly varying parameters (as in aerospace) or with significantly variable dead-time. If the next decade shows the same progress as the last, it promises to be an exciting time.

REFERENCES

1.   Allidina,A.Y., Hughes,F.M. and Tye,C., 1981,
        Proc.IEE, Vol.128, Pt.D, No.6, pp.283-291.

2.   Andreiev,N., 1981, Control Engineering, August.

3.   Astrom,K.J.", 1980, in 'Applications of Adaptive
        Control', (ed.) Narendra and Monopoli,
        Academic Press.

4.   Astrom,K.J.; 'Ziegler-Nichols auto-tuners', 1982,
        Report LUDFD2/(TFRT-3167)/01-025/(1982),
        Lund Institute of Technology.

5.   Astrom,K.J., 1983, Automatica,
        Vol.19, No.5, pp.471-486.

6.   Astrom,K.J. and Wittenmark,B., 1973,
        Automatica, Vol.9, No.2, pp.185-199.

7.   Belanger,P.R., 1980, in 'Applications of Adaptive
        Control', (ed.) Narendra and Monopoli,
        Academic Press.

8.   Bierman,G.J., 1977, 'Factorization methods for
        discrete system estimation', Academic Press.

9.   Cegrell,T. and Hedqvist,T., 1975, Automatica,
        Vol.11, No.1, pp.53-59.

10.   Clarke,D.W., 1980, in 'Numerical techniques for
        stochastic systems' (ed.) Archetti and Cugiani,
        North-Holland.

11.   Clarke,D.W., 1981, in 'Self-tuning and adaptive
        control' (ed.) Harris and Billings,
        Peter Perigrinus.

12.   Clarke,D.W., 1982, Opt.Control App. and Methods,
        Vol.3, pp.323-335.

13.   Clarke,D.W., 1982, Trans.Inst.M.C.,
        Vol.5, No.2, pp.59-69.

14. Clarke,D.W. and Gawthrop,P.J., 1975, <u>Proc.IEE</u>,
     Vol.122, No.9, pp.929-934.

15. Clarke,D.W. and Gawthrop,P.J., 1979, <u>Proc.IEE</u>,
     Vol.126, No.6, pp.633-640.

16. Clarke,D.W. and Gawthrop,P.J., 1981, <u>Automatica</u>,
     Vol.17, No.1, pp.233-244.

17. Clarke,D.W., Hodgson,A.J.F. and Tuffs,P.S., 1983,
     <u>Proc.IEE</u>, Vol.130, Pt.D, No.5, pp.217-225.

18. De Keyser,R.M.C. and van Cauwenberghe,A.R., 1979,
     'A self-tuning predictor as operator guide', IFAC
     Symposium on Identification and System Parameter
     Estimation, Darmstadt, FRG.

19. De Keyser,R.M.C. and van Cauwenberghe,A.R., 1981,
     <u>Automatica</u>, Vol.17, No.1, pp.167-174.

20. Dexter,A.L., 1981, <u>Automatica</u>,
     Vol.17, No.3, pp.483-492.

21. Dumont,G.A. and Belanger,P.R., 1978,
     <u>IEEE Trans.Autom.Control</u>, Vol.AC-23,
     No.4, pp.532-538.

22. Fjeld,M. and Wilhelm,R.G., 1981, <u>Control
     Engineering</u>,   October, pp.99-102.

23. Fortescue,T.R., Kershenbaum,L.S. and Ydstie,B.E.,
     1981, <u>Automatica</u>, Vol.17, No.6, pp.831-835.

24. Franklin,G.F. and Powell,J.D., 1980, 'Digital
     control of dynamic systems', Addison-Wesley.

25. Gawthrop,P.J., 1977, <u>Proc.IEE</u>,
     Vol.124, No.10, pp.889-894.

26. Gawthrop,P.J., 1980, <u>Proc.IEE</u>,
     Vol.127, Pt.D, No.5, pp.229-236.

27. Gawthrop,P.J., 1982, 'Self-tuning PI and PID
     controllers', IEEE Conference on Applications of
     Adaptive and Mutivariable Control, Hull.

28. Gawthrop,P.J. and Lim,K.W., 1982, <u>Proc.IEE</u>,
     Vol.129, Pt.D, No.1, pp.21-29.

29. Grimble,M.J., 1981, <u>Int.J.Control</u>,
     Vol.33, No.4, pp.751-762.

30. Halme,A., Ahava,O., Karjalainen,T., Torvikoski,T.
     and Savolainen,V., 1981, 'Implementing and testing
     of some advanced control schemes in a
     microprocessors Based process instrumentation
     system', IFAC Congress, Kyoto.

31.   Hodgson,A.J.F., 1982, 'Problems of integrity in
         applications of adaptive controllers',
         OUEL report 1436/82.

32.   Hodgson,A.J.F. and Clarke,D.W., 1982, 'Self-tuning
         applied to batch reactors', IEEE Conference on
         Applications of Adaptive and Multivariable
         Control, Hull.

33.   Isermann,R., 1981, 'Digital control systems',
         Springer-Verlag.

34.   Kallstrom,C.G. and Astrom,K.J., 1978, 'Adaptive
         autopilots for large tankers',
         IFAC Congress, Helsinki.

35.   Kurz,H., Isermann,R. and Schumann,R., 1980,
         Automatica, Vol.16, No.2, pp.117-133.

36.   Lam,K.P., 1980, 'Implicit and explicit self-tuning
         controllers', OUEL report 1134/80.

37.   Latawiec, K. and Chyra, M., 1983, Automatica,
         Vol.19, No.4, pp.419-424.

38.   Lim,K.W., 1982, 'Robustness of self-tuning
         controllers', OUEL report 1422/82.

39.   Ljung,L., 1977, IEEE Trans.Autom.Control,
         Vol.AC-22, No.4, pp.551-575.

40.   Ljung,L., 1978, IEEE Trans.Autom.Control,
         Vol.AC-23, No.5, pp.770-783.

41.   Moden,P.E. and Nybrant,T.,1980, 'Adaptive control
         of rotary drum driers', IFAC Symposium on Digital
         Computer Applications to Process Control,
         Dusseldorf, FRG.

42.   Morris,A.J., Nazer,Y., Wood,R.K. and Lieuson,H.,
         1980, 'Evaluation of self-tuning controllers for
         distillation column control', IFAC Symposium on
         Digital Computer Applications to Process Control,
         Dusseldorf, FRG.

43.   Narendra,K.S. and Monopoli,R.V. (ed.), 1980,
         'Applications of adaptive control', Academic Press.

44.   Peterka,V., 1975, Kybernetika, Vol.11,
         No.1, pp.53-67.

45.   Proudfoot,C.G., Gawthrop,P.J. and Jacobs, O.L.R.,
         1983, Proc.IEE, Vol.130, Pt.D., No.5, pp.267-272.

46.   Richalet,J., Rault,A., Testud,J.L. and Papon,J.,
         1978, Automatica, Vol.14, No.5, pp.413-428.

47.   Sandoz,D.J. and Swanick,B.H., 1972, Int.J.Control,
      Vol.16, No.2, pp.243-260.

48.   Schumann,R., Lachmann,K.H. and Isermann,R., 1981,
      'Towards applicability of parameter adaptive
      control algorithms', IFAC Congress, Kyoto.

49.   Smith,O.J.M., 1959, Instr.Soc. of America Journal,
      Vol.6, No.2, pp.28-33.

50.   Unbehauen,H. (ed.), 1980, 'Methods and applications
      in adaptive control', Springer-Verlag.

51.   Wellstead,P.E., Edmunds,J.M., Prager,D. and
      Zanker,P., 1979, Int.J.Control, Vol.30,
      No.1, pp.1-26.

52.   Whittle,P., 1963, 'Prediction and regulation by
      linear least-squares methods,
      English Universities Press.

53.   Wittenmark,B., 1973, 'Self-tuning regulators',
      Report 7312, Division of Automatic Control,
      Lund Institute of Technology.

54.   Yaglom,A.M., 1973, 'An introduction to the theory of
      stationary random functions'
      (translated by R.A. Silverman), Dover.

55.   Zanker,P.M. and Wellstead,P.E., 1979, 'Practical
      features of self-tuning', IEE Conference on Trends
      in On-line Computer Control Systems, Sheffield.

56.   Ziegler,J.G. and Nichols,N.B., 1942, Trans.ASME,
      Vol.64, pp.759-768.

Chapter 4

Real time computer control— CAD for digital controller design

A.S. Morris

4.1 INTRODUCTION

This chapter is concerned with computer implementation of classical techniques of control system analysis. Consideration is limited to computer aided design of single-input, single-output systems, for which software packages are readily available. Multivariable system design is still very much the subject of active research and whilst some software for the design of multivariable systems exists, it is not so widely available.

Classical techniques of control system analysis have been developed over several decades and are now well established and widely accepted. The frequency domain design methods of Nyquist (1), Bode (2), Nichols (3), and Evans' (4) root locus technique have proved remarkable successful for the design of single-input, single-output systems, and are now essential tools of the practising control engineer.

A common feature of these methods is the requirement to calculate the system gain and phase values for a range of frequency values and then to present these in some graphical form. System compensators are then designed by appropriate manipulation of this graphical information to achieve an overall system with satisfactory gain and phase margins. Any past student of control engineering will remember exercises in applying these techniques of system analysis and design which formed part of the course, and will be well aware of the rather laborious nature of producing such graphs. Although calculators have done much to reduce the arithmetic burden of calculating the necessary data, the process of committing this information to graph paper remains very laborious and time consuming.

Since the advent of the interactive minicomputer some ten years ago, much effort has gone into writing software which will allow a computer to analyse systems and produce information in the form of a Nyquist diagram, Bode plot etc. on a graphics display terminal connected to the computer. Some excellent computer-aided control system design packages have resulted from this work.

At the same time as the availability of computers has allowed the computerisation of control system design techniques, the digital computer has also been exploited as a very convenient, accurate and cost-effective means of implementing system control schemes. However digital computer control brings with it new problems of having to analyse a process as a sampled-data rather than continuous system, requiring some modification of the classical frequency domain design techniques. For instance, the left hand half plane stability region of the s-plane is transposed to the unit circle stability region in the z-plane for discrete systems, and in order to apply Bode methods the bilinear transformation from the z-plane to w-plane is often applied. Packages normally provide for transformation between the s, z, and w planes and allow analysis in each plane.

As well as offering classical frequency domain design facilities, many packages provide for time domain analysis. This reflects the importance in many systems of having adequate dynamic performance as well as good stability margins in their frequency response. Such time domain analysis algorithms always include step response computation and usually provide ramp and impulse responses as well.

Perhaps the one benefit of computer aided control system design packages which is most immediately apparent to the practising control engineer is his emancipation from the labour involved in the manual production of frequency domain graphs. However, the computer not only frees an engineer from the drudgery of using classical system design techniques: it also performs the analysis orders of magnitude faster. The benefits do not even end there, for the computer greatly diminishes the incidence of errors through replacing the error-prone human calculation of gain and phase data by a simple question and answer session about the system, where information entered is redisplayed for verification. This redisplaying by the computer of information entered by the engineer is very important. Any 'slips of the finger' in entering data at a keyboard are thereby made obvious and can be readily corrected.

Work on control system design packages has proceeded in a number of universities, though these have tended to be independent developments with little coordination between them being apparent. As a result, a number of similar packages are available which, whilst all offering a common core of the major design techniques, nevertheless differ appreciably in many ancillary features. There is a considerable difference also in the standards of documentation and testing of these various available packages, and some which are adequate for undergraduate student exercises in system design can break down when used as a tool in the analysis of more complicated real-life problems. This is unfortunate but a fact of life about much university-originated software, which is rarely marketed commercially but rather swapped from one university to another on the basis of personal relationships between individuals.

The particular package available in the Control Engineering Department at Sheffield is called TRIP. This was written at Delft University in the Netherlands and was kindly passed on by P.P.J. van den Bosch of that university. It is an excellent package, which is well documented and free of performance 'bugs' so far as our considerable use of it to date has shown. TRIP is written in Fortran and

implemented on a Perkin-Elmer 3220 computer at Sheffield.
    Whilst the rest of this chapter is devoted to a des-
cription of the features and use of this one particular
design package, the facilities available and procedures involved are very similar in most other such packages. The
material should therefore be viewed as a general tutorial on
the working concepts of computer-aided control system design,
with the approach required by TRIP well serving to illustrate
the techniques generally necessary with such packages. The
reader ought therefore to find this material to be of interest and useful whether or not TRIP is the particular package which he ultimately uses.

4.2 TRIP

    TRIP stands for TRansformation and Identification Program.
It provides facilities for transformation between alternative
forms of system representation, and identification of the
frequency and time domain characteristics of the system. Its
applicability is restricted to linear, single-input, single-
output, time-invariant systems. Full details of the package
can be found in the TRIP manual by Schouten (5).

4.2.1 Standard System Representations And Transformations

    Various forms of system representation are allowed, with
appropriate codes, as shown in Table 4.1 and Figure 4.1.
Transformations between these representations are provided,
as shown in Figure 4.1 and Table 4.2. Arrows in Figure 4.1
between system states denote possible transformations. The
absence of an arrow means that a transformation is not
possible in the package (even though it may be theoretically
possible).
    As shown in Tables 4.1 and 4.2, all system representa-
tions are defined by two-letter codes and all transformations
by four-letter codes. Transformation codes are defined by
the code letters of the initial system representation followed by the code letters of the destination system representation. Thus the code for the transformation from continuous transfer function form (SS) to discrete transfer
function form (ZZ) is SSZZ. Table 4.2 has been abridged to
show only some typical transformation codes. The codes for
all other possible transformations can be readily derived
by recourse to Figure 4.1.
    Consideration of the possible transformations revealed
by Figure 4.1 shows that, apart from the classical design
transformations from transfer functions to the time and frequency domains, some reverse transformations from the time
and frequency domains to transfer function form are also
provided. These 'black box' system identification procedures which operate on system time and frequency response
data are fully described in the TRIP manual (5) in respect
of the algorithms employed. Whilst these procedures are
available in TRIP, no further consideration will be given
to them in this chapter as they do not fall within the
bounds of the classical analysis techniques being discussed.

TABLE 4.1 Valid System Representations and Codes

Code	Representation
SS Transfer function H(s)	$\dfrac{K'(s-z_1)(s-z_2)\ldots\ldots(s-z_j)e^{-sT'}}{(s-p_1)(s-p_2)\ldots\ldots(s-p_i)}$ for i poles, j zeros and time delay T'
WW Transfer function H(w)	$\dfrac{K'(w-z_1)(w-z_2)\ldots\ldots(w-z_j)}{(w-p_1)(w-p_2)\ldots\ldots(w-p_i)}\left(\dfrac{1+w}{1-w}\right)^{\frac{-T'}{T}}$ for i poles, j zeros, time delay T', sample time T
ZZ Transfer function H(z)	$\dfrac{K'(z-z_1)(z-z_2)\ldots\ldots(z-z_j)e^{-T'/T}}{(z-p_1)(z-p_2)\ldots\ldots(z-p_i)}$
MA Continuous matrix model	$\dot{x} = Ax+Bu$; $y = Cx+Du$
MZ Discrete matrix model	$x(K+1)=\emptyset x(K)+\Delta u(K)$; $y(K+1)=C'x(K)+D'u(K)$
FR Frequency domain model	(Bode or Nyquist data)
TY Time domain model	(Step, ramp or impulse response data).

TABLE 4.2 Codes for System Transformation Operations (examples only)

Code	Transformation
SSZZ	Continuous transfer function H(s) to discrete transfer function H(z)
ZZSS	Discrete transfer function H(z) to continuous transfer function H(s)
SSSS	Open loop continuous transfer function H(s) to closed loop continuous transfer function with feedback: $\dfrac{H(s)}{1-KH(s)}$
ZZTY	Discrete transfer function model to time response data
etc.	

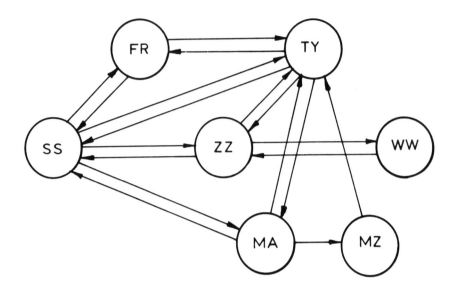

Fig.4.1   System representations and transformations

Seven common areas are reserved within the program for
each of the seven alternative forms of system description
defined in Table 4.1.   Thus whenever a system transformation
is computed, both the original and new forms are preserved
(until overwritten by a further transformation to the same
type of system description).   If therefore a continuous system is described to the package and subsequently a continuous to discrete transformation (SSZZ) is executed, this will
result in two representations being stored together in the
program, the continuous and discrete transfer function
models.   Two exceptions to this are the SSSS and ZZZZ transformations which convert an open-loop system representation
to closed loop, by applying feedback.   As there is only one
storage area for SS and ZZ models, the open-loop models
originally stored in these areas are overwritten by closed-
loop models.   The open-loop system representations are
thereby lost, as no inverse transformation back from closed
to open-loop is available.

4.2.2. Transformation Parameters

The execution of transformations between legal forms of
system representation is controlled by parameters.   These
parameters must be set up before the transformation is executed.   The parameters required for each individual transformation and their definition are described in detail in
Schouten   (5).   However, the following examples will serve to
illustrate the general form taken by parameters.

SSZZ
This transformation requires two parameters.
Parameter one (P1) defines the presence or absence of a
zero order hold. (P1=0 for no hold, P1=1 for zero-order
hold included).
Parameter two (P2) defines the sample time.

SSFR
This transformation requires four parameters.
Parameter 1 (P1) defines the type of frequency response
data required. (P1=1 for Bode diagram, P1=2 for
Nyquist plot).
Parameter 2 (P2) defines the frequency range scaling
method. (P2=1 for automatic choice of frequency range,
P2=2 for frequency range defined by parameters 3 and 4).
Parameters 3 and 4 define the minimum and maximum
values respectively of the required frequency range
(valid for P2=2 only).

4.2.3 Special Transformations

Apart from transformations between the seven forms of
system representation described, certain other transformations are provided for special purposes, as shown in Table
4.3. These cater for transformations which go outside the
bounds of the seven standard types. They either have an input of one of the seven standard system types and a special
output, or an output of one of the seven standard types with
a special input. PORO, for example, is a transformation with
a transfer function output (SS,ZZ or WW model) and an input
polynomial defined by the transformation parameters. This
allows a system transfer function to be entered as a ratio of
two polynomials instead of in factored form.

TABLE 4.3   Special transformations (subset only**)

Code	Transformation
PORO	Input of polynomials and transformation to H(s), H(z) or H(w) in factored form (SS,ZZ or WW model).
ROPO	Calculation of numerator and denominator poly- nomials from H(s), H(z), or H(w) transfer function in factored form.
ROLO	Calculation of root locus from H(s), H(z) or H(w) transfer function.
WWWW	Calculation of Bode diagram from H(w) transfer function.
EIGV	Calculation of eigenvalues from matrix model.
**	Other special transformations are also available- see Schouten (5).

4.2.4   Command Structure

Thus far, we have defined the structure of system representations and transformations, and the transformation parameters. Various commands are provided in the package to read in system data, define parameters, execute transformations, and display time and frequency response data. System structure data and parameter values can also be changed at any stage by entering an update mode.

Provision is made for using disc files to store and retrieve system models by model read and write commands. This facilitates experimenting with model changes designed to improve system performance, with the capability of readily returning to the original model where modifications made are unsatisfactory. This is particularly useful for storing open and closed loop forms of the same model.

TRIP allows storage of any of its seven model types. The model display mode allows superimposition on the same graph of two or more models stored in separate disc files. This is useful for comparing time or frequency responses obtained from different system models.

4.3   ANALYSIS OF CONTINUOUS SYSTEMS USING TRIP

The following example shows the capabilities of TRIP for analysing continuous system characteristics in the frequency and time domains. The transfer function of this example system is:

$$F(s) = \frac{7780}{s(s+20)(s^2 + 10s + 100)}$$

This is appropriate for entry into the TRIP package as an SS type model, either in polynomial form:

$$F(s) = \frac{7780}{2000s + 300s^2 + 30s^3 + s^4}$$

or in factored form:

$$F(s) = \frac{7780}{s(s+20)(s+5+0.866j)(s+5-0.866j)}$$

The first of these two alternative forms is preferable in this case, as it avoids having to calculate the complex poles arising out of the term $(s^2 + 10s + 100)$ prior to entering the model into TRIP.

Time domain responses can be calculated by transformation (SSTY) to time model form. TRIP can calculate step, ramp or impulse responses for any amplitude of input signal and over any time interval. The response will be open or closed loop according to whether or not the original open-loop system model has been converted to closed loop form by the SSSS transformation. Fig. 4.2 shows the closed-loop step response produced for the system.

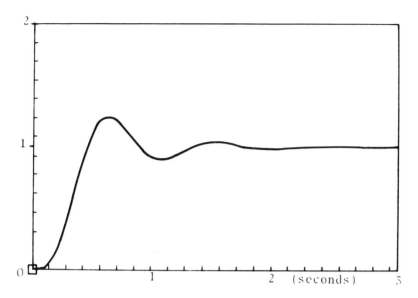

Fig. 4.2   Closed-loop step response of continuous
           system

Frequency domain responses are obtained in a similar
way, by transformation (SSFR) to frequency model form.
These can be displayed in either Nyquist or Bode form, with
user-defined frequency ranges. Figs. 4.3 and 4.4 show respectively the Nyquist and Bode diagrams produced. The gain
margin of 6.1dB and phase margin of 62º indicated are consistent with the form of the closed-loop step response
(Fig. 4.1).
    TRIP also enables computation and display of the root
locus. That produced for the example system above is shown
in Fig. 4.5.

4.4   ANALYSIS OF DISCRETE SYSTEMS USING TRIP

Discrete systems automatically arise when a continuous
process is sampled and controlled by a digital computer. As
the controlled process is usually modelled in terms of the
Laplace transfer functions of its constituent parts, it is
normally appropriate to commence analysis by entering the
continuous process transfer function into the TRIP package
and then allow the package to carry out the conversion to a
discrete representation. However, where a discrete transfer
function of the process is available, as a result of some
identification procedure for instance, the package allows
direct entry of the system model in z-transfer function form.
    As an example, a system having the continuous transfer
function

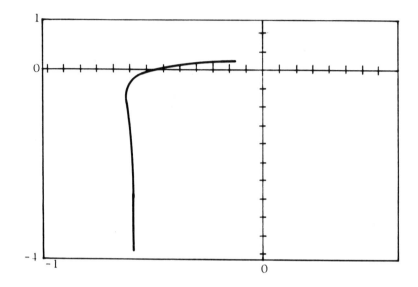

Fig. 4.3   Nyquist diagram from continuous system

$$F(s) = \frac{5}{s(s+2)}$$

will be used. This might for instance represent an idealised shunt field controlled d.c. motor. If the digital controller is represented as a sampler and zero order hold, and unity feedback is applied, the system block diagram becomes:

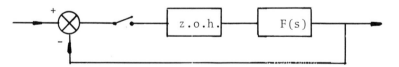

This model is suitable for entering into the computer as an SS type model. TRIP then offers the option of including a zero order hold automatically during the transformation (SSZZ) from a continuous to a discrete transfer function model.

Figure 4.6 shows the computed closed loop step response of the model. In this case, the overshoot of 26% is probably unacceptable.

The open loop z-transfer function of the combined sampler, zero order hold and process is given by

$$G(z) = \frac{0.0226(z+0.94)}{(z-1)(z-0.819)}$$

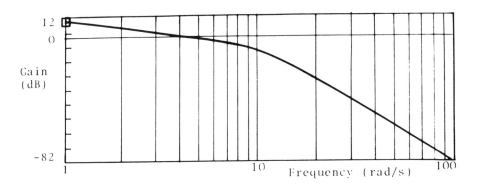

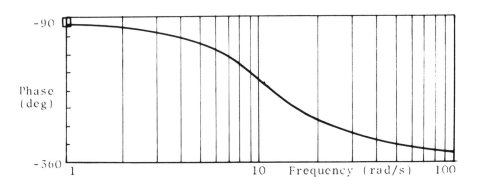

Fig. 4.4   Bode diagram from continuous system

An obvious line of investigation is to include a digital
filter such as

$$D(z) = \frac{5.7(z-0.819)}{z} = 5.7(1-0.819z^{-1})$$

This filter can be included in the model update mode by
appending the appropriate poles and zeros of D(z) to G(z).
     This clearly improves the system characteristics as
shown by the closed loop, unity step response in Figure 4.7.
         Alternative discrete system design methods in the
frequency domain are also available in the package in terms
of executing a bilinear transformation and drawing a Bode

plot in the w-plane.

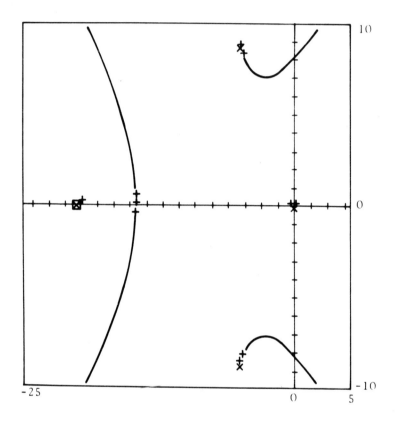

Fig. 4.5   Root locus plot for continuous system

4.5 SUMMARY

These two examples in the use of TRIP illustrate the
sort of facilities which control system design programs
typically offer and show their value in enabling system
analysis and design to be carried out quickly and easily.
The particular path through a package during system design
depends largely on personal preferences, and the versatility
of a package is measured in terms of the range of design
techniques offered.
Where design engineers do not already have access to
computer-aided, control system design facilities, packages
such as TRIP can be implemented on any computer system with

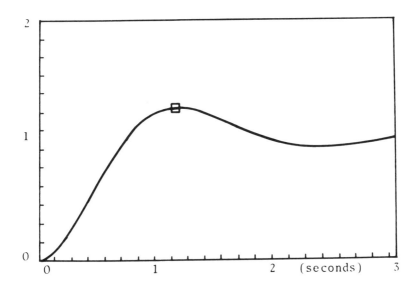

Fig. 4.6 Closed-loop step response of discrete system

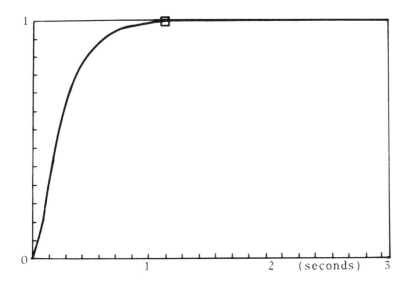

Fig. 4.7 Step response of modified discrete system

about 100 kilobytes of available memory and with some disc
file support for the storage of work files. This would preferably be a multi-user minicomputer with hardware floating
point support facilities. Alternatively, many microcomputer
systems are capable of handling such packages, albeit with a
severe execution speed penalty.

Apart from a computer, a graphics terminal is also required for such packages. The author has found both high
resolution (1024 x 780 points) raster scan terminals and
storage tube terminals (e.g. Tektronix) to be equally
suited to this purpose. However, lower resolution raster
scan terminals are not recommended, as the aliasing problem
(whereby inclined vectors are approximated to horizontal and
vertical steps) creates problems in this type of CAD work.

4.6 REFERENCES

1. Nyquist, H., 1932, 'Regeneration theory', Bell System
   Tech. J., 2, 126-147.

2. Bode, H.W., 1945, 'Network analysis and feedback amplifier design', Van Nostrand, Princeton, N.J.

3. James, H.M., Nichols, N.B. and Phillips, R.S., 1947,
   'Theory of servomechanisms, chapter four', McGraw-Hill,
   New York.

4. Evans, W.R., 1948, 'Graphical analysis of control systems', Trans. A.I.E.E., 67, 547-551.

5. Schouten, H.P.R., 1980, 'Trip manual', Delft University,
   The Netherlands.

Chapter 5

Construction of real-time software

S. Bennett

5.1.   INTRODUCTION

The past decade has produced a clarification and refine-
ment of the techniques for the design of robust computer
programs: it has also produced a greater understanding of
the complex nature of the activity of 'computer programming'. The changes are reflected in the growing use of the
term 'software engineering', and a recognition that software
is a 'product' which has to be designed, manufactured, and
maintained (Somerville (1)). It is also now widely recognised that good software is expensive to produce, particularly for real-time systems where high reliability is of
importance (see Chapter 9, section 9.1.1).
Attention has also been paid to providing clearer and
more precise definitions of terms used. One such term is
"real-time", this was originally introduced to distinguish
between "batch" processing and computations in which there
is a direct interaction between the processor and the real
world. The term real-time is used to indicate that the
computation is triggered by external events and that the
results of the particular calculation may depend upon the
value of the variable "time" at execution, or upon the time
taken to execute the computation. It is now realised that
real-time systems can be subdivided into two main categ-
ories: for one the computation may be assumed to be correct
if the mean execution time over a defined time interval is
lower than a specified maximum; for the other failure on any
one occasion to complete the computation within a specified
maximum time will constitute failure of the system (Civera
et. al.(2)).
A universal solution to the problems of real-time programming does not exist. In tackling the problems, however,
it is useful to have a clear understanding of the differences between various types of program.

5.2.   CLASSIFICATION OF PROGRAMS

Arising out of the work on the techniques for validating
programs - mathematical proofs of correctness - has come a
clearer understanding of the differences between various
types of program. Pyle (3), drawing on the work of Wirth,
has presented definitions identifying three types of

programming: (1) sequential, (2) multi-tasking, (3) real-time. The definitions are based on the kind of arguments which would have to be made in order to formally validate programs of each type.

5.2.1   Sequential Programming

In classical sequential programming, <u>actions</u> are strictly ordered as a time sequence: the behaviour of the program depends only on the effects of the individual <u>actions</u> and their <u>order</u>, the time taken to perform the action is not of consequence. Validation, therefore, requires two kinds of argument:
  (1) that a particular statement defines a stated action
  (2) that the various program structures produce a stated
      sequence of events.
It should be noted that we are not concerned here with how the process of validation is carried out, or even whether it can be carried out, but only with the arguments which would be required if we wished to validate the program.

5.2.2   Multi-task Programming

A multi-task program differs from the classical sequential program in that the actions it is required to perform are not necessarily disjoint in time: several actions may be required to be performed in parallel. We should note that the sequential relationships between the actions may still be important. Such a program may be built from a number of parts (processes or tasks are the names used for the parts), which are themselves purely sequential, but which are executed concurrently and which communicate through shared variables and synchronization signals.

Validation requires the arguments for sequential programs with some additions. The tasks (processes) can be validated separately only if the constituent variables of each task (process) are distinct.   If the variables are shared, then the potential concurrency makes the effect of the program unpredictable (and hence not capable of verification) unless there is some further rule that governs the sequencing of the several actions of the tasks (processes). It should be noted that the use of a synchronizing procedure means that the time taken for each individual action is not relevant to the validation procedure.   The task can proceed at any speed, the validity depends on the actions of the synchronizing procedure.

5.2.3   Real-time Programming

A real-time program differs from the the previous types in that in addition to its actions being not necessarily disjoint in time, the sequence of some of its actions is not determined by the designer, but by the environment; that is by events occurring in the outside world, events which occur in real time and without reference to the internal operations of the computer.   Such events cannot be made to conform to the inter-task synchronization rules. A real-time program can still be divided into a number of tasks, but communication between the tasks cannot necessarily wait for a synchronization signal: the environment task cannot be delayed. It should be noted that in process control applications the main environment task is usually that of keeping real time i.e. a real-time clock task. It is this task which provides the timing for the scanning tasks which gather information from the outside world about the process. In real-time programs, in contrast to the two previous types of program, the <u>actual time taken</u> by an action is an essential factor in the process of validation.

Consideration of the types of reasoning necessary for the validation of programs is important, not because we are seeking, as engineers, a method of formal proof, but because we are seeking to understand the factors which need to be considered when designing real-time software. It has been found by experience that the design of real-time software is a significantly more difficult task than the design of sequential software.

5.3.   STRUCTURE OF REAL-TIME PROGRAMS

An essential feature of real-time programs is that they are required to run continuously and hence the natural structural element is the "infinite" loop.

```
PROGRAM RealTimeControl;
BEGIN
      WHILE NOT (TheEndofTheWorld) DO
            BEGIN
                  ControlTask;
            END;
      END.
```

In addition to running continuously a real-time program has also to be synchronized to the outside world, the simplest way of achieving this is to use the technique of "polling". This is a method in which the program checks to see if an external event (or events) has occurred. Two approaches are possible: (1) if the event has not occurred the program continues with other actions before returning to check again; (2) the program continually repeats the check until the event occurs. The difficulty in using polling arises in ensuring that all the many tasks can be performed within a stated time. The advantage is that the program can be considered as a single task and its design and implementation is much simplified.

5.3.1.   Single Task Programs

An example of this approach is given below, it is assumed that the program has to (a) monitor the keyboard for input, (b) do some control (c) update a display and that these activities are carried out by the procedures Keyboard, Control and Display and that flags Keyflag, Controlflag and Displayflag are true when each activity has to be performed.

```
PROCEDURE ControlTask;
BEGIN
     IF Keyflag THEN Keyboard;
     IF Controlflag THEN Control;
     IF Displayflag THEN Display;
END;
```

A system constructed in such a way can be considered to work only if the time taken to process the longest computational unit is less than the maximum permitted service time (t_e) for an event. In the above example the worst case would be when all the events were active, i.e. when Keyflag, Controlflag and Displayflag were true and when the action specified in each was such that each module took its maximum computation time, then the total computational time would be given by:

$$t_{keymax} + t_{controlmax} + t_{displaymax}$$

and this would have to be less than the maximum service time for the event with the shortest maximum service time. Note that if the total time is not less than t_e then, in this example, it can be reduced by testing Controlflag twice in the loop, once after the test of Keyflag and again after Displayflag.

This simple approach to real-time system programming can be used in most languages providing they support character input/output and have facilities for checking that a key on the keyboard has been pressed. The input/output routines of some high level languages only provide for line input and output and in such cases the use of the standard INPUT or READ statements means that a return to the calling program is not made until the carriage return key is pressed on the keyboard. Similarly on output the standard output routine may assume that a carriage return and line feed is required after every output.

It is a requirement of most control algorithms that the process measurement is made and the new value of the controlled variable calculated at fixed time intervals. In the approach described above the time interval between computations of the controlled variable will not be fixed: it depends upon the various actions required. In a simple program with few different paths it is possible to determine all the paths through the program and either measure or calculate the time for each path, ballast coding is then added to make the computation time for each path equal, within some specified accuracy (Hine, Burbridge (4)).

The need for ballast coding can be avoided if some measure of time is provided, either in the form of a real-time clock or from an external interrupt. For example many systems now provide an interval timer, which would be set on exit from the Control module and, having tested Keyflag and Displayflag, the Control module would again be entered. It would have at the begining some code that caused the program to wait until the time interval had ended. In the example which follows the NextSampleTime is found at the end of the control loop by adding the SampleInterval to the current Time, the program then cycles round the REPEAT-UNTIL loop until it is time for the next sample.

```
        PROCEDURE Control
        BEGIN
            REPEAT
            UNTIL Time > NextSampleTime;
            ----
            ----
            Do Control
            ----
            ----
            NextSampleTime:=Time + SampleInterval;
        END;
```

This **single task (with timer) approach** provides an excellent engineering solution to simple real-time control problems and is widely used in small systems programmed at assembly level and increasingly in systems programmed using higher level languages. For many microprocessor families, development systems are available which provide BASIC, Pascal or other languages which can be used to develop programs of this type with subsequent loading of the code into ROM to form a simple self-contained controller (see section 5.4.2).

5.3.2 Multi-task Programs

Most programs are required to perform several clearly identified tasks and it is (or should be) standard practice in program design to consider the tasks as separate units with precisely defined interfaces between the tasks. This is fairly easy with sequential programming in that the tasks are used separately, in real-time environment the tasks will have to run in parallel and this leads to difficulties in defining the interface between tasks, since at any given time (or program action) it is not possible to predetermine the state of a task. There are many different approaches to this problem, but all rely on the use of some form of executive program or kernel, which may be very small and simple or may be part of a large operating system. We will consider first the simple foreground-background systems before dealing with larger real-time operating systems.

5.3.3. Foreground-background Systems

In most real-time systems a division can be made between tasks which have to be synchronized with the external environment - usually tasks involving data logging, direct digital control, sequence control or supervisory control - and tasks which perform a service - data reduction, operator communication, long term performance monitoring - which do not have to be tightly synchronized. This binary division leads to the idea of dividing the tasks into foreground tasks i.e tasks of high priority which are synchronized to the external environment and background tasks of lower priority. Many operating systems for real-time work are based on this simple concept e.g. the RT/11 operating system. In the simplest form only two tasks are permitted, one in the foreground and one in the background, but it is always possible to extend the number of tasks by using the polling techniques described in 5.2.1 above.

It is usually possible to adapt any standard sequential operating system to run a simple form of foreground-background system by making the foreground task into an interrupt routine. A consequence of this is that the foreground task has to be written partially in assembler, but since in many applications, particularly on the smaller computer systems, the control routines would be written in assembler anyway, this does not impose a great burden. It should also be noted that many of the control routines can be provided as library segments so that the coding required is simply that of providing the linkage, in addition it is usually possible to use many of the library functions and procedures provided with a high level language compiler and to call these directly from assembly level.

The widely used CP/M operating system can be used in this way with for example the Microsoft FORTRAN compiler. The background task is written in FORTRAN and the foreground task is written in the M80 assembly language making use of the Fortran library routines as and when required. The whole system is linked using the L80 linker to form a loadable module which can be loaded using the standard CP/M system.

For many simple systems the foreground-background approach using interrupt routines is adequate: the weakness is in the methods of sharing data between the tasks. In the absence of operating system support the only data sharing mechanism available is through the use of shared memory i.e. the use of shared or common variables. This is not always apparent since data is usually passed between the two tasks by means of parameters in procedure calls, however, unless interrupts are inhibited the effect is the equivalent of having the data held in a common area. The reason for this is that neither task has any knowledge of the state of the other task and if for example a controller has three parameters which are to be changed a procedure call

MODIFY(parameter1, parameter2, parameter3)

could be used. This procedure call does not represent one indivisible action but several actions which are required in turn in order to transfer the three parameters. An interrupt may occur between any of the several actions, the consequence could be that the control algorithm could be executed with one new parameter and two old parameters. In many DDC applications this would be of little consequence since it would represent only a transient disturbance to the system, it could be more serious if the change were to a sequence of operations. The potential for serious consequences is not great in small, simple systems (a good reason for keeping systems small and simple wherever possible), it is much greater in large complex multi-tasking systems.

The transfer of data between the foreground and the background task is a <u>critical</u> section of the program and should be an indivisible action which should be carried out by the operating system. In the absence of operating system support special routines can be provided:

```
PROCEDURE Modify(parameter list..........);
BEGIN
    InhibitInterrupts;
    TransferParameters;
    EnableInterrupts;
END;
```

By using a routine of the type shown the transfer of parameters to the control routine cannot be interrupted, however, a disturbance to the controller can still occur since the control action may be delayed and there is no way for the control task to indicate that it is a suitable time for the transfer of the information.

5.3.4   Real-time Multi-tasking Operating Systems

The programming of large real-time systems is considerably eased by the availability of real-time multi-tasking operating systems (the abbreviation RTMOS will be used). Many different types of RTMOS have been developed, the major restriction has been that they have been machine and vendor dependent. The reason for this is that in the past RTMOS have had to be written mainly in assembler code since they make use of many specific hardware features of the machine on which they run. With the development in recent years of languages such as C, Modula and Concurrent Pascal it is now possible to write operating systems in higher level languages with the minimum of assembly coding and this makes portability across a range of machines easier: as is indicated below it also makes the construction of special purpose operating systems a more economic proposition.
The essential features of RTMOS are:

* ability to monitor and change the states of the tasks,
* to regulate the exchange of information between tasks,
* interrupt handling.

Additional features are frequently present as part of the RTMOS, e.g. file handling routines, input/output routines, editors, compilers, loaders, librarians and various system management utilities, but these are not essential.
The major features required for task control are shown in figure 5.1. in the form of a state diagram. This shows the possible states of a task and the transitions from state to state. Not every RTMOS will have all the states shown, e.g. some simpler systems do not allow new tasks to be added while the system is running, all tasks have to be made known to the system by a process known as sysgen i.e. system generation which takes place off-line, the operating system and the tasks are then loaded together and the total system is run. The actual implementation of the various state transitions will also differ as will the rules under which the transitions take place.

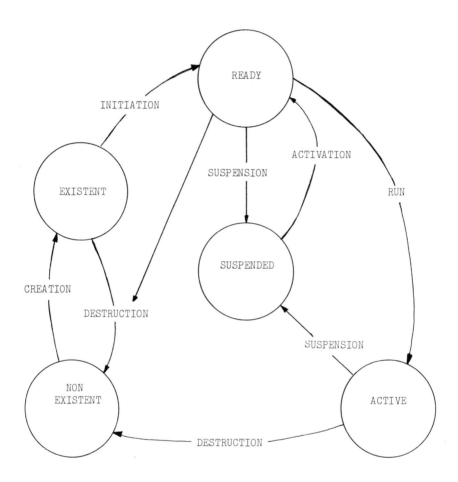

Fig.5.1   Task states and commands

Many RTMOS have language compilers (particularly FORTRAN) which have been enhanced to provide high level statements for manipulation of task states. Typical statements are:

TURN OFF TASK <n>
TURN ON TASK <n>,<{immediately, in x seconds}>
DELAY TASK <n>,<x seconds>
DELETE TASK <n>
ADD TASK <n>,<name>

The standard way of ensuring regulated exchange of data is to insist that information transfer between tasks is through the operating system. The operating system can then use a monitor to ensure correct access. RTMOS vary in the way in which inter-task communication is organised, some provide a GLOBAL COMMON facility in addition to the protected mechanism of supervisor calls, others insist that all communication between tasks is through the operating system.

Interrupt handling is crucial to the operation of real-time systems and is one of the most difficult areas of program construction and testing. The aim of handling interrupts within the operating system is to hide the details of the actual implementation from the application programmer. It is frequently adequate if the programmer has facilities to set a real-time clock such that events are initiated at preset time intervals. Another useful feature is the facility to declare that a task is to be executed immediately a particular interrupt signal is recognised, this enables an alarm task to be programmed at the application level rather than at the operating system or interrupt level.

5.4. CONSTRUCTION TECHNIQUES AND TOOLS

The tools used to construct real-time software fall into three main groups: (1) general purpose real-time operating systems and general purpose languages, (2) languages and systems for constructing applications software which combine the necessary operating system components with the specific application code, (3) specialised very high level languages for specific types of real-time applications. An example of the first category is the use of a standard operating system with say an assembler, or FORTRAN, or one of the older real-time languages such as CORAL or RTL/2. An example of the second category is the use of assembler, Modula or one of the versions of Pascal designed for real-time application to write both the operating system and the application. The third category is typified by say the CUTLASS system of the CEGB (see Chapter 9).

Regardless of the types of tools used it is usual to build, and test as fully as possible, the software on a 'development' or 'host' computer system which has more extensive facilities than the computer on which the software is to run (the 'target' system). Frequently the host and target systems will use the same processor, or use processors belonging to the same family, although this is not necessary and particularly with respect to microprocessor systems software is often developed on a different processor, in this case the development software is referred to as 'cross-support' software.

5.4.1. Use of General Purpose Tools

There was early recognition that many of the requirements for real-time control would be common across many applications, particularly in respect to the multi-tasking and that these could be handled by a general purpose operating system. The question then arises as to which language should be used for the application programs? In the 1960s the choice was essentially between assembler and FORTRAN, and because of memory size limitations, speed requirements, and the need to access all the hardware features of the computer, the pressure to write in assembler was strong. The provision of extensions to some versions of FORTRAN to give PROCESS FORTRAN i.e. a FORTRAN that provides the programmer with better access to the low level features of the computer hardware, and the development of real-time languages such as CORAL and RTL/2, has reduced the need to write in assembler. However, these languages are not entirely satisfactory (Young (5), Sandmayr (6)).

There have been several attempts during the last few years to develop good, general purpose real-time languages, the most comprehensive of these being Ada (see Chapter 6). The problems which arise, even when using languages specifically designed to meet real-time computing requirements, are that the specialist staff are still needed to write the applications software. This introduces the difficulty of engineering staff having to translate the requirements into a form understandable by computer specialists. Another disadvantage of general purpose high level languages is that the code generated is much larger than necessary for a given application. This is not important in large scale systems, but can considerably influence the costs of high volume microprocessor based systems.

One type of general purpose tool which is being used is real-time BASIC. The speed of program development using BASIC for small single board microprocessor based controllers is such that the extra cost due to the inefficiences of BASIC are offset when production runs are below the hundred level (Lees (7)).

5.4.2. Special Development Tools

In recent years there has been extensive development of special tools for writing various types of software. The aim of much of this development has been to provide a programming 'environment' which supports all aspects of software development. The minimum aims of such systems have been to provide editors, compilers and assemblers, library support, link editors and testing and debugging facilities. In the area of real-time control the development by Texas

Instruments and Digital Equipment Company of Pascal-based systems is one example, others are the development systems produced to support various microprocessors. Much of the power of these systems is in the support that they provide for debugging and testing of the software (and in some cases the hardware). The host processor normally remains connected to the target computer during the testing phase, and controls the testing. The host system keeps information regarding the source code and is thus able to provide detailed and meaningful error information. Again as with the general purpose languages, these tools require specialist knowledge and are not suitable for the application engineer to use directly.

5.4.3 Application Oriented Languages

Recognition of the fact that for a given area of application there will be considerable commonality between different systems implementations within the area, means that specialised systems for constructing software can be developed. Many special application oriented systems have been developed within the control field and are widely used. They can be divided into three main groups:
1. Program generators
2. Interpreters
3. Application environments.
They all have the common aim of enabling non-computer specialists to write the application software.

5.4.3.1 Program generators. In many process applications the structure of the software does not change significantly for many different implementations, the changes are e.g. in the number of control loops being used, in the addresses of the interface cards, in the calibration constants of the instruments. In these cases if the software is organised such that implementation dependent variables are accessed indirectly through a look-up table, then it is an easy task to modify such software, either manually or with the assistance of a program. As an example let us consider a system programmed in assembler which supports a number of three-term controllers, the system is assumed to be coded such that the number of controllers and the parameters are held in a table, the coding for the table could be as follows:

```
        ORG TABLE
; This    table must be loaded with correct data for
; implementation
IDENT:  DB 0        ; insert identification
;
; number of controllers
NCON:   DB 0        ; insert number of control loops
;
; parameters for loop 1
KP1:    DW 0
KP2:    DW 0
KP3:    DW 0
;
```

; etc.
Given knowledge of the location of the TABLE it is an easy
matter to arrange to put the appropriate values for the
implementation into it. Table driven software provides
flexible and easily implemented systems (Lees, (7)) and
systems based on this approach are widely used (Chapter 12,
Saunders (8)).

Many of the process control equipment manufacturers provide interactive software which allows the engineer to
specify the number of loops, loop parameters and other
features of a control system. This software sits on top of
a general purpose control system, probably written in assembler code and inserts the values in the appropriate places
in the tables of the underlying system.

More extensive modifications to a general applications
package can be made if re-compilation or re-assembly is
permitted. The procedure can be much the same, either
manually or with the aid of a program, changes to constants
are made within the general framework, and possible calls to
subroutines are added or deleted. In this case, however,
specialist programmers, who know the 'stock' and who can
make minor amendments if necessary, are usually involved.

5.4.3.2 Interpreters. Two forms of interpretive software
are to be found in process control applications, in one the
whole system is executed interpretatively, in the other the
time critical parts are actually written in assembler and
the interpreter acts partially as a program generator
filling in the table entries, and partially to enable the
user to add additional features to the program. Interpretative systems can provide an excellent development tool and
can provide an economic means of programming one-off
systems. They can, however, lead to clumsy and uneconomic
systems if used for applications widely different from those
envisaged by the designer (Lee, Nichols (9) Crawley Milling
et. al. (10), Pickett, Schutz, (11)).

5.4.3.3 Application environments. In addition to the
development of the general purpose real-time languages such
as Coral, RTL/2, Modula 2 and Ada, many languages and
language systems have been designed to support particular
application areas. The aim of such developments has been to
provide a vocabulary and syntax which is sufficiently close
to the normal usage of engineers working in the application
area to enable them directly to specify their requirements
in the language. The value of this approach is that the
user, rather than some intermediary, is responsible for
putting the engineering specification into a formal
language. Once the specification is expressed in a formal
language validation techniques can be used and the specification can be checked for inconsistencies.

Two approaches are used: in one the formal specification
is directly compiled or otherwise processed by a computer
system to generate the final code, in the other the formal
language specification is coded by specialist programmers
into some other language, which is then compiled. An example

of the first approach is the CUTLASS system (see Chapter 9), and of the second are the specification languages such as MASCOT, GEMMA, CADES (Sage (12)).

5.5   CONCLUSION

In the design and construction of real-time software, as in the construction of any software, the aims must be clearly defined and in recent years considerable progress has been made in providing formal systems, either in the form of improved languages for computers or in design languages and systems which meet the requirements for the expression of real-time systems. There is now available a wide range of tools for the construction of real-time software and the choice is very much dependent on the application. Sage (12) has suggested a very general division as shown below:

System size / Dominant Characteristics	Large system	Small system
High hardware unit cost	either extensive software system adapted to process or standard parameterised software and process "adapts" to system	only standard software likely to be economic
Low hardware unit costs	software implemented within hardware and extensive software development	software design critical and code optimization may be critical

It is in the large systems area that application languages and design languages are most used, however, manufacturers languages are rarely applicable in systems where low unit cost hardware is involved. For both large and small systems with low unit cost hardware the most viable approach is usually through microprocessor development systems preferably with the use of a high level language.

Real-time systems present difficulties both in design and in testing and it cannot be overemphasised that a simple approach to the structure of the software should be used. Whenever possible the system should be divided into modules and a separation between the actual real-time routines and other routines in the system should be made.

REFERENCES

1. Somerville, I., 1982, 'Software Engineering' Addison-Wesley, London. See also Myers, G.J., 1976, 'Software Reliability', Wiley, New York.

2. Civera, P., Del Corso, D., & Gregoretti, F., 1983, 'Microcomputer systems in real-time applications', in

Tzafestas, S.G., 'Microprocessors in Signal Processing, Measurement and Control', Reidel, Dordrecht.

3. Pyle, I.C., 1979, 'Methods for the design of control software', in 'Software for Computer Control', Proc. Second IFAC/IFIP Symposium on Software for Computer Control, Pergamon, Oxford.

4. Hine, D., Burbridge, L., 1979, 'A microcomputer algorithm for open loop step motor control', Trans. Inst. Meas. Control, 1, 233-239.

5. Young, S.J., 1982, 'Real Time Languages: Design and Development', Ellis Horwood, Chichester.

6. Sandmayr, H., 1981, 'A comparison of Languages: CORAL, Pascal, PEARL, Ada and ESL', Computers in Industry, 2, 123-132.

7. Lees, R.A., 1972, 'Building real-time software', Trends in on-line control systems, IEE Conf. Pub. No.85, 13-18.

8. Saunders, A., 1982, 'FOCUS: a process control system integrates the modern approach to process analysis and user-oriented software', Trends in on-line computer control systems, April, 1982.

9. Lee, R., Nichols, J., 1982, 'Process control BASIC simplifies programming', Instrum. & Control Systems, 55, 51-54.

10. Crawley-Milling, M.C., Hyman, J.T., Shearing, G.G., 1973, 'Interpretative software for a large one-off process', Software for Control, IEE Conf. Pub. No. 102, 63-67.

11. Pickett, M.S., Schutz, H.A., 1976, 'Interpretative execution of real-time control applications', ACM SIGPLAN 11, 78-87.

12. Sage, M.W., 1982, 'Developments in software technology', trends in on-line control systems, IEE Conf. Pub. No. 208, 119-124.

Chapter 6

Programming language requirements for process control

S.J. Young

6.1 PROGRAMMING LANGUAGE REQUIREMENTS FOR PROCESS CONTROL

In this section, the main requirements of a language suitable for programming real time Process Control systems will be discussed. Later sections will then examine one of these requirements, a multi-tasking capability, in detail by describing the way that multi-tasking is handled in some of the real time languages which are in use today.

To gain some insight into the sort of programming tasks involved in real time process control software, consider a typical medium sized system as illustrated in Fig. 6.1.

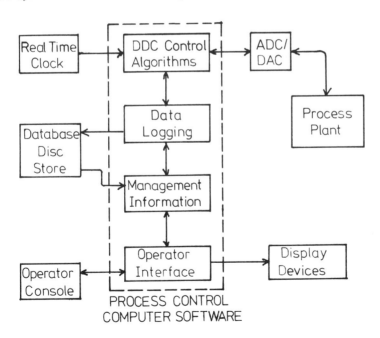

Fig. 6.1 Typical Medium Sized Process Control System

In this system, the computer is dedicated to controlling the operation of some process plant. It is interfaced directly to this plant via analogue to digital and digital to analogue convertors which enable it to measure the state of the plant and impose control over its operation. As the control algorithms used will require the state of the plant to be sampled at regular intervals, a real time clock is provided which interrupts the computer each sample period. As well as interfacing to the plant, the computer must also interface with human operators so that start-up and close-down sequencing operations can be activated and to enable the overall behaviour of the plant to be varied. Additionally, control engineers and managers must be able to monitor the operation of the plant. To meet this need, data logging is performed which stores information about the plant's operation in a database on disc. This information can then be accessed when required via a number of colour graphic display devices.

The software for the above system is naturally divided into distinct functions or tasks. In the example, four tasks have been identified: digital control, data logging, management information and operator interface. These tasks are represented in the software by processes which are executed in parallel, interacting where necessary to synchronise on certain events and to transfer information. Division of software into tasks simplifies design and development and makes it easier to meet the response time requirements of the system since important tasks such as the digital controller task can be assigned a higher priority than less urgent tasks such as the operator interface task. From this, it follows that the first requirement of a programming language for process control is that it should provide constructs for representing parallel tasks.

The second language requirement follows from the fact that process control software will be large and complex. In order to deal with this complexity, facilities must be provided for program modularisation. This means that the software should be broken up into small self-contained units, each unit being separately compiled and tested. Modularisation is important for many reasons. It aids program design, it simplifies modification and maintenance, and it allows the software to be developed by teams of programmers since each member of the team can work on his own module or modules without undue dependence on the others in the team.

The third language requirement is self-evident. Process control software must be reliable and the language used for the development of such software must give positive support to reliability both by its inherent security (i.e. its ability to detect programming errors at compile and run time) and by the provision of explicit constructs for handling error conditions which arise whilst the program is running.

The fourth language requirement arises out of the special nature of process control systems. Unlike general purpose computer systems, a process control system will have many special-purpose input/output devices such as ADC's, DAC's, real time clocks, etc. Because these devices will differ on each individual system, the language cannot provide built-in support for them. Instead they must be explicitly programmed as part of the overall software development. Hence, a good process control language should give explicit support for low level device programming (including interrupt driven devices).

Of the above four requirements, the multi-tasking requirement is probably the most important and certainly the most demanding. Hence, the remainder of this chapter will examine the way that this requirement is met by some of the main programming languages currently used in the process control area. The interested reader will find a full duscussion of all these requirements in Young (1).

Finally, however, it should be noted that 90% of any process control software system is not significantly different from software taken from any other application area. Hence, a language suitable for process control must also meet all the requirements which are now considered mandatory for any good computer programming language. For example, it should be readable, well-structured, portable, simple to learn and use, and efficient.

6.2   MULTI-TASKING IN TRADITIONAL LANGUAGES

Software which contains several concurrently executing tasks is said to be multi-tasking and the facilities provided by a language for this have a major effect on the ease of development, reliability and maintenance of process control software.

In the older real time languages, there is little explicit support for multi-tasking within the language itself. Instead, each task is represented as a separate procedure (or program) and a multi-task operating system (MTOS) is used to execute these procedures in parallel and to manage interactions between them. As a good example of this approach, RTL/2 is a language designed around 1972 specifically for process control and has a standard MTOS to support it (2).

In a multi-task software system written in RTL/2, a global data area is set up to define the procedure name, stack (i.e. local workspace), priority and initial state of each task. The MTOS then uses this information to execute each named procedure in parallel to form the required multi-task system. For example, the process control system described in section 6.1 would be defined in the following way

```
LET ntasks = 4;

ENT DATA tkdfn
    ARRAY(ntasks)PROC() tkproc:=(ddc,logger,opint,maninfo);
    ARRAY(ntasks)STACK tkstack:=(ddcstk,logstk,opstk,manstk);
    ARRAY(ntasks) BYTE tkprio:=(4,3,2,1);
    ARRAY(ntasks) BYTE tkstat:=(active,active,active,suspended);
ENDDATA
```

In RTL/2, the notation "DATA name ... ENDDATA" denotes a global block of data with a specified name (similar to COMMON in FORTRAN).

The preceding ENT keyword in the example simply makes the
following data block accessible in separately compiled program
modules. As can be seen, the procedure names, stacks, priorities
and initial statuses are each declared in a separate array. For
example, the first element of each array defines the characteristics
of the DDC (digital controller task) i.e. procedure name 'ddc', stack
space 'ddcstk', priority 4 (highest) and initial status 'active'.

The actual DDC task would then be represented by a conventional
globally accessible procedure. For example, in outline it might
look as follows

```
ENT STACK ddcstk 1000;        % 1000 bytes of workspace %

ENT PROC ddc();               % ENT means globally accessible %
   LOOP:
      readinputs();           % Execute an endless %
      computeoutputs();       % control loop

      --- etc.
   GOTO LOOP;
ENDPROC
```

When the MTOS is started, it examines the task definition arrays in
'tkdfn' and executes each named procedure in parallel. Thus, the
ddc task will start executing an endless loop, whilst at the same
time each of the other tasks is performing its own functions.

A major problem with any multi-task system is to ensure that
communication between tasks is safe and free from deadlock. In
RTL/2, tasks communicate by reading and writing into global shared
data areas. Mutually exclusive access to such areas is guaranteed
by the use of special flags called semaphores. Suppose that
semaphore S is associated with a shared data area B, then before a
task T can access B, it must call the procedure 'secure(S)'. This
procedure is implemented by the MTOS. When it is called, the MTOS
checks to see whether another task is currently accessing B and if
so, it suspends T until B is free, otherwise it allows T to proceed
immediately. When T has finished accessing B is must call
'release(S)' to let the MTOS know that B is free again. Similarly,
when a task T needs to wait until some event E has occurred, it
executes the MTOS procedure 'wait(E)'. Task T is then suspended
until some other process executes the MTOS procedure 'send(E)'
thereby signalling that the event E has occurred.

The use of these semaphore and signalling mechanisms is
illustrated by the following. Suppose that the ddc task
needs to transmit messages to the data logger task. It is
convenient to pass these messages via a bounded buffer defined by
the following array

```
ARRAY(bufsize)message buffer;
INT inx,outx,used := 0;
```

where 'message' is a suitable record structure for holding each
message and 'bufsize' gives the maximum number of messages which can

be held in the buffer. The integer variables 'inx', 'outx' and 'used' denote the array index values for storing the next message, retrieving the next message and the total number of messages in the buffer, respectively.

Given this array structure, the 'ddc' task could insert a message by the following operations

```
buffer(inx) := newmessage;        % Store the message %
inx := (inx + 1) MOD bufsize;     % Increment inx ready to %
                                  % Insert next message %
used := used + 1;                 % Increment used counter %
```

However, this code takes no account of the fact that the 'data logger' task may simultaneously be manipulating the same variables in order to retrieve a message. Hence, the two tasks must use semaphores to guarantee mutually exclusive access to the buffer. Furthermore, signals must be used to synchronise the tasks should the buffer become full or empty. The actual code required to insert a message into the buffer is therefore

```
secure(BufSem);              % Secure buffer semaphore %
IF used=bufsize THEN         % If buffer is full then %
    release(BufSem);         % Allow data logger to empty
                               buffer %
    wait(NonFull);           % Data logger will send(NonFull)
                               when %
    secure(Bufsem);          % its done this.  Get semaphore
                               Back %
END;
buffer(inx) := newmessage;   % Now insert new message %
inx := (inx + 1) MOD bufsize;
used := used + 1;
release(BufSem);             % Release buffer semaphore %
send(NonEmpty);              % Signal 'nonempty' since data
                               logger %
                             % may be waiting for it %
```

The comments alongside of this code should help explain how the insertion task is performed. Similar code would, of course, also be needed in the data logger task for retrieving a message from the buffer.

The above illustrates how multi-tasking is organised in traditional real time languages. Although the examples have concentrated on RTL/2, the general approach is typical and similar schemes are used with Coral (3), Pearl (4), Real Time Fortran (5) and many others. (Note, however, that Coral has recently been upgraded by the addition of a high level multitasking environment called Mascot (6)).

The merits of this approach to multi-tasking lie in the simplicity of its implementation in the sense that it involves no significant extensions to the language. However, it suffers severe drawbacks. The code for the message insertion operation given above illustrates how careful one must be to avoid making serious errors

in the program design. For example, it would be very easy to omit
the release operation within the IF statement thereby hanging-up the
entire system. The use of semaphores and signals have been shown in
practice to be highly insecure and error prone. The root of the
problem is that they are very low level mechanisms. Furthermore,
since the multi-tasking facilities are not part of the language,
there is little that the compiler can do to help in checking for
errors. Instead, any error checking which is possible must be done
by the MTOS at run-time and this leads to efficiency problems.

In recent years, it has become clear that the only way to improve
the multi-tasking facilities of a real time language is to make
multi-tasking an explicit language feature. This not only allows the
overall task structure to be more clearly shown in the program
but also allows higher level inter-task interaction mechanisms to be
provided. The first step in this direction came with the
introduction of processes and monitors (7). A good example of a
language which features these is Modula and this will be discussed
next.

6.3   CONCURRENT REAL TIME LANGUAGES

Modula is a Pascal-based programming language designed for small
process control systems (8). It was developed around 1976 and is
typical of the earlier concurrent languages. It provides specific
mechanisms for representing multiple tasks within a single program
and for allowing safe and secure inter-action between them.
Although only Modula will be described here, it should be noted that
many other very similar languages were developed about the same time
e.g. Concurrent Pascal (9), Mesa (10), Pascal Plus (11).

In Modula, processes (i.e. tasks) are denoted using an identical
syntax to procedures except that the starting keyword is PROCESS.
Processes may also be called just like regular procedures. However,
when a process is called, the calling program is not made to wait
until the process terminates (which may be never) but continues
immediately leaving both the calling program and the called process
executing in parallel.

As an example of process definition in Modula, the following
outline indicates how the example system of section 6.1 might be
described

```
MODULE Main;                    {main program heading}

    PROCESS ddc;                { define ddc task }
    BEGIN
        LOOP                    { .. as an endless }
            readinputs;         { loop..            }
            computeoutputs;
            -- etc.
        END
    END;

    PROCESS datalogger;         { define datalogger task }
    BEGIN
        --                      { code for datalogger here }
```

```
END;

PROCESS operator;        { ... and so on }

--etc.

BEGIN  main program
    ddc;                 {start each task by}
    datalogger;          {calling it}
    --etc.
END.
```

The meaning of the above should be clear from the comments. Each task is defined as a process with a statement body which defines what that process does. Usually this statement body will consist of a LOOP statement, as in the ddc task, which causes the process actions to be repeated endlessly. An actual instance of each process is then created by the main program by executing a process call statement for each defined process.

It is fairly clear that the Modula method of describing a multi-task system is an improvement on the earlier RTL/2 approach since the program text is more readable and there is no requirement to construct obscure task definition blocks. However, the real benefit of Modula becomes evident when tasks wish to communicate.

The RTL/2 message passing example was introduced primarily to show the difficulty of programming task interaction using primitive low level mechanisms such as signals and semaphores. In fact, this example also demonstrates the importance of proper program structuring. When a shared data area is used to provide a communication channel between two or more processes, the responsibility for accessing that data should lie with the data itself and not with the processes that access it. From this realisation has grown the concept of Monitors (7) or Interface Modules as they are called in Modula. An interface module contains a shared data area and a set of procedures for accessing that data. These procedures are entirely conventional except for one important difference - when they are called by several processes concurrently, the system guarantees that at most one interface procedure can be executed at a time. Since the only means an external process has of accessing an interface module's shared data is by calling an appropriate interface procedure, mutually exclusive access is thereby guaranteed without resort to low level semaphore mechanisms. Process synchronisation is still achieved by signals, but at least these can now be encapsulated within interface modules where their inherent insecurity can be localised.

As an example of this, the following interface module could be used by the ddc task to pass messages to the data logger task (c.f. the RTL/2 example in section 6.2)

```
INTERFACE MODULE buffer;

DEFINE put,get ;         {define externally accessible}
                         {interface procedures        }
CONST bufsize=64;
```

```
VAR buffer:ARRAY 1:bufsize  {declare the shared data area }
         OF message;       { - in this case,  }
    inx,outx,used:integer;  { a circular buffer }

    nonfull,nonempty:signal;    { declare signals for }
                                { process synchronisation }

PROCEDURE put (m:message);  {interface procedure for putting }
BEGIN                       {a message into the buffer }
    IF used=bufsize THEN
        wait(nonfull)       {if buffer full then wait ..}
    END;
    buffer[inx]:=m;         {insert message into buffer }
    inx:=inx MOD bufsize + 1;
    used:=used+1;
    send(nonempty)          {finally, signal non-empty in}
END;                        {case another process is waiting }

PROCEDURE get(VAR m:message);  {interface proc for getting }
                               {a message from the buffer }
BEGIN
    IF used=0 THEN
        wait(nonempty)      {if buffer empty then wait ..}
    END;
    m:=buffer[outx];        {extract message from buffer }
    outx:=outx MOD bufsize + 1;
    used:=used-1;
    send(nonfull)           {finally, signal non-full in}
END;                        {case another process is waiting }

BEGIN {main body}
    inx:=1;                 {these statements are executed}
    outx:=1;                {just once when program is }
    used:=0                 {started - they serve to initialise}
END buffer;                 {the interface module }
```

This module contains a circular message buffer and two access
procedures 'put' and 'get'. The ddc task would put a message into
the buffer by simply calling 'put(m)' and the data logger task would
extract the next message from the buffer by simply calling 'get(m)'
- neither task need worry about mutual exclusion or synchronisation
since this is all taken care of within the interface module. When
the 'ddc' task calls 'put', then if the 'datalogger' task is
currently executing 'get', the 'ddc' task is suspended until the
call to 'get' has completed (or a wait on signal statement is
executed), at which time the call to 'put' is allowed to proceed.
In this way, safe and orderly access to the shared buffer structure
is maintained.

   The Modula approach to process definition and interaction
represents a major step forward in multitasking language design.
Multi-task programs are easier to design, implement and test in
Modula since the process interaction protocols are encapsulated
within a single program unit (i.e. the interface module).
Furthermore, the protocols themselves are simplified since the low
level and difficult semaphore mechanism is replaced by the high
level interface procedure concept.

Despite the advances made by Modula (and similar languages), problems remain with the use of processes and monitors. Firstly, the low level and dangerous signalling mechanism is still relied upon for process synchronisation. Secondly, the process communication mechanism is firmly based on the concept of shared memory and this may be inappropriate for modern distributed computer systems where each process runs on a separate processor connected by a communication link rather than via shared memory. In the next section, the multi-tasking system provided by the very latest real time language, Ada, will be described to show how signals can be dispensed with using a model which does not rely on shared memory.

6.4 CONCURRENT PROGRAMMING IN ADA

As with Modula, several tasks may be defined in Ada within a single program (12). Each task has two parts: a specification and a body. The specification defines a task's entry procedures, if any, and the body defines what each task does. Entry procedures are used for inter-task communication in a similar way to the interface procedures of Modula described above, however, the underlying process model is different. In Ada, mutual exclusion and synchronisation are combined into a single mechanism called a 'rendezvous'. The basic idea of the rendezvous and the general format of task definition in Ada is illustrated by the following outline which shows a fragment of the process control example again

```
-- (A) Task Specifications

TASK ddc IS              -- ddc has an entry setparam
   ENTRY setparam(p:paramlist);
END ddc;

TASK operator;           -- operator has no entries

-- (B) Task Bodies

TASK BODY ddc IS
BEGIN
   --
   --
   ACCEPT setparam(p:paramlist) DO
      --
      -- update ddc control parameters
      -- from parameter list p
      --
   END setparam;
   --
END ddc;

TASK BODY operator IS
BEGIN
   --
   -- get new parameters from
   -- the operator
   --
   setparam(newparams);   -- update ddc parameters
```

```
    --
    END operator;
```

This example fragment shows the 'ddc' task and the operator
interface task. It is assumed here that part of the function of the
'operator' task is to accept commands from the human operator to
change the parameters of the control algorithms within the
'ddc' task. This is made possible by the 'setparam' entry defined
within the specification of the 'ddc' task. As noted earlier,
entries are a special kind of procedure used for task communication.
In this case, task 'operator' has no entries and task 'ddc' has a single
entry called 'setparam' with parameter p. The actions to be performed
by each task are defined by its body and each task executes concurrently with all other tasks.

When task 'operator' wishes to communicate with task 'ddc', it
calls the entry 'setparam' as shown. At this point task 'operator'
is suspended until task 'ddc' indicates that it is ready to accept
the entry call by executing an ACCEPT statement for 'setparam'.
When this occurs the rendezvous begins. Task 'operator' remains
suspended while task 'ddc' executes the statements within the body
of the ACCEPT statement. The parameter p is used to transfer the
new parameter values from the calling task to the accepting task (in
general an entry can have any number of parameters so there is no
limit on the amount of data that can be transferred in this way).
When the end of the accept statement is reached, the rendezvous is
terminated and both tasks continue independently. Finally, note
that if task 'ddc' had reached the accept 'setparam' statement
before task 'operator' had called it then task 'ddc' would have been
suspended until the call occurred.

The rendezvous provides a simple and elegant solution to both the
mutual exclusion problem and the synchronisation problem. Mutual
exclusion is assured because a task may only engage in one rendezvous
at a time and synchronisation is implicit in the entry call/accept
protocol.

There is, of course, much more to tasking in Ada than is shown by
the above example. A complete description is beyond the scope of
this chapter but the problem of non-determinism is important enough
to merit discussion. As noted above, once a task reaches an accept
statement then it commits itself to wait for a call on the corresponding entry no matter how long this may take. Clearly this is far too
restrictive for many programming problems. As a result, Ada provides
a SELECT statement which allows a task to accept one of several entry
calls depending on which calls are pending. As an example, the message
passing problem illustrated previously would be solved in Ada by introducing a new task containing the actual buffer with entries 'put' and
'get' for storing and retrieving messages from it. The 'ddc' task
would then send a message to the 'datalogger' task by calling the
entry 'put' in the buffer task, the 'datalogger' task would retrieve
it later by calling the 'get' entry. The code for such a buffer task
in Ada is as follows

```
TASK buffer IS
    ENTRY put(m:  IN message);
    ENTRY get(m:  OUT message);
END buffer;

TASK BODY buffer IS
    bufsize:  CONSTANT := 64;
    buf:  ARRAY(1..bufsize)OF message;
    inx,outx:  integer RANGE 1..bufsize;
    used:  integer RANGE 0..bufsize;
BEGIN
    inx:=1; outx:=1; used:=0;
    LOOP
        SELECT
            WHEN used<bufsize⇒
                ACCEPT put(m:  IN message) DO
                    buf(inx):=m;
                    inx:=inx MOD bufsize +1;
                    used:=used+1;

                END put;
            OR
            WHEN used>0 =>
                ACCEPT get(m:  OUT message) DO
                    m:=buf(outx);
                    outx:=outx MOD bufsize +1;
                    used:=used-1;
                END get;
        END SELECT;

    END LOOP;

    END buffer;
```

Ignoring the "WHEN .. ⇒" clauses for the moment, the task 'buffer' executes an indefinite loop. Within the loop is a single select statement containing two alternatives: an accept 'put' and an accept 'get'. Each time this select statement is executed there are three possibilities

1)   No entry calls are pending – the task is suspended until either entry is called at which point the appropriate accept statement is executed.

2)   A single entry call is pending – the corresponding accept statement is executed immediately.

3)   Calls are pending for both entries – one of the accept statements is executed at random.

The purpose of the "when .. =>" clauses is to 'guard' the alternatives of the select statement. In the example, 'put' entry calls may only be accepted when the buffer is not full otherwise overflow would occur. When the FULL condition becomes true, the accept 'put' alternative is closed and calls to that entry are ignored.

The 'buffer' task, therefore, controls access to the circular message buffer. It makes sure that buffer operations are executed strictly in mutual exclusion and deals with the 'boundary conditions'. As long as there is at least one call pending for which the corresponding accept statement is open, the task will remain active. When no entry calls are pending, the task is suspended until such a call occurs.

6.5   CONCLUSIONS

The preceding sections have traced the development of just one of the requirements of programming languages suitable for process control, namely the provision of facilities for multi-tasking. It has been shown that the traditional approach to providing multi-tasking by means of a multi-task operating system coupled to an otherwise purely sequential language does not give the necessary level of support for well-engineered software development. The inclusion of multitask facilities directly into the programming language, however, enables much higher level and more secure mechanisms to be designed. These allow multitask software to be implemented which is easier to understand, more reliable and quicker to develop than previous methods. The choice of a concurrent programming language would therefore appear to be mandatory for dealing with the level of complexity found in todays large-scale process control systems.

REFERENCES

[1]   Young, S. J.   1982.   Real Time Languages: Design and Development, Ellis Horwood, Chichester.

[2]   Barnes, J. G. P.   1976.   RTL/2: Design and Philosophy. Heydon, London.

[3]   Woodward, P. M. et. al.   1970.   Official Definition of Coral 66, HMSO, London.

[4]   Brandes, J. et. al.   1970.   PEARL: the Concept of a Process and Experiment-oriented Programming Language, Elektronische Dataverarbeitung, 10, p 162-175.

[5]   Kelly, E. A.   1970.   FORTRAN in Process Control: Standardising Extensions, Instrumentation and Technology.

[6]   Simpson, H. R. and Jackson, K.   1979.   Process Synchronisation in MASCOT. Computer J., 22, 4, p 332-345.

[7]   Hoare, C. A. R.   1974.   Monitors: an operating system structuring concept, Comm ACM, 17, p 549-557.

[8]   Wirth, N.   1977.   Modula: a language for modular multiprogramming, Software Practice and Experience, 7, p 3-36.

[9]   Hansen, P. B.   1975.   The Programming Language Concurrent Pascal, IEEE Trans Software Engineering, 1, p 199-207.

[10]   Geshke, C. M. and Satterthwaite, E. H.   1977.   Early Experience with MESA, <u>Comm ACM</u>, <u>20</u>, p 540-522.

[11]   Welsh, J. and Bustard, D. W.   1979.   Pascal Plus: Another Language for Modular Multiprogramming.   <u>Software Practice and Experience</u>, 9, p 947-958.

[12]   Young, S. J.   1983.   Introduction to Ada.   Ellis Horwood Ltd., Chichester.

Chapter 7

Computer control in
flexible manufacturing systems (FMS)

A. Wilkins

7.1 INTRODUCTION

Many companies have taken advantage of computer systems
to aid manufacture, inventory control, and other management
functions over the last ten years. Most implementations are
of standard manufacturing control software packages of pro-
prietary origin, developed by computer suppliers or software
houses, although some companies operate 'home-grown' systems.
The development of a control system for an FMS is probably
beyond the scope of most manufacturing organisations, owing
to the different technologies involved; a turnkey computer
system supplier such as Systime is well placed to assist such
developments, although currently the concept of a standard
FMS control package cannot be attained due to the diversity
of manufacturing scenarios. Not all computer suppliers will
be able to adopt this role, it will be limited to those software houses with an understanding of the manufacturing problems, with the determination to accept the technical risks,
with the ability to form a long-term partnership with their
client on a sound commercial basis, and probably also those
with microprocessor hardware and software experience.

7.2 THEORETICAL BENEFITS

The main purpose of FMS is to reduce production costs.
This is achieved in a variety of ways:
- Reduced manning levels.
- Increased use of production equipment and hence of capital
  expenditure. In the mechanical engineering environment,
  this means increased cutting time on machine tools.
- Ability of the production line to make parts of different
  types in different mixes concurrently.
- Automated parts handling between the various manufacturing
  processes.
- Computer-assisted scheduling, so that work is normally
  available to the machines at all times.
- Adaptability of the system to manufacture new components
  or products without substantial redesign.
  The use of robots (either stand-alone, or integrated
robotic arm) or automated pallet-loaders breaks the conventional man controlled cycle of the machines, so that production efficiency is increased to the maximum potential of the

equipment. This itself leads to a considerable reduction in manpower. The automated parts flow, whether by a fixed conveyor or a more flexible array of automatic or wire guided vehicles, eliminates the handling delays. Again, to take the machine shop example, the conventional throughput times of two to four months can easily be reduced to two to four days. This not only releases a substantial amount of cash tied up in work-in-progress, but also makes the whole process much more reactive to changes in demand. Indeed the entire FMS may be operated on a 'manufacture-to-order' basis instead of 'manufacture-for-stock'.

Other minor benefits include potential reductions in raw materials, enhanced safety, vastly improved management information (both real-time status and historical reports), and the ability to schedule very small batches economically.

All of these benefits can only be achieved by the sensible integration of computers and software into the manufacturing process. The key to the integration process is the ability of the system designers to interface the computer into the machinery, both electrically and for the passage of the appropriate data or messages. It is in this area that the lack of standards is a nuisance: each machine vendor may have his own standard, with little or no commonality between them; but this does not prevent the job being done, it simply creates more work and this will naturally reflect in a higher cost. Although the author would welcome a universal standard, it is currently felt that this is totally impracticable, not only due to the enormous variety of manufacturing equipment available for the spectrum of manufacturing processes, but also due to the considerable momentum of the various suppliers in their own directions.

The key to the usefulness of the FMS, once integration has been achieved, lies in the software. This cannot be attempted without a painstaking two-way dialogue between the vendor of the computer system and his customer, probably lasting several months, a water-tight specification, an intelligently designed system, and programming in modules for maximum flexibility and ease of testing the system.

7.3 FMS BUILDING BLOCKS

The example given pertains to a mechanical engineering shop-floor, but the principle applies to any manufacturing process. It is equally adaptable to welding or paint-spraying lines.

A conventional machine-shop comprises a number of stand-alone machine tools, and this modular concept applies to the design of an FMS also. The module in this case is not just the machine tool, but a machining cell comprising the machine tool, a robot-loading device, and mechanical interfaces to the conveyor or guided vehicle system for the input of workpieces and the output of finished or more finished parts. All of the components in the cell are interfaced to the computer system. This cell therefore forms the basic building block of the FMS. Of course the basic cell may be enhanced by the provision of accessories such as post-process gauging equipment, automatic tool changers, possible mechanical interfaces to a tool conveyor, or swarf removal and recovery conveyors. Equally the machine tool may be re-placed by an assembly machine, or by an automatic inspec-tion machine for quality control outside the basic manufac-turing cell.

The FMS'production line' is then assembled from a number of building blocks as above, the parts transportation system effectively connecting the modules mechanically and the control system connecting the modules electrically for distribution and collection of data, and hence functionally.

7.4   JUSTIFYING AND BUILDING AN FMS

An FMS will cost more than a conventional machine shop. Whether existing machine tools are used in the FMS or not, additional equipment is necessary, namely the robots, the parts transportation system, the computer system, and the software. The robots and conveyor mechanisms will have to be justified in each case, and the costs will depend on the types of component being manufactured. It would appear from a number of studies conducted to date that the costs of the computer, associated electronics interfacing, and software will total about 15 per cent of the overall cost.

The second point to bear in mind is that it takes a long time to implement the FMS. This is a reflection of the complexity of the system and the number of potential sup-pliers or contractors contributing to the system. Even before contracts are placed, many months, perhaps years, of rationalisation and planning work needs to be done. The development exercise itself should take two to four months of post-contract specification, followed by a similar period of internal system design by the software team behind closed doors. Subsequently the implementation will require any-thing from eight months to two years, although on the more complex systems, a usable FMS may be achieved before the full implementation is complete.

Thirdly, one of the contractors must assume the respon-sibility of project integration and management over and above the normal project management by the end user. This ensures that interprocess specifications are formalised and precisely specified and where communcation interface stan-dards do not exist they are created.

Lastly, the designer of the overall control system must ensure that he does not build any single point failure nodes into the system: for example, if the computer were to fail as computers do occasionally, then the whole machine shop will grind to a half.

7.5   CONTROL SYSTEM DESIGN

It is possible to conceive of a control system whereby all the mechanical devices (machine tools, robots, conveyors) are directly connected into a process computer. This suffers from the above mentioned single-point failure node.

A better approach is to use two computers, one acting as the 'live' controller and the other as 'standby.' This reduces the risk considerably, effectively squaring the

'up-time' of the computer system virtually to a 100 per cent availability. But there are still a number of inter-related deficiencies with this approach:
- All the signal I/O lines from each mechanical device (and there may be many of them - 50 or 60 is a typical number) must be cabled back from the shop floor to the computer room. This presents an unrealistic cabling cost.
- The same signal I/O lines must be terminated in I/O modules in the computer. For a large system the total number of I/O signals could total thousands, and this number may be beyond the capacity of the computer hardware.
- It is difficult to switch this number of connections bet-ween the live computer and the standby.
- The computer, however powerful, may have difficulty in polling round all the inputs within the time constraints of the system.
    For these reasons, the only sensible control strategy is to adopt a distributed processor system. The upper level of the control might be two minicomputers as previously des-cribed, connected by two-wire, four-wire, or fibre-optic interfaces to a network of microprocessors out on the shop floor near the equipment. The switching of the electrical connections is made very simple, and the switching process can even be automated for 'hot standby' applications through the provision of a 'watchdog' - an independent arbiter of the performance of both computer processors.
    Needless to say, where the machine is already intelli-gent - it may itself contain a micro or minicomputer, such as a CNC controller for a machine tool - then it may prove feasible to connect the equipment to the computer directly rather than through an additional microprocessor. The provisos are:
- The device must have a suitable serial port for connection to the computer (RS232, current-loop etc.)
- The device must have a defined structure for data'flow on that connection with data protection protocol.
- The machine's processor should be able to respond to com-puter initiated requests asynchronously from the main pro-cess that it is controlling.
- There should be adequate facilities for operator-to-computer dialogue, i.e. a readable display and alpha numeric keyboard.

7.6   WHY MICRO-PROCESSORS?

    Distributing microprocessors across a control system incurs numerous advantages to the system designer. These are:
- Each micro has about 30 per cent of the power of the mini-computer and hence the sum total of the computer power available is vastly increased with each of the micros operating in parallel.
- The micros can be locally sited, reducing cabling costs and putting operator-interaction adjacent to the machine.
- The approach is modular and gives very good resilience against failure. A breakdown of one micro does not affect operation of the entire factory. (In fact the micros are

supremely reliable compared to the electro-mechanical devices they control).
- The modular approach eases spares holdings and maintenance training.
- The micros can assist fault-finding through pre-programmed diagnostics.
- The micros allow easy common use of data protocols through-out the system.
- To a certain extent, the micros allow each cell to operate in the event of a main-computer black-out.
- The development timescale is shortened, since once the interface between minicomputer and microprocessor has been defined then separate project teams can work in parallel.
- All this is achieved at very low cost.
- Using Systime's range of Modular Micro family microproces-sor interfaces, the various different controllers can be rapidly put together from standard parts, in standard in-dustrial cabinets, leaving only the internal and external cabling to be specifically designed. The software modules are assembled similarly to promote rapid programming and because the micros are 'soft' devices they can be easily changed.

7.7   COMMUNCATIONS

Distributing the control system functions across a number of different processors assists the designer to put those control functions in appropriate physical places on the shop floor, with the supervisory minicomputers in an air-conditioned environment elsewhere. The task then is to con-nect together the various micros and minis to form a single control system. This leads to a discussion on communica-tions methods and protocols.

Distributed systems may be connected together either via a bus highway, or via a 'ring' type of communcation net-work, or by a 'star' type of network. Analysis of the traf-fic between the various devices led Systime to select the star connection as the most suitable for its FMS implementations. Each of the micros or CNC controllers is connected back via unique lines to a central point, the watchdog-controlled switching device, and thence to each of the two minicomputers. The communcations are therefore effectively point-to-point.

The machine shop environment is high in electrical noise, and long signal conductors can pick up electromagne-tic interference both low frequency and RF, and 'spikes'. In addition the large three-phase electric motors can exhi-bit non-unity power factors which cause deviations in ground, voltage locally. It is therefore essential to use an elec-trical signal which avoids referencing to ground, or to avoid electrical signals altogether. While much is being made of the merits of optic fibres, this technology does have its own drawbacks particularly the cost of interfacing, the cost of installation (grinding optical flats at fibre ends), and the necessity to avoid small radius curves. Systime therefore chose a combination of these techniques, using opto-isolators on both transmitted and received signals, with a 20mA current loop carried in conventional four-wire copper conductors. This method has been found to be most cost-effective and extremely reliable.

7.8 DECISION ON PROTOCOL

It remains essential, however, to check for errors in data transmission, no matter how reliable the communication medium since the data that is being passed around the system is critical. For example, if an error crept into a part-program being down-line loaded to a machine tool then, at best, scrap parts would be produced; at worst, considerable damage could be done to the machine itself.

After examining all the common data protocols in existence at the time (1980), it transpired that none was suitable for the purpose: one therefore had to be designed. It is a half-duplex protocol operating on asynchronous lines, with start and end-frames, parity and a CRC-CCTTT check-sum similar to Bi-Syne. Other suppliers to the SCAMP system agreed to use the protocol and implemented it on their CNC controllers. It guarantees that any transmission errors will be detected and the message in question re-transmitted. The equipment which could not be directly connected to the computers was front-ended by Systime micro-processors, and naturally these utilise the same protocol. There are 23 such additional devices on the SCAMP system.

Lastly there was the need to define the format of the data that was to make up the various messages, for example:
- Display text on the operator's screen.
- Send machine tool status back to computer.
- Load next block of part program into CNC
- Disable cycle-start

and so on. In all about 60 different message structures were found to be necessary.

7.9 SCAMP

Systime was one of ten major suppliers to the SCAMP system, which was formally announced in December 1982 after nearly three years development. A schematic diagram of the SCAMP system is shown in Fig. 7.1.

ACKNOWLEDGEMENT

The theme of this Chapter was presented by the author to the FMS conference of CAM -I in Milan in June 1983 by kind invitation of CAM - I and is reproduced here with their permission.

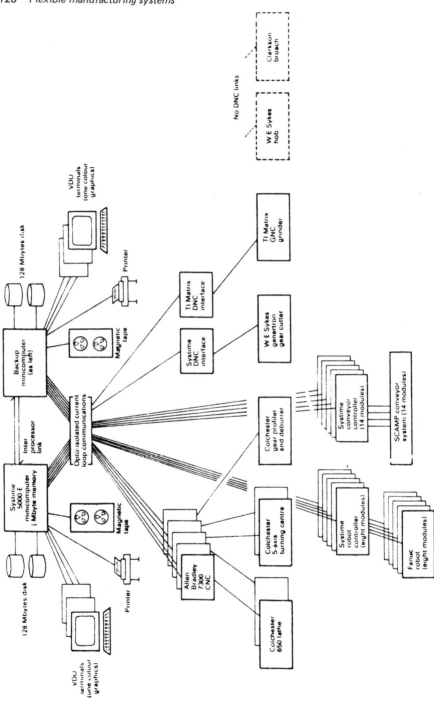

Fig. 7.1   Computer control hierarchy of the SCAMP FMS
as designed and supplied by Systime.

Chapter 8

Computer control of electrical power systems

M.J.H. Sterling

8.1 THE NEED FOR CONTROL

Power system control is required to maintain a continuous balance between electrical generation and a varying load demand, while system frequency, voltage levels and security are maintained. Furthermore, it is desirable that the cost of such generation should be a minimum. The variable nature of the consumer power demand necessitates fluctuations in the total generation in order that the power balance be maintained. Once more capacity than is available from a single set is required, the division of the load between generating plant becomes an important operational as well as economic problem, that must be solved continuously.

Fortunately, system frequency serves as an indication of any imbalance between load and generation and is used to control the power output of generators in the short term by way of fast continuously acting regulators, which detect deviations of the frequency from a pre-set value and act directly on the steam inlet valve. The initial division of the load fluctuations amongst the synchronised generating plant is consequently determined by the various parameters of these control loops. This situation is undesirable on economic grounds since the operational costs of generators invariably differ. As a result, it may be advantageous to run one or more sets in preference to other more expensive plant. Given the operational costs of all plant in service it should therefore be possible to allocate the available resources such that for a particular load the total production cost is minimised.

To a large extent the need for direct action to control network voltage levels has been overcome by the installation of automatic voltage regulating equipment. The security aspects of generation and transmission however, are at present the responsibility of grid control engineers, who rely on considerable operational experience together with off-line load flow studies.

Overall system control is based on a combination of manual intervention, fast continuously-acting feed back control of local loops for voltage regulation and speed governing together with a slower-acting open-loop feedforward-type of optimising control or generator scheduling based on predicted load demand. The optimising schedule for changes of bulk generation will usually include a coordination of generator costs and line losses subject to constraints on line and plant loading and security.

The control responsibility is divided basically according to the frequency of intervention required and to the time scale of the physical phenomena involved. Area level decisions may also include system voltage control by transformer tap positions and excitation control with an optimum scheduling of reactive power flow. Distribution of reactive power will not affect significantly system operating costs, but an optimum allocation may be important for maintaining steady-state system stability and voltage levels.

The requirements for control of frequency and power exchange or area regulation can be implemented by a secondary load-frequency control superimposed on the local speed governors. It provides automatic variation of generator set points for control of system frequency and tie-line power flows. The secondary control is autonomous, with each area responsible for its own steady-state power balance based on its own operating variables. It is usually implemented as an integral control action based on an area control error related to a linear combination of net change in tie-line power transfer and frequency deviation. It adjusts total generation to match the total load changes within the area and the scheduled interchange, and will also coordinate the interconnected operation and compensate for emergency generation changes in adjacent areas.

Thus the difference between generated and consumed power must be continuously monitored and control action applied to generation to restore the balance. The inertia of the rotating masses in the generating units provides the energy necessary for a temporary imbalance. An increase in system load is consequently met initially by a reduction in the kinetic energy of the system with an inherent speed reduction. However the speed of the generators determines the system frequency, thus frequency represents an indirect measure of the imbalance between consumed and generated power. The turbine control system must consequently adjust the control values to halt the continuous reduction of kinetic energy and speed, at which time the energy balance will have been restored.

The control loop, comprising the turbine control system (governor) and machine normally exhibits a linear relationship. As long as the consumption of the total network is equal to the sum of the outputs of the generating sets there is zero deviation from the target frequency. If the load on the system changes, the operating points of all machines move along their characteristic curves until the sum of the generated power is equal to the new load and balance is restored. Each individual generator accepts that proportion of the load change which corresponds to its characteristic curve. There remains a residual frequency deviation since the governors are essentially proportional controllers. However the frequency offset can be eliminated by altering the set points of the individual generator units.

Present-day power systems operating as interconnected grid networks have several advantages. Transfer of power between areas with predominantly hydroelectric, thermal or nuclear generating plant is made possible, enabling the advantage of each to be exploited and resulting in improved compensation of load fluctuations with reduced running costs. A reduction in the spare capacity of each inter-connected system is also feasible as a result of mutual assistance in the event of a fault.

Exchange of power between two adjacent networks is usually governed by a fixed programme so that during a given period of time a constant amount of power is exchanged. If the load on one system varies, the outputs of all generators in the grid are altered since each section of the interconnected system is involved in the change of load. The power flowing through the tie lines consequently deviates from the scheduled values. Hence, in addition to the frequency deviation there is also a variation in exchanged power. These differences can be corrected by alteration of the governor set points in both areas. It is therefore apparent that there are at least two levels of control action in the system control problem. Primary control is effected by the turbine governors which attempt to balance generated and consumed power with secondary, slower acting, control of set points by a system controller. It is the task of the system controller to maintain both the combined power transmitted between networks and also the system frequency at preset values. This function is normally referred to as load-frequency control (LFC).

8.2 EVOLUTION OF SYSTEM CONTROL

The prime objective of system control in any power system, whether interconnected or not, is the matching of generation to load demand, and in the short term is achieved by the turbine governors adjusting power input to the system in response to frequency deviations. On an isolated system this is the only type of control required to match generation with load and is called 'flat frequency control'.

The combined operation of the governors is, however, essentially proportional, requiring a sustained frequency deviation to produce a sustained change of power output from the turbine. Hence although the generation and load may be in equilibrium the frequency will no longer be at its scheduled value following a sustained load change.

The change in system generation required to restore the frequency to its nominal value is termed the 'area requirement'.

In the early stages of control development it was usually found possible to obtain satisfactory frequency regulation by setting the speed droop to zero on a suitable machine, usually one of the larger sets. The quality of frequency control with this arrangement was often improved by selecting other units to play a supporting role to the zero droop or master machine. Good frequency regulation was usually possible with this form of control provided that the governors were operating satisfactorily and the master machine was kept within its regulating range. The latter requirement resulted in very frequent manual adjustment of the governor set points on the other generation to keep the master machine within its limits.

The next step in the development of system control was the replacement of the zero droop machine by a frequency regulator, which performed essentially the same function but was capable of subdividing the regulating burden to several machines within a power station. The basis for the subdivision was often established according to the machine capacity but more sophisticated regulators could distribute load between machines on the basis of their relative efficiencies.

When all the regulating machines are in one plant it is comparatively simple to arrange for the desired division between units, but for remote stations to participate some form of centralised control is necessary. The frequency controller is then located at the central control point and telemetry provided to the various units and stations. It is then possible to select which units should be used for regulation at any given time, which is particularly useful in hydro-systems where water conditions may preclude the use of a particular station for regulation during certain periods of the year. Centralisation of control also necessitates extensive telemetry since it is essential that the load on the regulating units is known at all times, together with other plant information.

In addition to the need to spread the regulating burden over several plants, economic division of plant loading may be another reason for multiple plant regulation. It is frequently the more compelling reason on a pure thermal or mixed hydro-thermal system since there is considerable financial benefit in dividing the loads among the various units for maximum economy.

8.3   TIME SCALE OF SYSTEM CONTROL

The management and control of a power system is a complex process requiring interaction between many levels of the command hierarchy and on widely differing time scales. Fig. 8.1 shows the main elements of the control hierarchy and the approximate time scale on which each level operates. Naturally there will be considerable variation in the frequency of intervention for one level dependent on the means by which that level is implemented. Manual control will generally be slower than automatic control while digital control is, by nature, discrete and analogue control continuous with time. The availability of large scale process control computers has resulted in consideration of digital computer implementation of many levels previously under manual or analogue control. Furthermore the scale of problem representation, and consequently the complexity of the solution and control, has been increased in line with the power of the available computers. However there is still much scope for automatic control not only on fast time scales but also at the management levels.

Primary control at the lowest level of Fig. 8.1 is fundamental to the operation of the power system and has for many years received the greatest attention. The rapid response required necessitates local automatic equipment for control of such functions as voltage regulation, excitation control, and fault isolation. Historically this control was implemented by analogue devices but small digital systems based on micro or mini computers are beginning to be considered. The automatic adjustment of governor set points to maintain tie line flows and frequency, or load-frequency control as it is more commonly known, is now mainly implemented by online digital computers. Early schemes employed complex analogue equipment which although satisfactory for small networks did not have the flexibility of digital schemes. The frequency of control and the relatively simple computations needed were also ideally suited to online computer implementations.

The higher levels of control on time scales ranging from 10 minutes to 10 years are largely manually controlled at present, although the economic dispatch and plant ordering phases have been incorporated into some more advanced computer control schemes. The time scale on which this optimisation is implemented depends considerably on the technique for the optimum allocation of plant outputs. The manually calculated merit order schedule, currently used by most regions of the UK Central Electricity Generating Board, attempts to load the cheapest sets to their maximum output, reserving other more expensive plant for sudden unexpected load increases. Limitations on network operation, other than generator and group maxima and minima are usually excluded to reduce the complexity of the problem. Furthermore, the large variation of consumer load between day and night necessitates the start-up and shut-down of plant, in order to minimise the cost of providing stand-by synchronised generation. Not only must the online generation be

Time scale   Function   Implementation

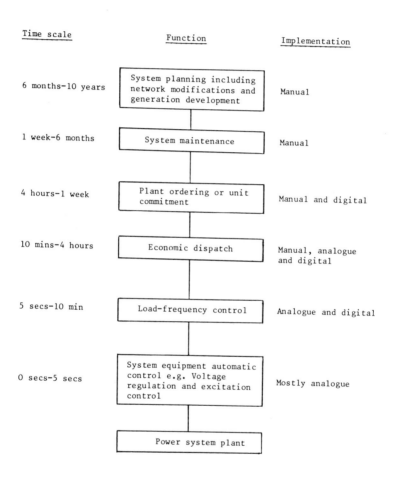

Time scale	Function	Implementation
6 months–10 years	System planning including network modifications and generation development	Manual
1 week–6 months	System maintenance	Manual
4 hours–1 week	Plant ordering or unit commitment	Manual and digital
10 mins–4 hours	Economic dispatch	Manual, analogue and digital
5 secs–10 min	Load-frequency control	Analogue and digital
0 secs–5 secs	System equipment automatic control e.g. Voltage regulation and excitation control	Mostly analogue
	Power system plant	

Fig. 8.1   Time decomposed hierarchical control structure

optimally distributed on a minute-to-minute basis, but the overheads associated with bringing plant in and out of service must be minimised over the long term. These two problems are usually considered separately such that in the generation dispatch problem, only synchronised plant is optimised, whereas in the plant ordering phase, sufficient generating capacity is made available to meet the estimated load and provide enough spare capacity for secure operation.

System planning and maintenance although manually implemented frequently require extensive offline computations to assess the effects of plant or network availability or expansion. Fortunately the large time scale enables these levels to receive adequate attention however, since many factors are often unknown, the conclusions drawn are not always correct.

8.4 ONLINE COMPUTER CONTROL

Many of the fundamental control functions needed to operate a power system, including the acquisition and presentation of information and the subsequent processing of that data, can in principle be realised by analogue based hardware consisting of electronic devices with fixed wired logic, chart recorders, mimic diagrams, telecontrol systems and numerous other devices. Indeed most power systems prior to the nineteen sixties operated satisfactorily with solely analogue type instrumentation and control, some schemes being very complex with provision for many of the features normally associated with modern control implementations. However within the last 10 to 15 years digital techniques have been increasingly used to supplement, and in many cases replace, discrete analogue hardware.

Naturally there must be an economic justificaiton for the introduction or improvement of any computer control scheme which can often be broadly classified into improvement of data processing, the man-process interface by way of graphical or alphanumeric displays giving more reliable and closer control, and implementation of closed loop real time control. Of these the data processing function is often the most easily justified and is a prerequisite for the other two areas.

Perhaps the main obstacle to the acceptance of digital computers in real-time applications has been concerned about their reliability. Early schemes would sometimes utilise several separate centralised computer systems, each with multiple processors, incorporating elaborate change-over devices in order to improve the overall reliability. However the present trend is for small scale computers to be integrated into all levels of system control in order to improve the quantity or quality of information and control. High integrity is still required but the system reliability can now be more easily tailored to the application, resulting in a more cost effective solution.

Present day computer involvement in power system operation is widespread and sophisticated computer control schemes have been commissioned in many countries. The majority of these schemes have a configuration corresponding to Fig. 8.2

A system diagram display board or mimic diagram can be very large and will usually dictate the layout of a control room whereas interactive CRT's can be located at each control desk and can be programmed to present network diagrams. A CRT can also be arranged to zoom on selected regions of a network to show enlarged and possibly more detailed network configuration with alphanumeric represen- tation of measured values such as voltage profiles, on line power flow and transformer loadings. A wide range of facilities is available to enhance the man-machine inter- face including light pen or joy stick interaction, blinking of selected display information and audible tones. Alarm information is often routed to a different set of displays and may be only alphanumeric. Although incremental plotters may be available for hard-copy of selected measured value variations with time, most instal- lations retain continuous multi-channel chart recorders.

A major advantage of a computer based tele-control system is that the validity of all control actions can be established. Attempts to open circuit breakers which would divide the network can be intercepted and the operator informed. Furthermore, even without automated dispatch, simple loading rates and generation limits can be tested prior to transmission of commands.

The integrity of the final system must not be jeopardised by the failure of the computer and consequently a dual computer arrangement is often specified. Each display controller drives one display unit on each console, thus failure of one computer or controller does not incapacitate a console completely. Should both computers fail limited supervision and control can be maintained through an emergency system. Manual addressing of outstations for display or control is possible but restrictive, however the reliability of the overall system should be high.

Timing in an online computer system is of vital importance for both events related to specific times of day and time intervals. A log of all alarms and control actions would normally be kept together with the time of day that each occurred. Scanning of inputs would, however, be time interval dependent. In consequence an accurate time reference must be provided which is independent of the mains frequency.

8.5   SOFTWARE ELEMENTS

The computer assisted control of electrical power

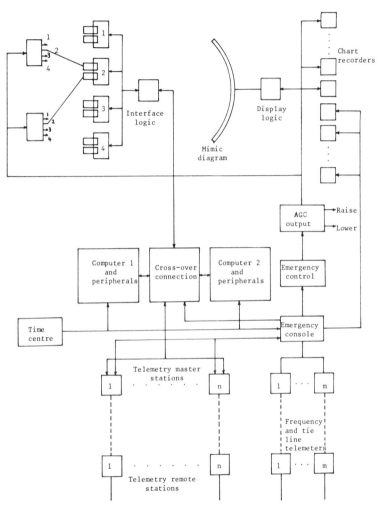

Fig. 8.2 Computer based telecontrol scheme

transmission and distribution systems represents a large scale real time data processing problem and demands an integrated approach to software design.

Fortunately, the complexity of the software can be reduced by considering the overall control as a series of semi-autonomous subsystems which communicate via a common database and task scheduling system.

8.5.1 State Estimation and Topology Determination

A prerequisite of any power system security monitoring or control scheme is a reliable data base in which the raw observations have been systematically processed in order to filter out the effects of uncertainty by inclusion of information on the network structure and measurement accuracy. In general the tele-metered data will contain small random errors associated with measurement or transmission noise and also a number of gross errors caused by equipment malfunction. It is the function of the state estimation and topology determination subsystem to eliminate the gross errors and filter the noisy measurements in order to obtain the most accurate and complete information possible on the present operating state of the network. A topology determination function is required to build up a nodal representation of the power system. However, the software cannot rely on the accuracy of the connectivity information which is available, and a data validation process is therefore required.

The validation may be performed simultaneously at a number of different levels. Data obtained from individual substations or groups of substations may be processed by a series of parallel substation validation tasks as shown in Fig. 8.3. The resulting partially corrected measurements may be further processed by an area validation task. Algorithms based on sparse linear programming provide a systematic approach to data validation and further details of this technique are given by Irving and Sterling (3).

If sufficient well placed measurements of voltage, current, active and reactive power flow are available in the network, the power system state (nodal voltage and phase angles) is well defined and the measurement set is said to be observable. An efficient algorithm for observ-ability detection is therefore an important adjunct to the state estimation subsystem, and can provide valuable assistance with meter placement decisions.

Provided that the network state is observable the state estimator performs the important roles of noise filtering and replacement of unavailable measurement data. The state estimator must also be capable of dealing with bad data in cases where correction at the data validation stage is not possible. Sparse linear programming estima-tors, Irving , Owen, Sterling, (2) are again applicable and can form a very useful alternative to the more conven-

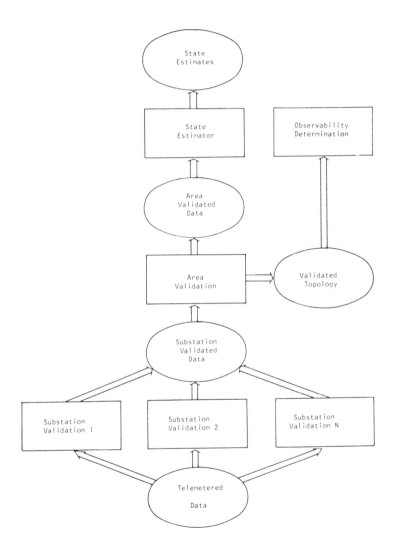

Fig. 8.3 State estimation and topology determination subsystem

tional weighted least squares estimation method used by
Schweppe and Handschin (5)

8.5.2 Monitoring and Prediction

The necessity for estimating the power system load
expected at some time in the future is apparent when it is
remembered that generating plant capacity must be
available to balance exactly any network load at whatever
time it occurs. In the long term the installation of new
plant and network expansion is dependent upon an estimate
of the future peak consumer demand up to several years
ahead. In the short term the variation of the system load
must be known in order that prior warning of output
requirements may be given to power stations, enabling
limitations on boiler fuel feed rates, and generator rate
of change of output constraints, to be observed. Furthermore, the economic schedule for the start-up and shutdown
of plant is dependent on an estimate of the network load
so that the cost of providing spinning spare capacity for
system security can be minimised. In a power system under
automatic computer control it is this short term projected
load which is used to calculate a generator dispatch for
which all operating limits are satisfied and the generation cost a minimum. Unfortunately, the consumer load is
essentially uncontrollable, although small variations can
be affected by frequency control and more drastically by
load shedding. The variation of the load does however
exhibit certain daily and yearly pattern repetitions and
the analysis of these forms the basis for load prediction
techniques. Methods using spectral expansion, Farmer (6),
and autoregressive moving average modelling, Sterling (1),
have been developed and are capable of predicting the
system load to within one or two percent over a time
period of up to four hours.
Accurate load predictions are only possible if a
reliable log of past load values is available. Fig. 8.4
illustrates the combination of raw load measurements with
area validated load data which is utilised in obtaining a
dependable log of past consumer loads. The load
monitoring subsystem is also able to detect any unexpected
loss or increase of load in the network and to provide
appropriate operator alarms and event logs.

8.5.3 Generation and Load Control

Generation control is an area in which major economic
benefits may be realised, especially in large scale
systems which are not simple to control manually.
Although the overall problem of generation control may be
expressed mathematically, the solution is beyond the scope
of currently available computing techniques. It is therefore customary to subdivide the overall problem into
subproblems which act over different time scales. Fig.

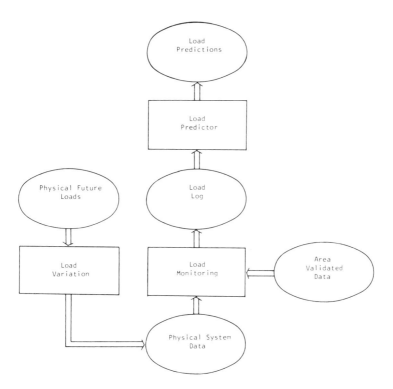

Fig. 8.4 Load monitoring and prediction subsystem

8.5 shows the interaction of unit commitment in the long term with economic dispatch in the medium term and with emergency rescheduling and load frequency control in the short term. Load shedding is also a necessary control option which is available in cases where generation control is no longer sufficient to maintain system security.

The unit commitment or plant ordering phase of control establishes the optimum pattern for starting up and shutting down generators, taking into account economic objectives and operational constraints. Presently available analytical methods based on mixed integer programming or dynamic programming are only computationally feasible for small systems; application to medium and large systems therefore implies the use of heuristic methods.

The economic dispatch function is concerned with the allocation of target output powers for generators in order to satisfy the predicted load demand at minimum cost, while remaining within operational constraints. This control problem is essentially predictive and is usually implemented on a time scale of five minutes upwards. A comprehensive solution which is able to include reactive power considerations and transmission losses has been developed using a quadratic programming technique, Sterling (1). For systems with a very large number of generators a simplified formulation is amenable to sparse linear programming solution, Irving and Sterling (4).

Load frequency control is required to regulate system frequency and scheduled tie-line interchanges. The standard classical control approach with exponential data smoothing is often adopted, and normally provides satisfactory performance.

During emergency conditions in which insufficient generation is available to meet system loads or where one or more unexpected plant outages have occured it is important to be able to rapidly reschedule generation and allocate the degree of load shedding required. It is vital that this phase of operation should be executed rapidly and modern computer control systems are increasingly being used in this area. Under emergency conditions the economic operation of the system has a lower priority than the minimisation of load shedding. However, emergency rescheduling methods, which are now available, generally assign artificial costs to each load supply point, allowing a priority order of load shedding and also enabling a trade-off between generation rescheduling and load shedding.

Although emergency resheduling gives an automatic indication of the required degree and location of load reduction, most applications require a more detailed analysis and further operator interaction before any load shedding takes place. Interactive programs have been developed which assign priorities and allowable load shedding fractions to each consumer demand point. Load may be

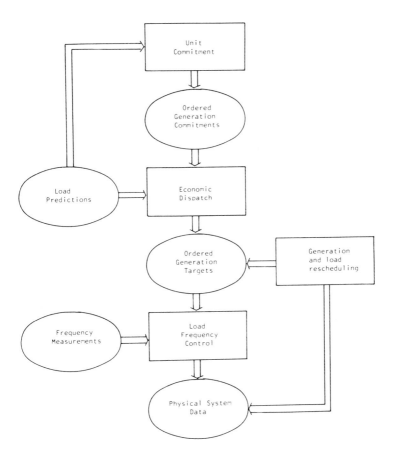

Fig. 8.5 Generation control and load shedding subsystem

reduced in a number of pre-defined stages and operator confirmation is necessary before any load shedding command is transmitted. Programs may be initiated either manually by operator selection or automatically by the detection of serious underfrequency or load/generation imbalance conditions.

8.5.4 Security Analysis

As an aid to the network control engineer it is possible to assess the effect of any scheduled or unexpected line or generator outages by means of a fast approximate loadflow method. This subsystem predicts the number and severity of any overloads which may result from the switching operation or breaker status change under consideration. Unfortunately, even applying the fast decoupled loadflow method proposed by Stott and Alsac (7) with efficient updating of outage solutions using the modified matrix technique, the solution time required for consideration of every possible outage may be excessive. It is therefore advantageous to perform a simplified analysis referred to as automatic outage preselection as shown in Fig. 8.6 which determines the subset of possible contingencies predicted to be most severe according to an overload performance index as used by Vemuri and Usher (8). The security assessment phase then proceeds to analyse the intact system and the preselected outage cases. Overloading in the intact system may often be corrected by generation rescheduling or in more severe cases load shedding. Potential overloads which are dependent on unscheduled plant outages are a more difficult case, and it is not yet clear whether they may be handled automatically.

Fault studies are a further aspect of security analysis, and are required to give the short circuit current levels for the present system topology and operating state. The operator may then determine whether any circuit breakers would exceed their rating under fault conditions, and if necessary implement topology changes to provide remedial action.

8.6   SOFTWARE COORDINATION AND SYSTEM SIMULATION

The software which has been described in previous sections can be coordinated to form an integrated system in the manner illustrated in Fig. 8.7. The configuration of the overall scheme highlights similarity with conventional automatic control systems. Information is monitored via the telemetry system, load monitoring, topology determination and state estimation subsystems. Feedback control is effected via load frequency control, generation rescheduling and load shedding, and feed forward control is implemented in the load prediction, security analysis, economic dispatch and unit commitment phases.

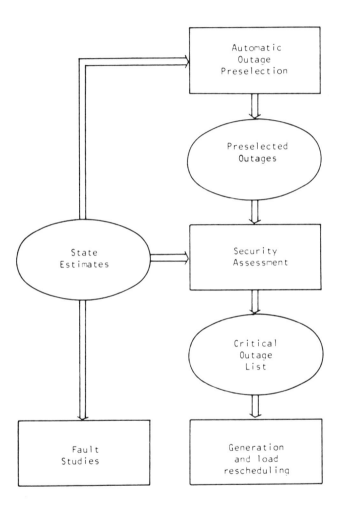

Fig. 8.6   Security analysis subsystem

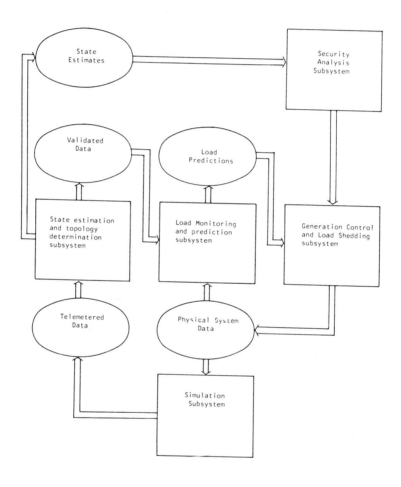

Fig. 8.7 Coordination of subsystems

Experience has indicated that in order to be robust the system must be highly modular in structure. Each task should communicate with others through shared memory areas with specified access privileges. The timing of task execution and synchronisation should be achieved as far as possible by the task itself and by reference to semaphores and event keys in shared data. Every task or subsystem ought to be capable of being initiated or aborted at any time without compromising the integrity of the overall control system (although various data may obviously become outdated).

A power system simulation facility is also a necessary component of an integrated software system for high level control of transmission or distribution networks. The simulation subsystem allows higher level control software to be tested and evaluated without recourse to 'live' telemetry data. It also provides a valuable tool for software diagnosis, operator training, pre-commissioning and feasibility studies.

Fig. 8.8 shows the major database elements and computational procedures required for simulation. The physical system data block contains information on the physical state of the network such as plant connections, equipment ratings, load conditions, and breaker status. The information is altered by automatic or manual control inputs, plant outages, consumer load variation, breaker operation, etc. The data includes a network representation in which individual busbar sections are modelled separately. For the purpose of network simulation using a mathematical modelling technique, a simpler description is required in which solidly connected busbars are collectively represented as nodes. The transformation of the connectivity data from busbar to nodal level is achieved by the exact topology determination module while the simulator applies a nonlinear algebraic model of the network in conjunction with a set of low order differential equations representing generator dynamics to produce telemetry information.

8.7   CONCLUSIONS

It will be evident from the foregoing sections that online computer control of electrical power systems is an extremely complex task which necessitates sophisticated control hardware and software structures. The incentives to achieve secure, economic operation of power systems are large with operating costs for the UK Central Electricity Generating Board being of the order of £4 x 10^9 p.a. Small improvements in efficiency consequently represent very substantial financial savings. The world market for improved system control is large but much research and development is still needed before totally automatic control schemes become a reality.

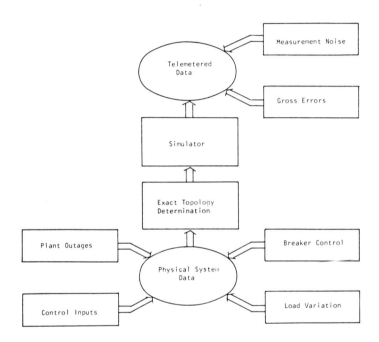

Fig. 8.8   Simulation subsystem

REFERENCES

1. Sterling, M.J.H., 1978, Power System Control, Peter Peregrinus, UK, ISBN 0 906048 01 X.

2. Irving, M.R., Owen, R.C., Sterling, M.J.H., 1978 Power System State Estimation Using Linear Programming, Proc IEE 125 (9) 879-885.

3. Irving, M.R., Sterling, M.J.H., 1982 Substation Data Validation, Proc IEE 129, (3) 119-122.

4. Irving, M.R., Sterling M.J.H., 1983 Economic Dispatch of Active Power with Constraint Relaxation, Proc IEE 130 (4).

5. Schweppe, F.C., Handschin, E.J., 1974, Static State Estimation in Electric Power Systems, Proc IEEE 62 (7) 972-982.

6. Farmer, E.D., 1963 A Method of Prediction for Nonstationary Processes and its Application to the Problem of Load Estimation. Proc. IFAC Congress, Basle.

7. Stott, B., Alsac, O., 1974 Fast Decoupled Loadflow, IEEE Trans Pas 93 859-869.

8. Vemuri, S., Usher, R.E., 1982 On-line Automatic Contingency Selection Algorithms. IEEE PES Summer Meeting paper no. 82 SM 413-3.

Chapter 9

DDC in CEGB power stations

M.L. Bransby

9.1 INTRODUCTION

This chapter describes some of the developments in computer software for control and instrumentation (C & I) applications which have taken place within the Central Electricity Generating Board (CEGB) over the last few years. The major part of this development has been performed by CEGB staff and, to date, use of the software has been almost exclusively confined to CEGB plant. Nevertheless, the circumstances behind this development are common to many industrial situations, and for this reason it is hoped that a description of the policy adopted will be of interest to control engineers in general.

Initially in this chapter the requirements that have led to the software development will be described and what are the broad objectives of this. Then the major features of the CEGB's CUTLASS software system (Maples et al (1)) will be outlined. This will be followed by two specific examples, based on power station applications, which illustrate the facilities provided for modulating and sequence control respectively.

9.1.1 The Cost of Control Software

Software development is expensive. In an Electric Power Research Institute report (2) published in 1982 it was stated that the full development cost of software for scientific calculations was between $10 and $40 per line of code. For C & I software for a process involving public safety, for example a nuclear power station, the stated cost was $300 to $700 per line of code. These figures include the costs of specification of requirements, preliminary design, detailed design, coding and testing, and it is interesting to note that detailed design and coding represents only around 20% of the total (Wolverton (3)).

Experience within the CEGB would confirm that production of control software for power station applications can be extremely expensive. For example, the resources required to develop and commission the software for a large power station display, logging and alarm system in assembler code could amount to some 70 man-years of effort, much of it involving specialist computer knowledge.

In view of such expenditures on C & I system software, the CEGB, in 1979, carried out a review of likely future C & I software requirements in the decade up to 1989. The life of a typical power station control system is perhaps 15-20 years before the equipment becomes obsolescent and there is a demonstrable economic case for replacement and enhancement. The first 500 MW boiler-turbine unit was commissioned in the CEGB in 1963 and in the following decade a further 44 units of nominally 500 MW or larger were built. The C & I systems on many of these units were therefore likely to require replacement in the decade under consideration. In addition, there was a case for control system refurbishment on some of the smaller, older units. A conclusion of the review was that, unless major efforts were made to reduce it, a total resource of around 700 man years might be needed for the development of C & I system software over the decade. There were insufficient available software specialists within the CEGB to provide the required level of resourcing, and this reflected a national situation which was thought unlikely to change in the immediate future. Consequently, in 1979, the CEGB committed itself to the adoption of CUTLASS as a standard software system for power station control applications in order to alleviate these two problems of high expenditure and shortage of computer specialists. A detailed discussion of some of the reasons which led to the development of this software system, and of some of the advantages of it, is given in the following sections.

9.2   THE OBJECTIVES OF CUTLASS

9.2.1 High Level Facilities

Many inexperienced programmers would be surprised by the high costs of software quoted above - particularly since they imply an overall productivity of 1 or 2 lines of code per man day. One reason (Wolverton (3), Chen (4)) for this is that many novice programmers have only written short programs. However, the time taken to produce software increases disproportionately with the size of program required. In general, the time to produce 10 programs each of 100 lines will be very much less than the time to produce one of 1000 lines. Furthermore, the time of production of a program of a given number of lines of code is relatively independent of the level of language used, and thus the writing of an assembler program of 1000 lines will take much the same time as an APL program of 1000 lines.

There is an obvious conclusion from this that, if it is required to program a particular function, it is likely to be most efficient to do it in a high level language which is tailored to the application and able to achieve it in a minimum number of lines of code. One of the most significant features of CUTLASS is that it provides language subsets specifically designed for the C & I applications frequently required in power stations. These subsets include:-

    Modulating Control
    Sequence Control
    VDU Display
    Data Logging
    Alarm Handling

Without doubt, the benefits of using these special-purpose language subsets compared with using a conventional, general-purpose language, such as Fortran, are very substantial.

A further benefit of adopting application orientated software is that it enables the application program development to be done by engineers rather than software specialists, and this has reduced the pressure on a limited manpower resource. Furthermore, because the engineers who understand the plant needs are doing the programming, effort need not be spent in communicating their ideas and experience to computer programmers who may be unfamiliar with the plant problems involved.

Of course, software specialists are required for the production of the CUTLASS system software and of the language subsets. However, the specification of the facilities provided is done, after careful investigation of the needs, by engineers. Thus CUTLASS is basically designed by engineers for use by engineers. Because of this it is a natural medium for communication between engineers.

Much power station control software can have significant operational implications if it fails, and therefore must be exhaustively validated. This generally involves testing of the software by a team of engineers different from that which wrote it. Obviously here the ease with which CUTLASS can be understood by engineers is most important.

9.2.2 A CEGB Standard

In the 1979 policy review it was identified that over twenty different types of software had been used in the various power-station and transmission-system control, display and instrumentation computers installed at that time. These types included assembler languages (which had been the only practical option in the earlier equipment), higher level languages such as CORAL, and some CEGB developed systems - much experience on these being later incorporated in CUTLASS. Following the review, the CEGB committed itself to the long term adoption of CUTLASS as the standard software system for all new C & I applications. It is turning out that it is also beneficial to convert existing software systems to CUTLASS at appropriate points in their life cycles.

The adoption of CUTLASS as a CEGB standard offered several advantages. First, it allowed the cost of writing and testing the CUTLASS system software and language subsets to be spread over a large number of projects. Software testing and reliability is important, particularly for nuclear power stations (Geiger et al (5)). It is considered to be preferable to adopt one standard system, in which all changes are properly monitored and tested and which has wide application on many fossil-fired power stations, rather than to adopt a number of different manufacturer's software systems.

A second advantage of a standard software system is that it can also allow application program development costs to be spread over several projects. Control structures employed on particular loops are similar at very many power stations, similar data needs to be logged and similar VDU displays and alarms need to be available. Thus, in principle, CUTLASS application programs produced for one power station should be relatively easily adapted for another. At the present time, with CUTLASS still quite a new product, this opportunity has not been fully grasped, but it offers great potential future benefit.

A third advantage of adopting CUTLASS as a standard is that it has allowed an efficient and co-ordinated training programme to be developed. This increases the cross-fertilisation of ideas between different locations and reduces the reliance on particular individuals. At some older power station computer installations, knowledge of the now obsolescent hardware and software resides in just one or two individuals. If these people move to different jobs, it can be a long and expensive exercise to train others to replace them. Refurbishment of such systems with CUTLASS can ease long term maintenance and improve staff efficiency.

9.2.3 Hardware Independence

It is not sensible for the CEGB to limit itself to a single computer manufacturer for all its numerous C & I applications. This would take it out of a competitive market situation, make it sensitive to a particular manufacturer's performance, and would not allow maximal advantage to be taken of technological advances. It was therefore decided in the design of CUTLASS that the software should, to a large extent, be machine independent.

There are three hardware elements in a power station CUTLASS application - namely the plant interface, the target computers and the host computer. In a system installed in 1981 for boiler modulating control (Bransby (6)), these elements comprised around 70%, 20% and 10% of the cost respectively. Providing a choice of manufacturer's equipment is thus most important for the plant interface equipment, and least important for the host computer.

The plant interface equipment takes electrical signals from plant (logical and analogue) and converts them into a form that can be accessed by the target computer. In a modulating control application, the target will generate variables to be output to drive plant actuators or to be displayed on meters on the control desk. The conversion of these to plant level electrical signals will also be done in the interface.

At present, CUTLASS can operate with 7 different makes of plant interface equipment and the addition of new types of interface equipment is designed to be straightforward. Thus, where appropriate, advantage can be taken of future innovations in this area.

A CUTLASS target computer is one which actually runs compiled CUTLASS programs on-line. So that CUTLASS can run on a variety of makes of target computer, much of the software required to be installed in the target has been written in CORAL 66. These components can, in principle, be run on any computer with a CORAL 66 compiler.

It is not appropriate to write all the target software in CORAL. In some areas it would give an unacceptable loss of efficiency. In other areas, for example handling of peripheral interfaces, it would be impractical. However, the software required to be written in the target's assembler code has been minimised and amounts to about 15% of the total. CUTLASS currently runs on DEC PDP/11 and Intel 8086 targets and implementation on other computers will be achieved in due course.

The generation of target software is done in the host computer. This involves a considerable amount of file manipulation, compilation of programs and other executive functions. At present this organisational work can only be done on DEC host computers. The difficulty with the host software is that much of it makes use of DEC's RSX operating system. Conversion to another manufacturer's operating system would be a long task, yet would give little saving in terms of total hardware costs on a typical power station project, and the task would have to be completely repeated if a third operating system was later chosen. One possible outcome here is that, in the future, the host software might be rewritten in some widely available operating system, such as Unix.

9.3   FEATURES OF CUTLASS

So far, the three main objectives that the CEGB had in developing CUTLASS have been described. The first objective was to provide high level facilities tailored to power station C & I applications so that programming could be done by engineers with a minimum effort. The second objective was to produce a CEGB standard in order to maximise the return on investment in system software development, to ease long term maintenance, and to provide a system which is quality-assured on CEGB plant. The third objective was to produce a system which would run on a variety of manufacturer's equipment to allow diversity of supply. The chapter shall now continue by discussing some of the basic features required in a computer system used for plant control applications, and how they are provided in CUTLASS.

9.3.1 Timing of Activities

For economic reasons, it will frequently be desirable to implement a number of control loops in one target computer. These loops will often need to be run at different repetition rates. For example, furnace pressure control on a power station must be run at least every 2s because the process can be subject to large, fast disturbances (Faubert et al (7)). The actuator to control the fan will also be fast acting - perhaps with a 0-100% travel time of 10 secs. A positioning loop running every 100ms or faster will be required to achieve a positional resolution of 1%.

On the other hand, steam temperature control every 10s may be adequate since the process dynamics are sluggish (Dunnett and Wells (8), Wallace and Clarke (9)). However, in order to improve linearity and provide feed-forward correction of disturbances, a cascade control structure is appropriate. The inner loop of this might run at a 2s repetition rate and drive a positioning loop running every 500ms to give 2% resolution on a 25s actuator.

If it was required to implement both the steam temperature control and the furnace pressure control in the same computer, then two control 'schemes' would be required, one consisting of two tasks, and one of three tasks. The arrangement is illustrated in Fig. 9.1.

In other areas of computer control it is also necessary to perform more-or-less regular activities. For example, in the sequence start-up of an electrical fan there will be a maximum acceptable delay in responding to a switch indicating low bearing oil pressure, and this will determine the run rate of the sequence control task.

Other functions of a target computer may necessarily occur at irregular intervals. For example, in a distributed computer network, requests for data from one processor can occur at any time in the processing cycle of another. Similarly, operator requests for VDU format changes can occur at any time.

The implication of these requirements are that the target computer must have a multi-tasking, time-and-priority-scheduling executive to organise the execution of the regular and irregular tasks it is performing. These executive operations should be, as far as possible, transparent to the application programmer. In CUTLASS very simple program statements, similar in form to those used in Fig. 9.1, are available to control the running of tasks. The underlying executive software is called Topsy-2 (Jervis (10)) and a copy of this resides in every target computer.

9.3.2 Data Types

1.   FURNACE PRESSURE CONTROL SCHEME

1A TASK PRESSCON RUN EVERY 2 SECS

This task reads in the furnace pressure, compares it with the set value and produces a demanded number, N, of 100ms raise or lower drive pulses to the actuator on the induced draught fan.

1B TASK PRESSPULSE RUN EVERY 100 MSECS

Whenever the slower task Presscon runs, this task copies the number, N, into a local store. If the contents of this store exceed zero, the raise output for the fan actuator is activated and the local store is decremented by one. A similar effect on the lower output is achieved with a negative value in the store. Thus the result is that the appropriate output is activated for 100N ms.

2.   STEAM TEMPERATURE CONTROL SCHEME

2A TASK OUTLETCON RUN EVERY 10 SECS

This task reads in steam temperature at the boiler outlet, compares it to the set value and produces a set point for superheater inlet temperature.

2B TASK INLETCON RUN EVERY 2 SECS

This task compares the set point of superheater inlet temperature with the measured value to produce a number, M, of raise or lower pulses to the spray control valve.

2C TASK SPRAYPULSE RUN EVERY 500 MSECS

Similar to the task Presspulse except acting on the spray valve and producing 500M ms of drive.

Fig. 9.1   Software Structure Requirements

In CUTLASS, all variables are defined as being of one particular type, i.e. logical, integer, real or text string, or as a combination of types, i.e. a record. As in other structured languages, the formal declaration of this information greatly increases the clarity of the code.

In addition, all CUTLASS variables are classified according to the scope of their useage. Local variables are internal to a single task. There are few restrictions on use and, for example, a variable may be calculated at one point and recalculated at a later point in the same task. Local variables have minimal attributes and take up little memory storage.

Common variables can be transferred between tasks in the same scheme. For example, in Fig. 9.1, the set-point superheater inlet temperature is calculated in task OUTLETCON and used in task INLETCON, and this would be a real common variable. Protection features are built in to the rules of common data access. Most importantly, only one task can write to (i.e. calculate the value of) a common variable, though any number of tasks in the same scheme can read it. Whilst at first sight restrictive, this rule forces controlled and obvious data flows, which is essential when there are several tasks running at differing rates.

Global variables can be transferred between different schemes, possibly in different target computers. Again, in-built protection will prevent more than one scheme writing to the same variable - though this is allowed if the variable is specified as a multi-write global. Whereas the names of locals and commons are not stored in compiled programs in the target, the names of globals are stored so that users can check, and in some cases alter, their values. The user who owns each global is also defined in order to prevent inadvertant unauthorised modification of important data.

The advantage of the data typing used in CUTLASS is that it results in formalised and obvious program structure, and software can be more easily understood, tested and modified by later users.

9.3.3 Bad Data

A minor apparent disadvantage of data typing is that it requires long data declarations at the head of every scheme. The concept of bad data, on the other hand, results in better program structure and also more compact code. It is therefore doubly advantageous.

In most C & I applications, many variables in the software derive from the plant interface equipment. The possibility exists that these inputs may become faulty and it may easily be deduced that they are faulty.

As an illustration of this, many plant signals derive from plant transducers and should lie in the range 4-20mA. Therefore, if the variable measured in the computer falls much below the value corresponding to 4mA, it is an indication that the transducer has failed. Any plant variable outside its acceptable range can, therefore, automatically be evaluated as 'bad'.

What action should be taken by a control scheme receiving bad data? For modulating control schemes, one ultra-safe response would be to always put the scheme into the manual mode. However, this would be over-conservative if the bad signal did not directly affect plant and was just used for operator display.

As an example, consider a hypothetical multi-mode modulating control scheme. Suppose control mode A was selected if a temperature was above 30°C or a fan was running. If the fan actually was running, it would be correct to operate in mode A whatever the value of temperature, even if it was bad.

To automatically achieve such rational action, bad data has been built into the arithmetic of CUTLASS. Thus, if there was running code equivalent to the statements

```
A:= B + C
E:= D / A
```

and B = 1.0, C = 2.0 and D = 3.0, then E would clearly take value 1.0. However, if B had value bad, both A and E would have value bad. Thus bad data propogates through the arithmetic.

Similar rules apply to logic variables. Thus, the expression

```
MODEA := (TEMP > 30.0) OR FANRUN
```

would give a value of true for MODEA if TEMP was bad and FANRUN was true; it would give a value of bad if FANRUN then became false. Other rules of this tri-state logic become self evident if the value bad is interpreted as "don't know".

As well as propagating within a single scheme, bad data can propogate between schemes. Suppose a global variable OK is generated in scheme FRED and read and used in tasks in schemes JOE and BILL. Suppose also that the executive cannot run a task in FRED within a reasonable time of its requested run time because other, higher priority tasks have consumed all the processing capacity. Now the Topsy executive will "time-out" FRED, and schemes JOE and BILL will read OK as bad. They will automatically take safe default action.

One of the subtle aspects of bad data is that often one can ignore it and just write programs that perform correctly with normal good data. In the great majority of circumstances the software will run safely and sensibly if the data goes bad. As will be seen, in modulating control schemes, the link between bad data and control modes assists in this.

9.3.4   Blocks and Functions

CUTLASS provides, in each language subset, a number of blocks or functions particularly tailored to that subset. There are also common language components which can be used in any subset.

Typical common language components are the FLOAT, EXP or steam table functions, and the MXANIN (multiplexed analogue input) or WDOG (watchdog) blocks. In the modulating control (DDC) subset, typical blocks are INCPID (incremental proportional, integral and derivative controller) or AUTOMAN (auto-manual).

Proper treatment of bad data is built into all blocks and functions. In addition, some extra blocks and functions are specifically provided for handling bad data. For example, the statement

```
EAVE OUTPUT A INPUT B, C, D
```

calculates A as the arithmetic mean of B, C and D, and if any of these variables is bad, A is bad. If B, C and D were signals deriving from replicated plant transducers, it may be desirable to continue control. The statement

AVE OUTPUT A INPUT B, C, D
calculates A as the mean of B, C and D, and if B were bad,
A would be the mean of C and D.

9.3.5 Control Modes

Many of the blocks in the modulating control subset
operate differently at different times according to the
"mode" of the task in which they are running. These are
termed history-dependent blocks. There are four modes:
Match, Manual, Auto-Normal and Auto-Constraint.
In Match mode, all history-dependent blocks are
initialised. All integrators are set to their initial
conditions, and history values internal to all blocks are
cleared of bad data. This is similar to an initialise mode
on an analogue computer.
In Manual mode, all "controller" type
history-dependent blocks remain tracking their initial
conditions, whilst "filter" type history-dependent blocks
are active. Consider the statement
    Y:= FIRST (X, TC)
representing a first-order low-pass filter with time-
constant TC - or rather the sampled data equivalent of it.
In Match mode, Y would be set equal to X. In Manual mode,
Y would be calculated according to
    $Y(n) = a Y(n-1) + b X(n)$
where a and b depend on TC, and the filter would be active.
Filter blocks are also active in the Auto-Normal and
Auto-Constraint modes.
In the Auto-Normal mode, all controller-type blocks
become active. Thus integrators accumulate and PID's
control.
Auto-constraint is a mode designed to prevent integral
wind-up of controller blocks when a control limit is
reached. The integral terms in the controllers are frozen
but the proportional and derivative terms remain active.
The mode selection is user controlled. When a scheme
is first enabled (i.e. set running) it goes through all
tasks twice in Match mode. This clears bad data and
initialises all stores. Only with two passes can it be
certain that all bad data fed between the tasks are
cleared. During these Matches the task run rate is
ignored.
The whole scheme is also forced into Match mode if any
controller-type plant outputs receive bad data. If bad
data has propogated this far in a scheme then, for
security, initialisation is necessary. Plant outputs used
only for display do not cause this scheme-wide Match, and
only the one output affected goes to a default state.
After its two Match passes, whether the scheme is in
an Auto or Manual mode depends on the logic input to the
AUTOMAN block : if true the scheme runs in Auto, if false
or bad it runs in Manual. Typical coding is
    OK:= BUTTON AND (TEMP> 70.0)
    AUTOMAN OK
In this illustration, the variable, BUTTON, derives

from a digital input connected to an auto-manual selection button on the operator's control desk.   If this is not a latching button, a software latch will be required.

The selection between Auto-Normal or Auto-Constraint depends on the logic input to the CONS block : if true the scheme runs in Auto-Constraint, if false or bad it runs in Auto-Normal. This input would normally be set according to a plant variable, say an actuator position, going outside limits, for example
    STOP := (ACTPOS $>$ MAX) OR (ACTPOS $<$ MIN)
    CONS STOP'
Constraint situation represent one of the most awkward modulating control programming problems. The CONS block is appropriate in some of the more common situations but, unfortunately, explicit programming of constraint response is sometimes necessary.

The powerful blocks, with associated bad data handling and mode control, have proved extremely versatile for programming modulating control schemes.   There is a similarity with the modules and mode control found on analogue computers and, like them, solutions of realistic problems can be achieved speedily.

9.3.6   Interprocessor Communications

There are several obvious advantages in distribution of a C & I system among several computers.   Firstly, it reduces the impact of computer failure and can eliminate the need for standby computers.   As an illustration of this, one modern, Kalman-filter based, steam temperature control system (Wallace and Clarke (9), Williams and Waddington (11)) saves around £7 per hour compared with manual control.   If the computer suffers five 2-hour failures per year (a pessimistic estimate in a well designed system with trained maintenance staff) the cost of these would be £70.   This would not justify the expenditure of £5000 or so on a back-up processor.   Obviously, this argument relies on there being a sufficiently wide distribution of the controls that the operator can successfully take over if any one processor fails.

A second advantage of distributed control is that it reduces the pressure on processor time and memory - not that the latter is a problem nowdays.   It matters little that there is a processing-time overhead in using a high-level language like CUTLASS rather than machine code. As suggested earlier, the savings in program development time far outweigh the cost of extra hardware.

A third advantage of distributed control is that it simplifies future replacements as this can be done in stages.   The CEGB is currently investigating the refurbishment of the C & I systems for those boiler-turbine units which have a single, centralised data-logging and control computer.   Typically, these computers each access several thousand plant inputs.   The replacement of these computers in a way which allows sufficient time for thorough testing, yet incurs minimal plant unavailability, presents a severe technical problem. Such problems are greatly reduced in distributed computer systems.

Given, therefore, that a large number of computers are going to be used in a complete power station C & I system (67 for the three units of Drax Completion) the question arises of how data should be transferred between them. For the quantity of data concerned, the most economic proposition is some form of data link. CUTLASS will currently operate with serial line links (Bransby (6)), parallel (HDLC) links (Harding (12)) and software for driving Ethernet is under development. The communications protocols used include checking of transmitted data with retransmission after failure, and on-line network reconfiguration to take account of failed links or newly installed links (Jervis (10)).

Whilst the detailed organisation of the interprocessor communications is of great interest to the software specialist, it should be transparent to the applications programmer. In CUTLASS, statements such as

CONNECT GLOBAL1 TO CPU3 EVERY 5 SECS

cause the appropriate data transfers to be arranged. The bad data and global access rules apply between the processors as detailed earlier.

Other features of the CUTLASS software are written assuming a distributed configuration. One example of this is the procedure used for keeping back-up copies of the software running in a target computer. This is necessary since, for reasons of cost, RAM memory is often used in target computers, and the contents of this will be lost if there is a memory power supply failure. Even on a power station this eventuality cannot be avoided!

There are two approaches to power supply failures : avoid them or protect against them. The former can be attempted by using power supplies from more than one independent source, one of which may be derived from batteries; this can never be completely reliable. Ultimately, therefore, protection against supply failures is required, and this is best achieved by storing copies of the target software on non-volatile media such as discs or tapes.

To provide disc stores on every target computer would be very expensive. The policy adopted in CUTLASS is, therefore, to provide disc stores on the host computer. If loss of power supply to any target's memory occurs, when the power is reconnected, the target system software and compiled schemes are automatically reloaded down communications links from the host. The reciprocal facility to this is that, whilst software is being built up in the target computer, it is possible, at any stage, to make a back-up copy of the target's memory on to the host computer's discs. These back-up facilities are also useful if the target power supply has to be disconnected for maintenance purposes.

9.3.7 User Aids

There are several other facilities in addition to those already described which are required to produce a working CUTLASS system. Some of these will be outlined.

The "Targetcon" facility is provided on the host computer to enable the user to build up the CUTLASS system software to go into each target. This comprises the Topsy executive, the compiled subroutines representing blocks and functions, and the communication and peripheral drivers. This software differs from target to target depending on the language subsets to be supported, the type of plant interface, whether hardware floating-point arithmetic is available etc. Targetcon consists of a preliminary "question and answer" session followed by a phase in which the basic target memory image is constructed.

The next phase is to produce data files defining the users to have access to the particular target and the global variables they require. These data files, and the basic target image, are loaded down the communications lines into the target computer.

Source files of CUTLASS schemes are then built up on the host using an appropriate editor. These can then be compiled using the CUTLASS compiler. During this process it is checked that all global variables used do exist in the target. After successful compilation, the object code may be loaded into the target using the CUTLASS installer.

At this stage, use is made of the CUTLASS monitor. This allows authorised engineers to set schemes running (enable them), stop them (disable them), or if necessary remove them from the target altogether. The engineer can also look at the values of local, common or global variables to ensure correct operation. He will also be able to make on-line alterations to particular global parameters for tuning purposes.

9.4   EXAMPLES

9.4.1   Mill Feeder Control

It is now appropriate to look at two detailed examples of CUTLASS programming. The first of these relates to the modulating control of the coal feed to a coal pulverising mill (Williams and Waddington (11)).

On a large coal-fired power station, there will typically be 8 to 10 coal mills which are used to crush coal to a powder as fine as flour prior to it being blown down pipework and into the furnace for combustion. Finely pulverised coal can be highly combustible and, to ensure safe operation, it is vital that the fuel/air ratio in the pipework is not too low. At the same time, the ratio should not be so high that the coal dust drops out of the air stream and accumulates in the pipework.

On a vertical-spindle coal mill, which is the type considered here, the air flow through the mills is controlled so that the total heat produced in the furnace corresponds to the demand for electrical power. The coal feed to the mill must be controlled to follow the air flow in such a way as produces the desired fuel/air ratio.

Unfortunately, there is no instrumentation which can reliably and continuously provide on-line measurement of the mixture strength in the pipework. However, this can be deduced from the impedance offered by the mill to air flow through it. The control policy adopted is thus to control to a preset "mill ratio" where this is defined as

$$\text{mill ratio} = \frac{\text{mill differential pressure}}{\text{primary air differential pressure}}$$

Here primary air differential pressure is a measure of air flow, and mill differential pressure is a measure of pressure dropped across the mill as air flows through it.

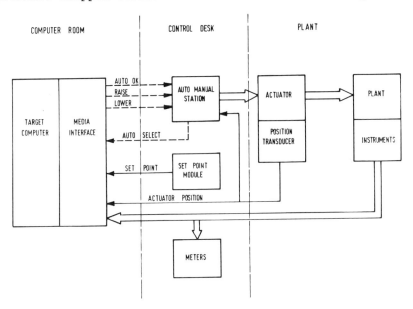

Fig. 9.2 Arrangement of Typical Control Loop.

The arrangement of computer hardware is shown in Fig. 9.2. The target computer is connected to the plant interface equipment which receives signals from plant and from the control desk. The computer sends out 3 digital signals to the auto-manual station on the operator's control desk. The AUTO-OK signal drives a light to indicate when auto control can be selected. When the operator presses the button on the auto-manual station, the AUTO-SELECT digital input is set, and the computer starts to generate appropriate raise and lower drives to plant. In this particular example there is no set point module on the desk, though one is shown in the figure.

A complete CUTLASS scheme based on that implemented at Thorpe Marsh Power Station is shown in Fig. 9.3. It is apparently very long, but this is largely because of extensive commenting. This is essential in software which

```
[002.00
DDC SCHEME AMILLFEED
            ;The purpose of this scheme is to maintain the air/fuel ratio
            ;within the mill to a desired and safe operating condition.
            ;This is achieved by the adjustment of the actuator on the
            ;coal feeder which varies the fuel quantity input to the mill.
            ;The primary parameters for the control of the air/fuel ratio
            ;are the mill and primary air differential pressures.
            ;Version 1.00  Written for Unit 2  F S Peach 4 Oct 83
            ;Version 2.00  Stripped down for publication  M L Bransby 9 Dec 83

            ;Declare global data
GLOBAL
            ;Globals preset by the Monitor and used by this scheme.
REAL    RGAINS[GN1]
INTEGER IGAINS[GN2]
            ;Communication globals - to primary air fan scheme.
LOGIC   FAUTOA
            ;Declare common data
COMMON
REAL    MDY                         ;Filtered mill differential pressure
REAL    PADY                        ;Filtered primary air differential pressure
LOGIC   M                           ;Flip flop flag
INTEGER N                           ;Increments to be sent
            ;Declare IO information as common presets
INTEGER A1:=0,CH1:=2                ;Mill diff
INTEGER A2:=0,CH2:=3                ;PA diff
INTEGER A3:=4,CH3:=3                ;Mill motor current
INTEGER A4:=20                      ;Feeder actuator position
INTEGER DI1:=50,B1:=13             ;Auto-Man button
INTEGER DO1:=64,B3:=9,B4:=7,B5:=8  ;Auto status,lower,raise
;*******************************************************************************
TASK FEED PRIORITY=210 RUN EVERY 5 SECS
            ;This task performs the main control functions


            ;Declare local data
            ;Real parameters from global array RGAINS[ ]
REAL    K                           ;Gain (%/mbar of mill diff)
REAL    TI                          ;Integral time (secs)
REAL    TD                          ;Derivative time (secs)
REAL    TF                          ;Roll off time (secs)
REAL    VMIN                        ;Min actuator position (%)
REAL    VMAX                        ;Max actuator position (%)
REAL    SC                          ;Scale (% actuator movement/pulse)
REAL    RATIO                       ;Desired mill diff/PA diff ratio
REAL    MMCOP                       ;Mill motor current running (amps)
            ;Real inputs from Media
REAL    MD                          ;Scaled mill diff
REAL    PAD                         ;Scaled PA diff
REAL    MMCX,MMC                    ;Raw,scaled mill motor amps
REAL    VX,V                        ;Raw,scaled actuator position
            ;Derived real variables
REAL    ERROR                       ;Pressure error from desired
REAL    DX0                         ;Incpid block output
REAL    REM                         ;Demanded output not yet sent
REAL    DX                          ;Incpid output + any remainder
REAL    VDOWN,VUP                   ;Actuator pos distance from bottom,top
REAL    DX1                         ;Limit block output
REAL    SENT                        ;Output being sent-not used
```

Fig. 9.3 page 1 Example DDC scheme

```
              ;Integers from array IGAINS[ ]
INTEGER NMIN,NMAX              ;Min,max no of pulses
              ;Derived integers
INTEGER N2                     ;Pulses to be output
              ;Logics from digital inputs
LOGIC   AMB,AMBX               ;Auto manual button
              ;Derived logic variables
LOGIC   GDSCH                  ;Good signals
LOGIC   MMRUN                  ;Mill motor running
LOGIC   OK                     ;Auto available
LOGIC   AUTO                   ;Auto available and selected
LOGIC   HI,LO                  ;Limit block outputs-not used
;------------------------------------------------------------------
START
MXANIN'MED CARD A3 CH3,MMCX    ;Read mill motor current
ANIN'MED A4,VX                 ;Read actuator position
DIGIN'MED CARD DI1 B1, AMBX    ;Read auto manual button
              ;Scale the analogue inputs into engineering units
MD:=(MDY-0.1)*70.0/0.8         ;Scale mill diff 0-70 mbar
PAD:=(PADY-0.1)*7.0/0.8        ;Scale PA diff 0-7 mbar
MMC:=(MMCX-0.1)*120.0/0.8      ;Scale mill amps 0-120 amps
V:=(VX-0.1)*100.0/0.8          ;Scale act. pos. 0-100%
              ;Invert digital inputs so that closed Media contacts show true
AMB:=NOT(AMBX)
              ;Preset control parameters set under Monitor
K:=RGAINS[1]
TI:=RGAINS[2]
TD:=RGAINS[3]
TF:=RGAINS[4]
VMIN:=RGAINS[5]
VMAX:=RGAINS[6]
SC:=RGAINS[7]
RATIO:=RGAINS[8]
MMCOP:=RGAINS[9]
NMIN:=IGAINS[1]
NMAX:=IGAINS[2]
              ;For the scheme to be able to operate in auto it is necessary
              ;that all the inputs from plant and all the globals set using
              ;the Monitor are good. It is possible to check each variable
              ;explicitly, but this is heavy. The alternative approach is to
              ;note that the final control output from this task, N2, is only
              ;good if all the variables used to generate it are good. This
              ;may therefore used to check all the inputs in one go. This
              ;works whatever the mode of the scheme.
GDSCH:=GOODINT(N2)
              ;The mill motor must be running before auto available is displayed
MMRUN:=MMC>MMCOP
              ;Calc the auto available flag for display on the desk A/M station
OK:=GDSCH AND MMRUN
              ;The scheme will be put into Auto-Normal mode when auto is available
              ;and auto is selected on the desk.
AUTO:=OK AND AMB
AUTOMAN AUTO
ERROR:=RATIO*PAD-MD                        ;Compute mill diff. error
              ;The mbar pressure error is the input to the controller. the
              ;output from the controller is % movement per mbar error.
DX0:=INCPID(ERROR,K,TI,TD,TF)      ;Feeder controller
              ;Summate the output change demanded this tick with that demanded
              ;in previous ticks, but not sent due to the actuator rate limit,
              ;quantisation or minimum movement.
```

Fig. 9.3   page 2 Example DDC scheme

```
DX:=DX0+REM                             ;Total % movement wanted this tick
        ;The summator output is passed to a look-ahead limit.Here the
        ;demanded movement is compared with the movement required to
        ;reach an actuator max or min limit so that these are not exceeded.
VDOWN:=VMIN-V                           ;Distance to bottom
VUP:=VMAX-V                             ;Distance to top
LIMIT OUTPUT DX1,LO,HI INPUT DX,VDOWN,VUP
        ;The incs block receives the limit block output of demanded
        ;movement and converts it into a number of 320ms drive pulses.
INCS OUTPUT N2,SENT,REM INPUT DX1,SC,NMIN,NMAX
N:=N2                                   ;Write pulses to common
        ;Generate a flip flop flag to indicate to the FEEDPULSE task
        ;when this task has run.
FLIPFLOP M
        ;The master pressure controller is not allowed to vary the primary
        ;air flow demand unless this scheme is on auto as this could lead
        ;to an incorrect air/fuel ratio.
FAUTOA:=AUTO                            ;Write scheme status to global
        ;Set the digital output to the desk auto-manual station.
        ;                 false,true,bad
DIGOUT'MED OK CARD DO1,B3 CLEAR,SET,CLEAR       ;Output to AM station
ENDTASK
;*************************************************************************
TASK FILTER PRIORITY=220 RUN EVERY 1 SECS
        ;This task reads the mill and PA diff signals five times faster
        ;than used in the control task and filters them to remove noise.

        ;Declare local data
REAL    MDX                             ;Raw mill diff
REAL    PADX                            ;Raw PA diff
REAL    TMD                             ;Mill diff filter time const (secs)
REAL    TPAD                            ;PA diff filter time const (secs)
;-----------------------------------------------------------------------
START
TMD:=RGAINS[10]
TPAD:=RGAINS[11]
MXANIN'MED CARD A1 CH1,MDX              ;Read mill diff
MXANIN'MED CARD A2 CH2,PADX             ;Read PA diff
MDY:=FIRST(MDX,TMD)
PADY:=FIRST(PADX,TPAD)
ENDTASK
;*************************************************************************
TASK FEEDPOS PRIORITY=230 RUN EVERY 320 MSECS
        ;Due to restriction on multi-write to common we cannot pulse N.So
        ;put N1 into a buffer and reset this to N each time FEED task runs.

        ;Declare local data
LOGIC   M0                              ;Change flag
INTEGER N1                              ;Pulses to be output
;-----------------------------------------------------------------------
START
M0:=CHANGE(M)
IF M0 TRUE THEN
N1:=N
ENDIF
PULSE'MED N1 CARD DO1 LOWER B4 RAISE B5
ENDTASK
ENDSCHEME
```

Fig. 9.3 page 3 Example DDC scheme

is critical to safe operation of plant and which will be maintained by various personnel during its life. The following brief explanations of some of the statements may clarify detail

1. MXANIN' MED CARD A3 CH3, MMCX
    Read the variable MMCX from multiplexer card A3, channel CH3. Media plant interface equipment is used.

2. DIGIN' MED CARD DI1 B1, AMBX
    Read the variable AMBX from Media digital-input card DI1, bit B1.

3. DXO:= INCPID (ERROR, K, TI, TD, TF)
    Incremental three-term controller with input ERROR, output DXO, gain K, integral action time TI, derivative time TD and high frequency roll-off time-constant TF.

4. LIMIT OUTPUT DX1, LO, HI INPUT DX, VDOWN, VUP
    If the input DX is less than VDOWN, set DX1 to VDOWN and set LO true. If DX is greater than VUP, set DX1 to VUP and set HI true. Otherwise, set DX1 to DX, and set HI and LO false.

5. INCS OUTPUT N2, DX2, REM INPUT DX1, SC, NMIN, NMAX
    Convert the demanded movement, DX1 to an integer number, N2 of pulses each expected to produce a movement SC. However, the size of N2 is constrained not to exceed NMAX, and, if the size of N2 would be less than NMIN, set it to zero. The value of the pulses sent (SC.N2) is DX2, and the output demanded but not sent (DX-DX2) is REM.

6. FLIPFLOP M
    The variable M alternates between true and false each time the task runs.

7. DIGOUT' MED OK CARD DO1, B4 CLEAR, SET, CLEAR
    The variable OK drives the Media digital-output on card DO1, bit B4. If OK is false, the output is cleared; if true, the output is set; and if bad, the output is cleared.

8. MDY:= FIRST (MDX, TMD)
    Filter MDX with first-order lag with time-constant TMD seconds.

9. MO:= CHANGE (M)
    If M changes, MO is true; otherwise it is false.

10. PULSE' MED INPUT N1 CARD DO1 LOWER B4 RAISE B5
    If the integer N1 is positive, the raise output (Card DO1, bit B4) is set and N1 decremented by 1. If N1 is negative, the lower output is set and N1 is

incremented. If Nl is zero, neither output is set.

Whilst the example given here is basically very simple, it does illustrate that realistic control functions can be achieved in very few lines of active code (excluding housekeeping details) and are easy to understand. As has been mentioned earlier, programs which are short and structually simple will be quick to develop. In fact, the complete process of designing, developing and commissioning the original mill feeder control program, on which this example was based, took around 2 man weeks. For a more complex modulating control example the reader is referred to Bransby (6).

9.4.2   Fan Start-Up Sequence

So far, this paper has concentrated mostly on aspects of CUTLASS relating to modulating control. Now the practically very important topic of sequence control will be discussed. A simple, every-day example of a sequence system is that used for traffic light control.

Here a simple sequence application will be described. It is concerned with the start-up and shut-down of a large electrically-driven fan and associated oil pump (which supplies lubricating oil to the fan shaft bearings), and might form part of the overall sequence for a complete coal mill.

As shown in Fig. 9.4, the pump and fan can be set running by closing contactors in their electrical supplies. These contactors can be activated from the control computer via its digital outputs. A pressure switch detects whether the oil pressure is satisfactory and the switch status can be monitored by the computer. A control module is provided on the operator's panel and this provides two status indicating lights and a switch with which he can initiate fan start-up and shut-down.

Sequence control involves carrying out a number of discrete actions in a preferred order to achieve the start-up and shut-down of plant. Each successive action depends on the final objective and the current state of the plant. Thus, in the present example, the operator's switch determined the objectives - namely "start" or "stop". If "start" is selected, the oil pump should be started, and, once oil pressure is established, the fan should be started. If the oil pressure subsequently falls, due, for instance, to a leak developing, the fan should be stopped and the alarm lamp lit.

The first stage in realising a sequence control program is to produce a functional specification; that is, a definition of the rules relating the required control actions to the observed plant condition. Ideally, the specification format should assist the designer in producing a rigorous specification, and be readily translated into an equivalent program.

For this reason, the CUTLASS sequence subset relates to a specification method based on algorithmic state

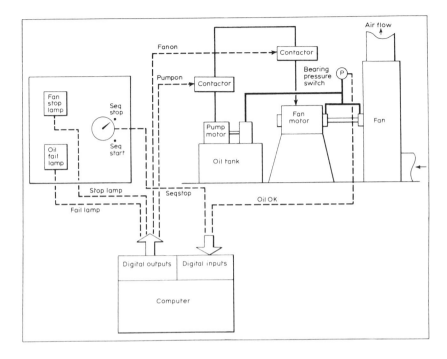

Fig. 9.4 Arrangement of fan, control desk and
computer equipment

machines (ASMs); that is, a controller, or 'machine',
having a finite number of indentifiable states
corresponding to all possible conditions pertaining during
a given sequence. This specification method can be used
whether the final implementation is to be by hardware or
software and is likely to be adopted as a standard within
the CEGB.

To use the method, the first step is to identify all
the possible states and the control actions associated with
each state. In the present example, there are four states,
namely SHUTDOWN, STARTPUMP, RUNNING and OILFAIL, and the
outputs to be set in each state are shown in Fig. 9.5. To
aid understanding, each output is given a meaningful name.

From the figure it is seen that, in the SHUTDOWN
state, neither the pump nor the fan is supplied with power,
the oil-fail lamp is off, and the fan-stop lamp is lit. In
formalising the sequence, each plant output is represented
by a logical variable, such as STOPLAMP. Setting the
physical output ON corresponds to the logical variable
having a value TRUE, and OFF corresponds to FALSE.

The next step is to define the conditions which cause
a transition from one state to another. These conditions
will generally depend on the plant inputs, which indicate
the current plant status. For example, selection of
"sequence start" by the operator, when in the SHUTDOWN
state, will cause a transition to the STARTPUMP state.

Physical Variable	Desk 'Fan Stop' Lamp	Desk 'Oil Fail' Lamp	Electrical Power to Pump	Electrical Power to Fan
Logical name	STOPLAMP	FAILLAMP	PUMPON	FANON
SHUTDOWN STATE	On	Off	Off	Off
STARTPUMP STATE	Off	Off	On	Off
RUNNING STATE	Off	Off	On	On
OILFAIL STATE	Off	On	On	Off

Fig. 9.5 Conditions for setting plant outputs.

The information regarding the states, the control outputs and the conditions for transition can be represented by the ASM chart shown in Fig. 9.6 which is, in effect, a complete specification for the sequence. By convention, the outputs required to be on, or TRUE, in each state are indicated, but those required to be off, or FALSE, are not.

Reference to Fig. 9.6 shows that, when in the STARTPUMP state, there are three ways of changing to another state. Selection by the operator of "sequence stop" causes a transition to SHUTDOWN; establishing satisfactory oil pressure within 30 seconds causes a transition to RUNNING; failure to establish oil pressure within this period causes a transition to OILFAIL. The sequence will remain in the STARTPUMP state if none of the above conditions apply.

Fig. 9.6 also shows the CUTLASS sequence language statements equivalent to the ASM chart presentation, there being an obvious correspondence between the two. This ensures that the translation from the specification to the equivalent CUTLASS program is unambiguous. As with the ASM chart, the language statements only define those outputs which are to be set TRUE. The system software environment, within which the statements operate, ensures that all the remaining outputs are set FALSE.

Further program statements are required to produce a working CUTLASS program for this example. Task run rate and priority must be declared, as must the variables used. Also the two digital inputs, SEQSTOP and OILOK, must be read in, and the four digital outputs, STOPLAMP, FAILLAMP, PUMPON and FANON must be set. These statements are included in the program in Fig. 9.6 but, since this is only an example program, commenting has been minimised.

Practical power station sequences are generally much

```
[001,00
SEQ SCHEME LUBEOIL

TASK FANSEQ PRIORITY=220 RUN EVERY 2 SECS

            ;Define digital inputs as locals
LOGIC SEQSTOP    ;Position of desk switch
                 ;True for sequence stop
                 ;False for sequence start
LOGIC OILOK      ;Oil pressure switch
                 ;True when pressure satisfactory
            ;Define digital outputs as locals
LOGIC STOPLAMP   ;Desk fan-stop lamp.True lights it
LOGIC FAILLAMP   ;Desk oil-fail lamp.True lights it
LOGIC PUMPON     ;Pump contactor.True runs pump
LOGIC FANON      ;Fan motor contactor.True runs fan

START
            ;Read Micro-C digin
DIGIN'MC CARD 4,1 SEQSTOP 2,OILOK

ENTERASM SHUTDOWN

STATE SHUTDOWN  ──────────────────────────
WHEN SEQSTOP FALSE NEXTSTATE STARTPUMP
STOPLAMP:=TRUE

STATE STARTPUMP  ─────────────────────
WHEN SEQSTOP TRUE NEXTSTATE SHUTDOWN
WHEN OILOK TRUE NEXTSTATE RUNNING
WHEN SECS(STATETIME>30) TRUE NEXTSTATE OILFAIL
PUMPON:=TRUE

STATE RUNNING  ───────────────────────
WHEN SEQSTOP TRUE NEXTSTATE SHUTDOWN
WHEN OILOK FALSE NEXTSTATE OILFAIL
PUMPON:=TRUE
FANON:=TRUE

STATE OILFAIL  ──────────────────────
WHEN SEQSTOP TRUE NEXTSTATE SHUTDOWN
FAILLAMP:=TRUE
PUMPON:=TRUE

ENDASM

DIGOUT'MC 5 1,STOPLAMP 2,FAILAMP 3,PUMPON 4,FANON
ENDTASK
ENDSCHEME
```

CUTLASS SCHEME

ASM CHART

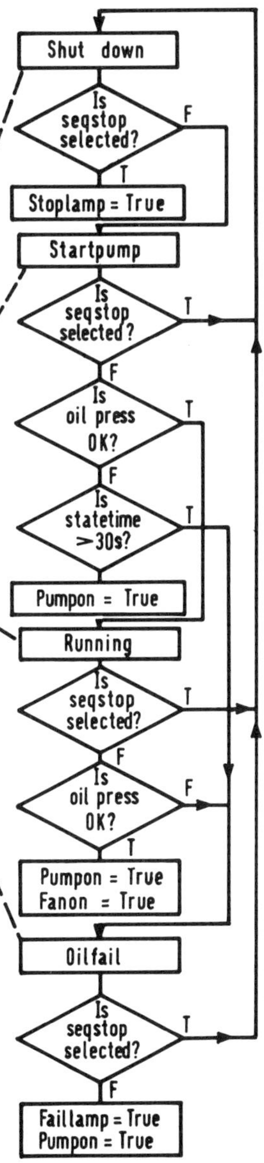

Fig. 9.6 Fan Control Sequence

more complex than this example. A complete mill sequence
involves around 100 states, whilst all the sequences for
large power station water treatment plant might involve a
total of 1000 states. For these large systems the use of
ASM's offers significant advantages (Collier (13)) over the
more widely used ladder diagrams. ASM's provide an
unambiguous, rigorous and efficient method of specifying
sequence systems (Blackledge (14)) which can be directly
converted to computer code. They are also easy to
commission, and lend themselves to automatic testing
procedures.

9.5   CONCLUSIONS

Much more could be said about the software
requirements for power station C & I applications - in
particular about the topics of VDU displays, alarm analysis
and history recording - however, space does not permit.
There could also be considerable discussion of the merits
of other C & I software languages and how they compare with
CUTLASS. Perhaps, if the writing of CUTLASS were to start
now - or in 5 years time - rather than as it did, 4 years
ago, minor details in the software might be quite
different. However, the fundamental requirement for a
high-level, machine-independent, CEGB-standard software
system for on-line control applications would not have
changed, nor would the software features that this implies
have changed. Moreover, if the CEGB had delayed, all the
problems which led to the creation of CUTLASS would have
become more severe. The development of CUTLASS and its
widespread application - in 26 major C & I projects at
power stations to date - has done much to alleviate these
problems, and has made an effective contribution to the
reduction of the CEGB's operating costs. The minimisation
of these is one of the Board's primary objectives.

ACKNOWLEDGEMENTS

The author wishes to emphasise that the development of
CUTLASS has been a collaborative project involving many
people from a variety of departments within the CEGB.
The chapter is published with the permission of the
Director General of the North Eastern Region of the CEGB.

REFERENCES

1.   Maples, G.C., Bransby, M.L. and Collier, D., 1983,
     CEGB Research, 14, 35 - 44.

2.   EPRI NP-2646, 1982, 'Validation of Real-Time Software
     for Nuclear Plant Safety Applications'.

3.   Wolverton, R.W., 1974, IEEE Trans. Computers, C-23,
     615 - 636.

4. Chen, E.T., 1978, IEEE Trans. Software Eng., SE-4, 187 - 194.

5. Geiger, W., Gmeiner, L., Trauboth, H. and Voges, U., August 1979, IEEE Computer, 10 - 18.

6. Bransby, M.L., 1982, 'Distributed Computer Control at Thorpe Marsh Power Station', IEE Symposium 'Microcomputer Applications in Power Engineering', Newcastle, England.

7. Faubert, F.M., Leus, A.F. and Srodawa, R.M., 1977, 'Furnace Implosion - A Model Study and Field Test, River Rouge Unit No. 3'. Proceedings 3rd Power Plant Dynamics, Control and Testing Symposium, Knoxville, Tennessee, USA.

8. Dunnett, R.M., and Wells, R., 1980, Proc. IEE, 127, 7 - 12.

9. Wallace, J.N., and Clarke, R., 1983, IEEE Trans. Automatic Control, AC-28, 416 - 427.

10. Jervis, P., 1980, 'The Design of Systems in a 'CUTLASS' Environment', IEE Symposium 'The Design of Distributed Microprocessor Systems'.

11. Williams, A.H. and Waddington, J., 1983, CEGB Research, 14, 16 - 24.

12. Harding, M., 1983, Electrical Review, 212, 21 - 23.

13. Collier, D., 1982, 'The Use of Highly Structured Languages for the Sequence Control of Power Station Plant', IEE Symposium 'Microcomputer Applications in Power Engineering', Newcastle, England.

14. Blackledge, P., 1983, Proc. IEE, 130, 185 - 189.

Chapter 10

Reliability in computer control of turbine-generator plant

P.A.L. Ham

10.1 INTRODUCTION

In recent years, the field of application of digital techniques, particularly involving microprocessors, has expanded very widely, and in a number of these instances the most important aspect of the design specification is what may loosely be termed the "Reliability". Indeed, in an industrial context this is becoming one of the most frequently considered factors in design, being both related to, and often as important as cost, and to an increasing degree forming part of a Contractual obligation by the Supplier.

Such considerations are of prime importance where some hazard to life or health could be involved, or where the financial or other penalties of a failure or malfunction could be high. Accordingly, the industrial sectors which have taken the lead in these matters are : aerospace, both military and civil, nuclear and conventional power generation, oil and gas production facilities and traffic control, particularly air and rail.

Improvements in device technology, as well as manufacturing and testing techniques have given a progressive advance in basic hardware reliability, whilst some progress has been made in the area of software preparation and validation. These factors alone, however, are not adequate to satisfy the most critical applications. Consideration must thus be given to system design methodologies, particularly those involving redundancy and self-checking techniques, to give the performance required.

Before any meaningful progress can be made, however, it is necessary to define by what criterion the reliability of a control system is to be assessed, and to determine a quantitative means by which the reliability may be measured or predicted. Whereas, in simplistic analyses, the time interval between failure of any kind is the easiest measure to derive, it is possible to recognise three broad classes of system in which other criteria may be more appropriate:-

10.1.1 High-Integrity Systems

In general terms, the system is required to be "Fail-Safe". More specifically, failures should not lead to an increase in hazard and, desirably, all failures should lead to a controlled degradation in performance rather than a total collapse. Virtually all the systems in 10.1.2 and 10.1.3 below will have these requirements also.

10.1.2 High-Continuity Systems

Such a system is required to operate on a continuous basis, and the factor of interest is therefore for what proportion of its life will it not be available, or alternatively how likely is it to successfully complete a life of given duration.

10.1.3 Protective or Standby Systems

Systems of this kind are only invoked in an emergency; it is therefore of interest as to how likely they are to be non-available when called into service.

The actual measurement of Reliability, however defined, requires observation of a number of systems over a period of time to establish statistical significance. For obvious reasons this is not practicable in the design of a new system, and predictive methods are employed. Figures so derived may be subject to wide variation depending on the assumptions made, but comparisons between, say, a number of alternative system architectures can be regarded as much more accurate, on a relative basis, since many assumptions will be common.

10.1.4   Definitions of Reliability

For a full exposition of the statistical concepts upon which Reliability theory is based, and the derivations of the terms in common use, the reader is referred to the literature (Humphries (1)),(Green and Bourne (2)). An important consideration is the way in which reliability can be built up (Crombe and Merrill (3)) and this is reflected in the available statistical data (IEE Inspec.(4)), (Wright (5)). In summary, the most generally useful expressions are as follows:-

10.1.4.1 Mean Time Between Failure (MTBF). This is the reciprocal of the Failure Rate (λ) for a complete equipment based on summated data for all the component parts. It is used in the context of repairable systems; for non-repairable systems the Mean Time To Failure (MTTF) is used.

10.1.4.2 Availability. This is the proportion of an equipment's life for which it is out of service due to a fault. Sometimes referred to as the Forced Outage Rate (FOR), it is of particular value in the context of 10.1.2 above.

10.1.4.3 Failure On Demand (FOD). This is the probability that a system, normally dormant, will fail to operate when called upon to do so. It is of particular value in the context of 10.1.3 above.

10.1.4.4 Mean Time to Repair (MTTR). An estimate of the statistically likely repair-time must be made in order to calculate the Availability.

10.1.4.5 Mean Time to Test (MTTT). An estimate of the statistically likely test interval must be made in order to calculate the FOD.

10.2   REDUNDANCY AND FAULT TOLERANCE

In a system of any degree of complexity, the MTBF will not represent a true picture of the reliability of the equipment as perceived by the environment in which it operates. Not all component failures will be immediately revealed, and not all will lead to an immediate total failure or even some observable performance degradation. Indeed, for reliable systems according to the definitions above, means must be found to enable them to continue to perform their functions (or as many such functions as can be preserved to give continuity or safety) in the presence of the widest possible range of individual component failures.

A system demonstrating this property may be described as Fault Tolerant (Bennetts (6)), (Depledge (7)) and in the most demanding contexts is generally implemented by systems incorporating multiple hardware paths or channels. This does not exclude the use of software techniques which may also involve redundancy, or which may otherwise confer the ability to recover from certain error conditions as a purely software-based procedure such as, for example, a repeated execution. The so-called Fault-Intolerant approach is no more than an attempt (ultimately impossible) to incorporate perfection into the complete design and manufacturing process.

10.2.1   Improvement to be gained by Redundancy

The degree of improvement which may be anticipated with various levels and forms of Redundancy has been estimated in a safety context (5) and is illustrated in Table 10.1, with certain qualifications.

TABLE 10.1   Approximate relative failure probability, or probability of a Failure On Demand, for various system configurations.

Type of System.	Failure Probability.		
Single-Channel System:	1.0	to	0.01
Single-Channel System with Fault-Detection:	0.3	to	0.003
Redundant System with Similar Channels:	0.05	to	0.0005
Redundant System with Partial Diversity:	0.01	to	0.0001
Redundant System with Full Diversity:	0.001	to	?

10.2.1.1 Implications of Number of Channels. It is assumed that all redundant channels are fully active and, for 3-channel or higher systems, have equal authority. Two-channel systems are a special case, one usually being in control, and the second being run as a HOT STANDBY. It is not generally possible, in two-channel systems, to compare the outputs in order to determine which is correct, and the changeover initiation must therefore rely on watchdog timers and other internal fault-detection means. Systems with three or more channels can employ majority-voting methods.

10.2.1.2 Implications on MTBF. The improved performance only applies to the overall system, and reflects the success in masking individual channel failures. The total number of failures actually experienced, however, is at least n-times as large with an n-channel system. It will be clear that systems with more than three active channels carry an additional overhead in terms of total failures, and for this reason are not common practice.

10.2.1.3 Conditional Features. An improvement on the scale indicated will only be achieved if the redundant system has no COMMON-MODE FAILURES, i.e. single faults which affect, or can propagate to, all channels simultaneously. Defences against this type of situation are largely centred upon procedural rigour in design, manufacture, test and maintenance (Bourne, et al.(8)). The beneficial results will only be achieved if particularly effective maintenance is carried out, to ensure that a faulty channel is repaired promptly and hence operation with the full degree of redundancy restored.

10.3   THE MINIMISATION OF FAULTS DUE TO SOFTWARE ERRORS

Whilst the achievement of Fault-Tolerant systems is virtually synonymous with hardware redundancy, the avoidance of errors due to software is an important consideration. A successful approach will involve consideration of a number of related factors.

10.3.1   Transient Phenomena

Power-supply-borne transients or Radio Frequency Interference (RFI) can corrupt readings from peripherals, interfere with the operation of the system bus and directly or indirectly lead to corruption of data held in RAM. It may be taken as axiomatic that suitable protection is vital in any high-reliability application.

It may be true that a limited amount of corruption arising in RAM may be successfully cleared by the use of Error Correcting Code (ECC) systems (see below) but it would be unwise to assume that errors induced in RAM by interference phenomena would necessarily be confined to single bits and therefore capable of correction by conventional ECC techniques.

It has been found advantageous to prepare software in such a way that all data held in RAM is automatically updated or re-validated at regular intervals, so ensuring that random errors from any cause are systematically cleared. Wherever possible, vital data such as interrupt vectors are best located in ROM, whilst input data from peripherals is best acquired by polling, rather than by raising an interrupt upon a change of state. Wherever an interrupt routine is essential, it should be associated with a timeout procedure to initiate a reversion to a predetermined state if the interrupt does not arise as expected.

10.3.2 "Hard" Memory Errors

"Hard" errors are caused by irreversible defects in the memory component, and can cause a repeated malfunction every time the faulty memory cell is accessed. The nature of the malfunction will be indeterminate, depending on whether the faulty cell forms part of an address, a data word, or a flag etc. Since it must be assumed that such a defect may lead to a complete system failure, it is advisable to incorporate a separate Watchdog-Timer in each system or channel to initiate a controlled shut-down in this eventuality.

The incidence of such errors is significantly less than that of "soft" errors, and it is reported (Lucy (9)) that current designs of 64K dynamic RAMs exhibit a "hard" failure rate of approximately 0.02% per 1000 hours (at 55°C). Such errors can be detected by a simple RAM test of, for example, the "Walking-Ones" pattern. This may be carried out as a production test, after ageing, but perhaps more usefully, can be built into a processor system as part of the start-up procedure, thereby ensuring that there are opportunities for detection and reporting at intervals.

Where Read Only Memory (ROM) is used to store program, it should also be assumed that "hard" errors can take place. Whilst it seems to be generally accepted that ROM is more reliable than RAM, there is a shortage of adequate references on the matter, and there is equally very little information on the life and mode of degradation for data stored in UV-erasable ROM.

It is, however, relatively easy to perform a simple test on ROM by carrying out a CHECKSUM, formed by an arithmetical addition of all the bits which are stored in the "high" state in a particular section of memory, and checking whether the resultant number complies with expectations. Such a test may well be carried out in production or built into the start-up procedure as above.

10.3.3 "Soft" Memory Errors

"Soft" errors are caused by the spontaneous change of a bit from a high to a low state or vice-versa. Such occurrences are in most cases caused by alpha-particles (helium nuclei) generated in the packaging material of the chip itself and, although most significantly associated with dynamic RAMs, may also affect static RAMs. More recently, packaging materials have been improved, designs have been changed to increase the storage charge level, and protective coatings have been developed to absorb the energy of alpha particles. It was reported in 1982 (9) that the best current designs of 64K dynamic RAMs exhibit a "soft" failure rate of 0.1% per 1000 hours (at 55°C) and that, on a per-kilobit basis, 64K RAMs are 3.5 times as reliable as 16K RAMs.

Problems due to errors of this kind may largely be overcome by the periodic re-validation of all data held in RAM as has already been referred to above. In a military context, reliable memory operation is still obtained by the use of core storage which is not subject to alpha-particle errors and also has the merit of being non-volatile. In systems where a significant amount of semiconductor RAM is required and where reliability is nevertheless of some concern, two approaches have been used:-

10.3.3.1 Error-Correcting Codes (ECC).

The "soft" error problem may be alleviated by the use of extra memory bits in each word, to provide a form of encryption which will allow both error detection and correction (Peterson (10)). Hardware is now available in which such systems are transparent to the user, and an MTBF improvement factor of between 20 and 100 times may be expected.

Simple parity-checking is markedly inferior in overall performance, and it can be shown that (9) a parity-protected memory demonstrates a failure rate which is typically some 11% inferior to that with no parity checking, as a result of the extra hardware required. However, a parity error does not lead to automatic error correction, but only to a re-try, re-start or shutdown procedure; a parity-checking routine may thus be regarded as a means to confer Failure-to-Safety rather than true Fault Tolerance.

The effects of ECC are beneficial overall only because the improvements due to error correction outweigh the penalties due to additional hardware. The "overhead" associated with ECC grows rapidly as the data word gets smaller; for a 32-bit word, the minimum overhead is quoted as 19% but for an 8-bit word, as much as 50%. As well as this, however, costs are higher and both access times and power consumption are increased. Depending on the application, there will thus be some point below which the installation of ECC will not be justified. Some authorities have put this as high as a 512K byte memory capacity, and clearly ECC is not justified at all in small systems.

10.3.3.2 Error Recovery Techniques. Methods of recovering system operation after a fault have been investigated for asynchronous systems and theoretical concepts have been devised (Campbell, et al., (11)). In the context of small, real-time micro-processor controllers, a multi-level approach has been investigated which uses, amongst other things, program copies or alternative algorithms in memory (Stewart and Preece (12)). Since the holding of replicated copies in a single memory space could be construed as a potential Common Mode Fault, a fully redundant structure is technically superior.

10.3.4   Programming Faults

It must be assumed that Programmers will generate code which contains a certain proportion of latent errors or "bugs". Where a Compiler is employed to translate high-level code into machine code, it should be remembered that the Compiler itself is yet another program which, until well-proven with the target processor, may be assumed to contain errors which could in turn lead to the production of faulty code. Some approaches to this problem are indicated below:-

10.3.4.1 Management Procedure and Software Aids. Much has been made in recent years of techniques such as "Structured Programming" to achieve more reliable, not to say comprehensible code. This is but one aspect of the drive towards better planning and discipline in the software-preparation process. It is sometimes thought that the property of "Structure" is the prerogative of particular languages, but even for Assembly-Language programming much benefit may be derived from the formulation of a program using logical principles in which a subdivision into self-contained "modules" forms an inherent part. On a wider front, formalised design reviews, software audits, reliability assessments, document substantiation and program validation analyses may be carried out at regular intervals.

More specific attempts have been made towards error-free software by defining Quality Assurance procedures (IEEE 730-1982 (13)) and by the development of software tools which are intended to block initial coding errors (Barnes (14)).

It has been reported (9) that the application of "error-free" software engineering principles of this kind has resulted in an error rate of much less than 1 error per 1000 source code lines, the industry average being considered to be 3 to 5. Since the rate is thought to be independent of language, this tends to argue the case for high-level languages, but in cases where compact coding and minimum run-times are sought, the use of Assembler may still be justified. The ease of change often quoted in connection with high-level languages is no necessary advantage in systems associated with safety, where great effort is made to ensure that software cannot be changed by anyone but duly authorised persons under strict administrative control.

10.3.4.2 Coding Procedures. An alternative approach in which the use of high-level languages is assumed, involves a technique described as "dual coding" (Geller

(15)). In this, a "Reference language" is used in addition to a "Target language" to generate code.

10.3.4.3 Predictions of MTBF for Software. It is not often considered that an MTBF for software is a quantifiable parameter, but some effort has been expended to obtain such predictions. One method, known as an "Execution Time" model, employs early observation of failures during the development phase of a program to predict future behaviour (Musa,(16)(17)), assuming an exponential distribution of much the same form as that used for hardware.

Methods for relating the results to real-time are very complex, and it would seem that such techniques are only of relevance in very large software projects.

10.4 THE IMPLEMENTATION OF RELIABLE CONTROL SYSTEMS

10.4.1 Levels and Types of Redundancy

In implementing a reliable system by means of redundancy, it is essential to adopt a hierarchical approach and provide redundancy only where it is of most value. In the control of Steam Turbines, for example, the control of speed and certain protective functions are implemented in TMR form, but less vital features such as variable rate-of-change are only implemented in a higher level Interface processor which communicates with all three TMR channels (Ham (18)). In general, many forms of multiple-processor systems may be envisaged, but in a reliability context the following are of most value:-

10.4.1.1 Distributed Processing. In this configuration, the tasks are subdivided between processors so that failure of one leaves an adequate range of total system functions still available; this ensures a gradual degradation of performance rather than sudden total system failure. An Interface processor combined with a TMR section (as above) illustrates this form of redundancy.

10.4.1.2 Modular Redundancy. In this configuration, each system of processor performs (or is able to perform) all the possible tasks in parallel with its fellows; the ultimate control action is obtained by some form of MAJORITY-VOTING.

10.4.2 Provision of Fault-Detection

As has been previously mentioned, it is essential to keep a redundantly structured system in good repair; such a system is also one which masks faults so that consideration must further be given to the provision of comprehensive automatic fault-detection or diagnostics in order that maintenance can be initiated in a timely manner. The following techniques are widely used in many such systems:-

10.4.2.1 Validity Checking. This covers Transducer out-of-range checks and excessive rate of change of variables, for example, and may be hardware or software oriented.

10.4.2.2 Cross-Channel Comparison. This is especially valuable in TMR or higher order systems, and enables a faulty channel to be identified and suppressed. It does not, of itself, determine the causative defect.

10.4.2.3 On-Line Proof Testing. This is particularly appropriate to processor based systems, where test routines can be run in apparent concurrency with the main control program.

10.4.3 Distribution of Functions Between Hardware and Software

Many of the considerations described above are not new, and have been applied over a number of years in analogue electronic systems in nuclear and aerospace contexts, as well as in Turbine control. With the introduction of processor-based control, it becomes possible to implement the reliability-

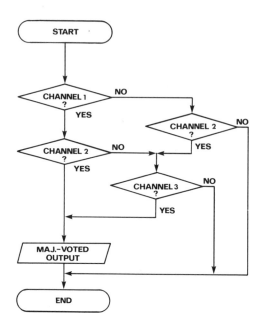

Fig.10.1 Flowchart for software majority-vote

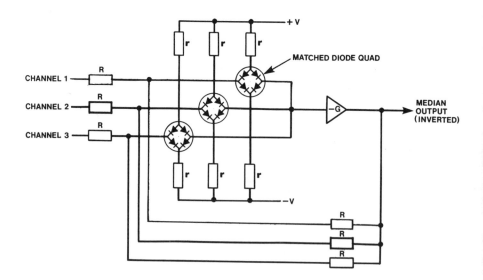

Fig.10.2 Median-selection circuit for modulating signals

enhancing features such as Majority-Voting or Fault-Detection in either hardware or software. A decision must be made as to the most effective assignment, and this is an area for a fine measure of engineering judgement. Whatever may be the possibilities in terms of ingenious software techniques, it is thought desirable, for ultimate safety reasons, to enclose a software-based system with an overriding hardware trap, such as a Majority-Voter or a Watchdog-Timer.

Consideration must also be given to the amount of hardware or software devoted to fault-detection, since this itself will produce errors. Work on software fault rates (9) (16) (17) suggests strongly that it would be unwise not to place some limit on the amount of software as well as hardware devoted to diagnostics within a system.

An empirical rule which has been followed in Turbine control is to not allow the number of hardware components or lines of code devoted to diagnostics to exceed that used to implement the main control function. A small fraction - say 10% - could be considered an effective design.

Examples related to Turbine-Generator control are given later in the text; these are all time-critical applications in which service-routine intervals of 10msec. are usual. This has led to the following design precepts:-

10.4.3.1 Programming. Short, modular programs are stored in Object Code in ROM.

10.4.3.2 Peripherals. Special interface peripherals have been designed where better noise immunity can be gained, or the load on the processor can thereby be reduced, so minimising program run-time.

10.4.3.3 RAM Usage. The data located in the relatively small amount of RAM used is re-validated at regular intervals (mostly every service routine.)

10.4.3.4 Fault-Detection. Internal software checks on data and internal cross comparisons are backed up by cross comparisons and watchdog-timers in hardware.

10.4.4 Majority-Voting Techniques

There are numerous pitfalls to be avoided in the design and implementation of redundant systems; a system wrongly-structured can prove in practice to be worse in all important respects than a single-channel implementation. In particular, it is necessary to avoid Common-Mode Faults, maintain separate channel integrity for input data, and employ appropriate Majority-Voting methods.

In TMR systems, the techniques of Majority-Voting are particularly important, and can be carried out in a number of ways:-

10.4.4.1 Hardware Logic Voting. This may apply to relay-contact signals or Logic voltage levels. A Two-from-Three procedure may be readily devised.

10.4.4.2 Software Logic Voting. This will be carried out on single bits i.e. Flags; the procedure is also straightforward as shown in Fig. 10.1.

10.4.4.3 Voting on Modulating Signals in Hardware. Two main methods have been employed in the past, based on (a) the formation of an Average against which each individual channel is compared, with a subsequent switch-out of any one which deviates by more than a pre-set amount (Ham (19)) and (b) the selection of a Median value from the presented signals (Ham (20)). Any system involving switching is likely to produce instantaneous level changes in the output control signal, for which reason there is a long-standing preference for Median-Selection, an embodiment of which used in Turbine-Generator control is shown in Fig. 10.2. Because a Voter is effectively a single-channel device, it is advantagious to be able to use several in parallel; this is possible in Turbine control since Steam Valves are grouped rather than used singly.

10.4.4.4 Voting on Modulating Signals in Software. The integrity of plant input

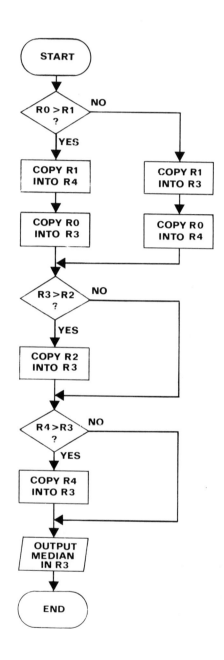

Fig.10.3 Median-selection flowchart for modulating signals

data may sometimes be improved by a Median-Selection carried out in software, as shown in Fig. 10.3.

10.4.5 Minimisation of Channel Divergence

In any multi-channel system, complete input separation together with the effects of marginally different clock frequencies, quantising errors, etc., will tend to cause modulating outputs to diverge; in systems which require a true integration the problems can be fundamental (Padinha (21)) but in industrial controllers it may well be feasible to employ a more suitable algorithm corresponding to a long time-constant. Assuming this to be the case, and that the errors described in Section 10.3.2 and 10.3.3 are dealt with by separate means, then the remaining errors can be categorised as follows:-

10.4.5.1 Errors which are Constant with Time. Arising from discrepancies in input data, these can be tolerated if they lie within certain limits, otherwise a Voting operation could be carried out as in 10.4.4.4.

10.4.5.2 Errors which Increase with Time. These typically arise from parameter reference values (i.e. setpoints) which require to be incremented or decremented at regular intervals, and where small errors become summated. These can be minimised by a correction algorithm resident in each channel, which has access to the corresponding parameter values in the other channels. At set intervals (i.e. after a setpoint change) the algorithm adds a small correction to the 'outer' levels to cause each to converge towards the Median, as in Fig. 10.4.

10.4.5.3 Errors on Start-up. The Start-up Routine must include means to set all reference values to safe initial values.

10.4.5.4 Post-Servicing Errors. A Routine must be included to harmonise all reference values in a channel just returned to service, this being conditional upon the other two channels being in agreement.

10.4.6 Provisions for Inter-Channel Communication

In order to implement the procedures indicated in 10.4.5.1 to 10.4.5.4 above, it is necessary that secure inter-channel communications be provided. Whilst parallel bus structures or byte-serial methods may be employed, such as the IEEE 488 interface, a superior reliability is likely to result from the use of asynchronous bit-serial links (Cox (22)), due to the smaller number of connections involved. Error-Correction methods may be included, but may not be necessary as a simple parity-check and re-transmit routine can generally suffice.

In Turbine-Generator control, a standard Hardware Module has been developed which incorporates four serial ports, so permitting a range of redundant system structures to be implemented.

10.5 CASE STUDIES

The following two examples of TMR systems are in use for the protection and control of Steam Turbine and allied equipment.

10.5.1 An Overspeed Trip System

A device intended to shut down a piece of rotating machinery if the speed exceeds a pre-set value is shown in the block diagram of Fig. 10.5. It consists of three, entirely separate probes operating with a toothed wheel, each feeding to a Speed Detection Module. Duplicate power supplies are provided for the system as a whole.

The Speed-Detection Modules are hardware-based, and are all interfaced with a monitoring processor. This enables an accurate time versus tooth count to be transferred to the processor at 10msec. intervals to enable shaft speed to be computed. The Modules further incorporate a hardware level detection system, based on a particular tooth/time count to detect Overspeed. This does not rely on

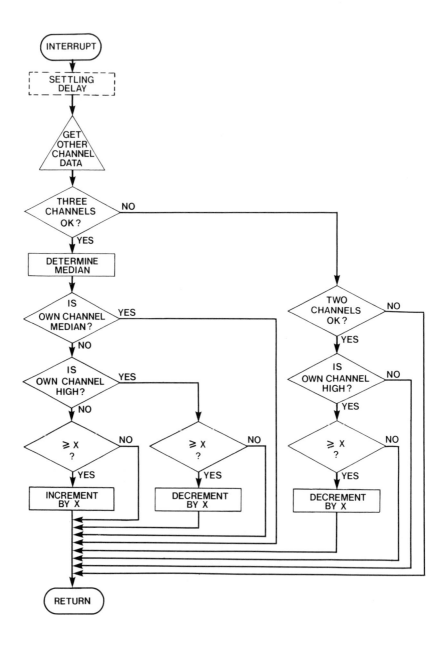

Fig.10.4 Flowchart for TMR divergence minimisation

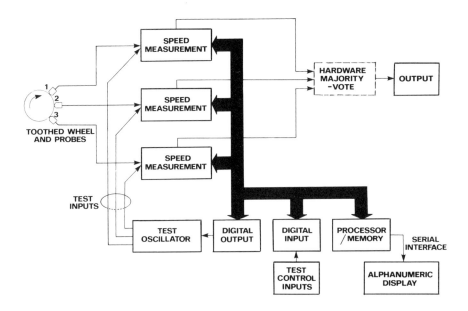

Fig.10.5 A TMR Overspeed Trip System

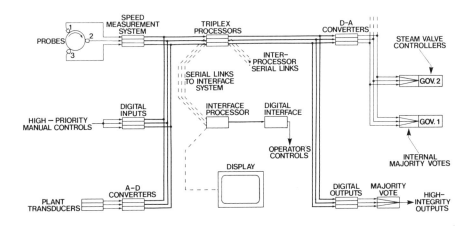

Fig.10.6 A TMR Turbine Control System

correct processor function.

The core of the system, wherein the maximum reliability is needed, is therefore only a proportion of the Speed-Detection Modules. The single Processor/Memory is thus devoted to continuous on-line diagnostics and manually-initiated automatic on-line testing. This leads to a very small number of unrevealed faults, and as a result, the following performance parameters are obtained.

	Assumed Manual Test interval:-	10 weeks
	Assumed proportion of Speed Detection total Module Faults which are Unrevealed:-	30%
then,	Probability of Failure on Demand =	5.9×10^{-6}
	For a Single-channel system (assuming means could be found to carry out on-line tests), FOD =	1.72×10^{-3}

In this case, therefore, a TMR system has improved the failure probability by over three orders.

10.5.2 A Digital Electrohydraulic Governing System

This system comprises a full TMR control system for Steam Turbines (18) and is shown in Fig. 10.6. It incorporates not only a speed controller operating down to almost zero, but also controls the synchronised load and allows pre-programmed load changes and load/frequency characteristics to be established. It further acts to protect the turbine against a variety of undesirable operating conditions, such as poor condenser vacuum or sudden loss of load. A number of steam valve sequencing modes can be employed and linearisation is carried out, particularly relating to the steam mass-flow characteristics.

The more vital of these functions, including a Manual back-up control, are resident in each of the three channels, whilst those of a lower priority, such as control of loading rate, for example, are resident in the single Interface Processor. Safety functions, such as signals to trip the machine, are brought out on separate channel outputs and majority-voted in hardware whilst the steam valve controllers, of which there may be up to ten, are provided with separate majority-voting systems fed from individual D to A Converters.

The system thus has the ability to run for short periods with one main channel out of service, and one or more steam valves closed. It also has a number of levels of controlled degradation in performance following a series of faults, and is, for all foreseeable faults, fail-safe, i.e. it will shut down rather than overspeed.

The Forced Outage Rate for this system depends on the particular specification in terms of number of valves and scope of control functions but is typically calculated as a few minutes per annum.

REFERENCES

1. Humphries, M., 1982, 'The Application of Reliability Techniques to Instrumentation Systems', SRS/GR/55, UKAEA.

2. Green, A.E., and Bourne, A.J., 1972, 'Reliability Technology', Wiley, London.

3. Crombe, R.C., and Merrill, R.A., 1981, 'Industrial Process Control, Instrumentation Systems Reliability Assurance Program, Reliability Growth and Field Results', Proceedings of Third National Reliability Conference; Joint Organisers NCSR, Culcheth, Warrington and IQA, 53 Princes Gate, London.

4. 'Electronic Reliability Data', 1981, IEE Inspec./NCSR.

5. Wright, R.I., 1982, 'Microprocessor Hardware Reliability', SRS/GR/50, UKAEA.

6. Bennetts, R.G., 1978, 'Designing Reliable Computer Systems', Electronics & Power, 24, 845-851 and 25, 51-56.

7. Depledge, P.G., 1981, 'Fault Tolerant Computer Systems', Proc. IEE. 128, 257-272.

8. Bourne, A. J., et.al., 1981, 'Defences against common-mode failures in redundancy systems'. SRD/R/196, UKAEA.

9. Lucy, D., 1982, 'Choose the Right Level of Memory Error Protection', Electronic Design, Feb.18, 37-42.

10. Peterson, W.W., 1961, 'Error Correcting Codes', MIT. Press., Camb., Mass.

11. Campbell, R.H., et.al., 1983, 'Practical Fault Tolerant Software for Asynchronous Systems'. IFAC Safecomp '83, Cambridge, U.K. (Pergamon), 59-65.

12. Stewart, T.R., & Preece, C., 1982, 'Fault Tolerance as a Feature of Digital Governing', Proc. 17th UPEC Conference UMIST 1-6.

13. IEEE Standard 730-1982, 'Software Quality Assurance Plans', IEEE Service Centre, Piscataway, N.J.

14. Barnes, D., 1983; 'Software Reliability'. Electronic Design, April 14, 172-180.

15. Geller, G.P., 1983, 'Coding in two languages boosts program reliability', Electronic Design, March 31, 161-170.

16. Musa, J.D., 1980, 'The Measurement and Management of Software Reliability', Proc. IEEE, 68 No. 9, 1131-1143.

17. Musa, J.D., 1979, 'Validity of the Execution Time Theory of Software Reliability', IEEE Trans. On Reliability, R-20, 181-191.

18. Ham, P.A.L., 1982, 'The Application of Redundancy in Controllers for High Capital Cost or High Integrity Plant', IEE Conference : 'Trends in On-Line Computer Control Systems'. Pub. No. 208, 14-17.

19. Ham, P.A.L., 1966, Brit. Pat. No. 52932/66, 'Improvements in or relating to electric circuits'.

20. Ham, P.A.L., 1975, Brit. Pat. No. 1555123, 'Improvements in and Relating to Logic Circuits and Control Systems Incorporating such Circuits'.

21. Padinha, H.A., 1972, 'Divergence in Redundant Guidance, Navigation and Control Systems', IBM No. SSE-01-006, IBM Electronics Systems Centre, Owego, N.Y.

22. Cox, H., 1979, 'The Advantages of Pure Bit Serial Interfaces for Microcomputers and Other Controllers', IEE Conference : 'Trends in On-Line Computer Control Systems'. Pub. No. 172, 26-28.

Chapter 11

Computer control of longwall coal-cutting machines

J.B. Edwards

11.1   INTRODUCTION

Quite apart from the conventional benefits of computer
control generally, underground longwall coal cutting can reap
enormous benefits from the application of such control. This
is because the vertical steering of coal cutting machines is
a fundamentally unstable process in the absence of large data
storage facilities in the controller which are normally
available only to the digital computer. This chapter sets out
to demonstrate this point and to highlight other important
advantages to be derived from digital control. The basic
requirements for possible digital schemes are determined
through a consideration of the process equations and the
associated practical problems are explored.

11.2   GEOMETRICAL MODEL OF THE SYSTEM

Figs. 1 to 5 show diagramatically those features and
variables of a modern longwall coal cutting machine (and the
associated mechanical systems) essential to the modelling of
its vertical steering characteristics. As shown in Fig. 3.,
the machine makes repeated sweeps, or passes, along the coal
face of length, L, extracting on each pass a volume of
material $= L W_d D$, where W_d and D are the drum width and
diamter respectively: assuming perfect horizontal steering.*
As indicated, the machine rides on the semi-flexible structure of an armoured face conveyor (a.f.c) of the scraper-
chain type, and the cutting drum may be ranged up and down
continuously in an attempt to keep the drum within the
boundaries of the undulating coal seam.

Also as shown, in a process normally termed the <u>pushover</u>,
the a.f.c structure is snaked forward horizontally onto the
newly-cut floor between passes, its front edge taking up a
profile, in the vertical plane, similar to that of the cut-
floor alongside the new face. In this way, on pushover, the
a.f.c undergoes a tilt-change, at any point along its length
(and in the face-advance direction), dependent upon the
deflection, J, previously applied to the steering boom in the
vicinity of the point in question. The tilt-change results

---

*i.e. assuming that the drum is fully embedded to a depth
W_d in the coal face on each pass

from the fact that the overall width, W_c, of the conveyor
trays, or pans, is invariably greater than that of the drum
i.e.

$$W_c > W_d$$

Fig. 4 illustrates in end-elevation the tilting of the conveyor brought about by steering action.

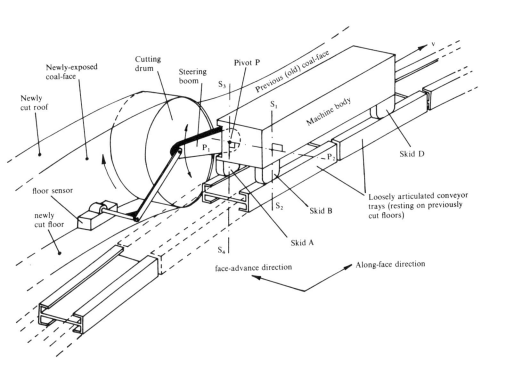

Fig. 11.1   Three-dimensional view of power-loader
and conveyor structure

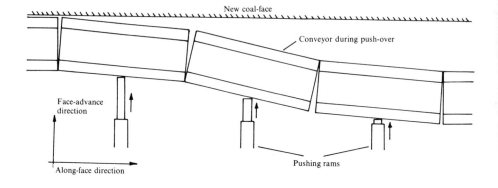

Fig. 11.2   Conveyor being advanced between cuts

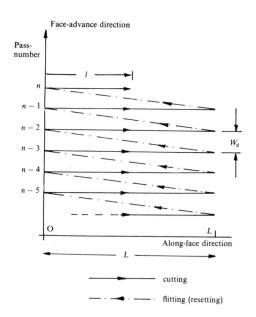

Fig.11.3   The system of unidirectional longwall coal
mining (schematic plan view)

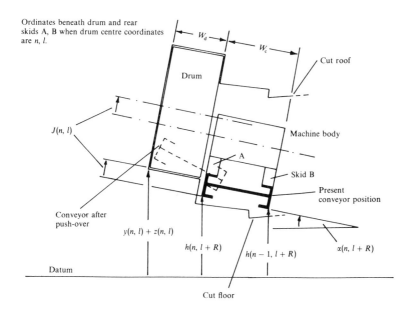

Fig. 11.4   End elevation

The relationships of primary importance in modelling the steering system are basically geometrical involving variable heights and tilts which are functions of <u>two apparently</u> <u>independent</u> variables: n, the pass number and ℓ, the distance <u>travelled</u> along the face.   In the interests of simplicity we shall consider the special case of nearly-equal drum and conveyor widths, viz:

$$W_c = W_d + \varepsilon \qquad (11.1)$$

the positive distance, ε, whilst ensuring the tilt-change effect on pushover, being small enough to permit the approximation

$$W_c \simeq W_d = W \qquad (11.2)$$

in developing the geometrical model.   On this assumption, mere inspection of the side-and end-elevations of Figs. 5 and 4 reveals that, for small angular changes, the following relationships exist between the heights and tilts of the cut-floor, seam and conveyor:

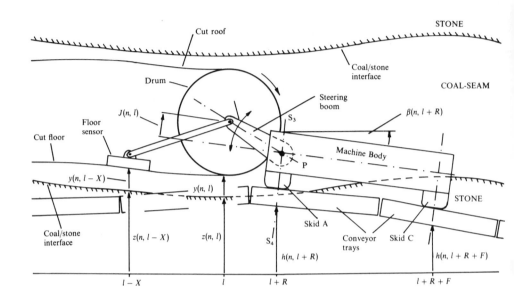

Fig. 11.5   Side elevation showing process variables
            (all measured on the extreme face-side
            of the system).

$$y(n,\ell) + z(n,\ell) = h(n,\ell + R) + W\,\alpha(n,\ell + R)$$

$$+ R\,\beta(n,\ell + R) + J(n,\ell) \qquad (11.3)$$

and
$$\alpha(n,\ell) = \{h(n,\ell) - h(n-1,\ell)\}/W \qquad (11.4)$$

$$\beta(n,\ell) = \{h(n,\ell) - h(n,\ell + F)\}/F \qquad (11.5)$$

where $y(n,\ell) + z(n,\ell)$ is the height of the cut floor at the
new face wall, $h(n,\ell)$, that of the conveyor's front edge,
$h(n-1,\ell)$ that of the rear edge, $z(n,\ell)$, the height of the
lower coal-stone interface and $J(n,\ell)$, the linear deflection
of the steering boom from its null position. $\alpha(n,\ell)$ and
$\beta(n,\ell)$ denote (in radians) the face-advance and along-face
tilts of the machine respectively and are calculated on the
assumption that the three skids A,B, and C (Fig. 1) are in
permanent contact with the a.f.c. The system parameters R
and F denote the fixed offset distances between the drum and
rear skids and between front and rear skids respectively.
Equations of somewhat greater complexity could clearly be

developed for the more general situation of unequal drum and
conveyor widths.

The multipass process model is incomplete without a description of how the armoured-flexible conveyor moulds itself
to the cut floor upon which it rests. Unfortunately, no
simple formula will accurately describe this 'conveyor-
fitting' process and, for its simulation, an elaborate optimisation program is needed which minimises the total potential energy of the conveyor without allowing it to penetrate
the cut floor or contravene the limited angular freedom
built into the joints between neighbouring conveyor trays.
For simplicity therefore we shall assume the conveyor to be
perfectly flexible (- the so called 'rubber-conveyor'
assumption) so that

$$h(n+1,\ell) = y(n,\ell) + z(n,\ell) \qquad (11.6)$$

11.3   PERFORMANCE UNDER DIRECT CONTROL FROM A PRESENT-PASS COAL SENSOR

In Figs. 1 and 5, a nucleonic sensor is shown detecting
the thickness of the coal floor (or ceiling) left at a fixed
distance X behind the cutting-drum.

The nucleonic sensor[3] incorporates a radio isotope,
the backscattered radiation from which is detected by a scin-
tillation crystal and photomultiplier housed with, but
shielded from, the isotope. The amount of backscatter received increases with increasing thickness of the coal layer
between the sensor and the floor (roof) stone due to the
density difference between coal and stone. Sensors detecting
the natural gamma emissions from coal (which differ from
those produced by stone) are also now in use and enjoy the
advantage of not requiring close contact with the cut floor
(roof). Sensors of either type usually involves a smoothing
filter of time-constant T_1 to smooth out the random component
of the weak backscattered radiation received by the detector,
so that the measurement $y_m(n,\ell)$ produced by the transducer
when the drum is at position n,ℓ, is related to actual coal
thickness by the first-order differential-delay equation:

$$d \, y_m(n,\ell)/d\ell = (1/X_1)\{y(n,\ell-X) - y_m(n,\ell)\} \qquad (11.7)$$

where distance-constant X_1 is related to T_1 by the equation

$$X_1 = V \, T_1 \qquad (11.8)$$

where V is the machine velocity, here assumed to be constant.
Alternatively, equation (11.7) may be written in the operational form:

$$y_m(n,\ell) = y(n,\ell-X)/(1+X_1 D) \qquad (11.9)$$

where $D \equiv d/d\ell$ $\qquad (11.10)$

The measurement from the coal sensor may be compared in an
analogue controller with a desired (reference) coal thickness

signal y_r and the error used to actuate the drum steering boom via a suitable gain k_h. The tilt signal $W\alpha(n,\ell+R)$ may also be measured by means of a pendulum transducer to provide a degree of 'rate feedback' (gradient being the rate-of-change of height) via another gain k_g so that the analogue control law may take the form

$$J_d(n,\ell) = k_h\{y_r - y_m(n,\ell)\} - k_g W\alpha(n,\ell+R) \qquad (11.11)$$

where $J_d(n,\ell)$ is the demanded drum deflection signal applied to the electrohydraulic servomechanism which drives the drum steering boom. This servomechanism will also involve some time-constant T_2 so that, the actual-and demanded-drum-deflections will be related thus

$$d\ J(n,\ell)/d\ell= (1/X_2)\{J_d(n,\ell) - J(n,\ell)\} \qquad (11.12)$$

where $\qquad X_2 = V\ T_2 \qquad\qquad\qquad\qquad\qquad (11.13)$

or, in operational form

$$J(n,\ell) = J_d(n,\ell)/(1+X_2D) \qquad\qquad (11.14)$$

Unfortunately, although gains k_h and k_g can be chosen to yield a stable performance on any <u>single-pass</u> of the process, over a series of passes, simulation of the system equations reveals a progressive deterioration of the system performance under analogue control, i.e. control of the sort described by equation (11.11). This is illustrated by the step responses shown in Fig. 6 for the system parameters k_h = 0.8, k_g = 1.0, X = 1.25m, X_1 = 0.6m, X_2 = 0.165m, R = 0*.
The process is therefore said to be 'single-pass-stable', but 'multipass unstable'. A simplified explanation of this multipass instability is given below but for a more thorough treatment the reader should consult references (1) and (2):
For simplicity set R = 0 and neglect the transducer and actuator time constants T_1 and T_2 so that $X_1 = X_2 = 0$, i.e. $y_m(n,\ell) = y(n,\ell-X)$ and $J_d(n,\ell) = J(n,\ell)$. Suppose also that k_g is set = 1.0 to completely offset the effect of α on y. (this is in fact the best value of k_g that can be chosen). The system variables y_r and z will also be neglected since these are only external disturbances on the system and do not therefore affect its stability. Combining all the process and control equations we thus obtain the simple result that

$$y(n,\ell) = y(n-1,\ell) - k_h y(n,\ell-X) \qquad (11.15)$$

or, after taking Laplace transforms in s w.r.t ℓ we get

*
The setting of R=0 actually applies to a so-called fixed-drum machine (rather than the ranging-drum machine shown in Fig. 1), where steering is accomplished by raising and lowering of the entire machine body by the steering jack and the drum is fixed with respect to the machine body. R > 0 only worsens the system performance on analogue control.

$$\tilde{y}(n,s) = \tilde{y}(n-1,s) - k_h \tilde{y}(n,s)\exp(-Ls) \qquad (11.16)$$

so that

$$\tilde{y}(n,s) = G(s) \tilde{y}(n-1,s) \qquad (11.17)$$

where

$$G(s) = 1/\{1+k_h \exp(-Xs)\} \qquad (11.18)$$

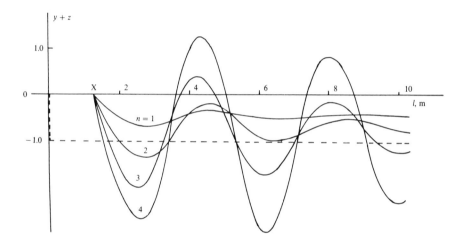

Fig. 11.6   Simulated response of rubber-conveyor
model to unit downward step in coal-seam

Each successive cut-floor profile $y(n,\ell)$ is therefore dis-
turbed by its predecessor via the overall transfer-function
$G(s)$. Now the system $G(j\omega)$ is a resonant system since, from
equation (11.18)

$$|G(j\omega)| = 1/\{1+k_h^2+2k_h\cos(\omega X)\}^{0.5} \qquad (11.19)$$

so that $|G(j\omega)|$ oscillates with increasing ω between the
limits

$$G_{min} < |G(j\omega)| < G_{max} \qquad (11.20)$$

where

$$G_{min} = 1/(1+k_h) \tag{11.21}$$

and $\qquad G_{max} = 1/(1-k_h) \tag{11.22}$

Now k_h will always be set between the limits of zero and unity to ensure single pass stability so that

$$G_{max} > 1.0 \tag{11.23}$$

The resonance peaks G_{max} in $|G(j\omega)|$ will occur when $\cos\omega X = -1$, i.e. when

$$\omega = \pm i\pi/X, \quad i = 1,3,5 \ldots \tag{11.24}$$

and, with each pushover, the process therefore repeatedly exites itself at these frequencies via a gain exceeding unity, so leading to a progressive increase in the system's stored energy at these frequencies, thus producing multipass instability.

It can also be shown that varying X_1, X_2 k_g and R(> O) fails to eliminate this inevitable instability caused by delay X. The only cure lies in the use of a different form of control which is now examined.

11.4   PREVIOUS PASS (STORED-DATA) CONTROL

If the measured coal thickness signal were derived from a sensor located at co-ordinates n-1,ℓ when the drum is located at n,ℓ, i.e. if the sensor was to be sited alongside the drum but in the previous rather than the present pass then equation (11.7) would be replaced by

$$dy_m(n,\ell)/d\ell = (1/X_1)\{y(n-1,\ell) - y_m(n,\ell)\} \tag{11.25}$$

with the result that equation (11.15) now becomes

$$y(n,\ell) = y(n-1,\ell) - k_h(y(n-1,\ell))$$

or

$$y(n,\ell) = (1-k_h) \ y(n-1,\ell) \tag{11.26}$$

so that G(s) is now modified to simply an algebraic constant

$$G(s) = (1 - k_h) \tag{11.27}$$

and $|G(j\omega)|$ is clearly less than unity at all frequencies provided $k_h < 2.0$. The process intercoupling the successive cut-floor profiles is therefore now non-resonant and the multipass system is stabilised. Including the reference signal we get

$$y(n,\ell) = y(n-1,\ell) + k_h\{y_r - y(n-1,\ell)\} \tag{11.28}$$

or $\qquad y(n,\ell) = k_h\, y_r + (1 - k_h)\, y(n-1,\ell)$ (11.29)

so that, in-steady state, when $y(n,\ell) = y(n-1,\ell)$

$$y(n,\ell) = y_r \qquad\qquad (11.30)$$

as desired.

The inclusion of reasonable values for X_1, X_2 does not seriously affect the stability of this modified system.

Unfortunately, to site a coal sensor at location $n-1, \ell$ is generally impractical since it would mechanically interfere with the conveyor structure if floor-mounted or the roof-support canopies if roof-mounted. The alternative is therefore to again employ a present-pass sensor i.e. one located at $n, \ell-X$, but to store its data within a digital computer for nearly an entire face length (for a distance $L-X$ to be precise) before using the data for drum position control.

The features of the necessary computer control scheme are now examined.

11.5 DISCUSSION OF COMPUTER-CONTROL SYSTEM REQUIREMENTS

11.5.1 Sampling Rates

For digital control sampling is, of course, necessary and the question of sampling rate is crucial. The sampling of the measurement signal $y_m(n,\ell)$ must be distance-based rather than time-based in this application to allow for the possibility of variations in machine speed. Indeed the machine is frequently stopped at irregular intervals along the face whilst obstructions (due perhaps to roof-fall or temporary misbehaviour of the roof supports following the conveyor) are cleared. For this reason, the controlling computer must be interrupt-driven, the interrupt signals being derived from a solid-state switch actuated by the toothed haulage sprocket of the machine. This sprocket engages the links of a fixed haulage chain stretched along the entire coal face or the teeth of a rack mounted along the a.f.c structure. The distance between sprocket teeth is generally less than the desired sampling interval, ΔX, by a ratio of between 2 and 4:1.

Clearly the value of ΔX must be very much less than sensor delay X, otherwise the sampling interval itself will create multipass instability and computer control would offer no improvement. A non-infinitessimal value of X is nevertheless acceptable provided

$$\Delta X \ll X_p \quad (=1.5X\text{ typically}) \qquad (11.31)$$

i.e. $\qquad \Delta X = \text{, say,} 0.05\, X_p$ (11.32)

where X_p is the length of a single tray of the a.f.c. Clearly natural frequencies $i\pi/\Delta X$, $i=1,2,3\ldots$ would not be propagated from pass to pass if condition (11.31) is satisfied since tray rigidity would prevent the a.f.c. from following such high frequency oscillations. The same is not true for an angular natural frequency of π/X (which represents a cyclic frequency of $1/2X$) since X and X_p are of similar magnitude and detailed studies[4],[5] of semirigid conveyor behaviour have confirmed the a.f.c's inability to iron out such low-frequence resonance.

11.5.2   Storage Requirements

The total number N of samples of the single function $y_m(n,\ell)$ to be stored in the computer between passes is therefore

$$N = L/\Delta X \qquad\qquad (11.33)$$

where L is the face length, and the ratio L/X_p may be as high as 200, i.e.

$$L/Xp = \text{, say, 200, maximum} \qquad\qquad (11.34)$$

so that from (11.32) and (11.34) we see that some $200/0.05 = 4000$ bytes of data storage at say 8-bits per byte for 0.5% accuracy are necessary in the controlling computer. Of course, our analysis has assumed that the a.f.c bridges only one pass and two stored functions $y_m(n,\ell)$ and $y_m(n-1,\ell)$ would be necessary if two passes were bridged, so doubling the data storage required to 8000 bytes. The data storage requirement would be increased by a similar increment if the computer were also to hold a slowly-updated statistical model of seam-disturbance function $z(n,\ell)$ for the purposes of feedforward control.

Yet a further 4 k-bytes would be needed if discrete integral action from cut-to-cut were to be incorporated in the control algorithm in addition to the existing proportional and derivative (tilt) **feedback** terms. Whilst not used in present prototype computer control systems underground, there exists a good case for integral action which is considered in Section 11.7.1.

11.5.3   Local Computer Control

Now 16,000 bytes of storage space is a trivial requirement for a central remote control computer located at the colliery surface (perhaps 1 to 3 miles from the underground coal face) because of either its large core store, or failing this, the accessibility of bulk storage in the form of magnetic tape or disc. For a microcomputer implementation mounted on the coal cutter itself however, bulk storage is out of the question because of the arduous coal face environment resulting from heat, dust, water, vibration and the need for intrinsic safety* of electronic control equipment

* Intrinsically safe equipment is roughly defined as being incapable of creating a spark capable of igniting methane under any deliberate or accidental short-circuit or open-circuit condition.

underground. Under these circumstances 16,000 bytes of core
storage for data alone is difficult to achieve within the
extremely confined space limitations imposed.
    Further restrictions imposed by machine-mounting the
computer controller involve the man-machine interface. There
is no possibility of allowing operator or engineer communication via the normal peripherals such as visual-display
units or teletype keyboards which are completely prohibited
for reasons of their fragility and non-intrinsic safety.
Only a few pushbutton controls and a simple one-line digital
display is all that can generally be accommodated on the
limited front panel area available so allowing very little
scope of altering controller parameters or controller structure on-line. Tuning the control system is therefore difficult and errors in system design extremely expensive to
correct.
    Machine mounted local control is nevertheless the format
adopted on present prototypes although transfer of data to
the surface for graphical vdu display and off-line analysis
is in operation.

11.5.4   Remote Computer Control

    Remote control from the surface is feasible and readily
eliminates the foregoing limitations but brings with it its
own difficulties. Sampling rate need not be a serious problem as regards the data links interconnecting the machine
and computer. Typically some 12 analogue variables (or
their equivalent) require transmission   including ℓ itself,
$y_m(n,\ell)$, $\alpha(n,\ell+R)$, $\beta(n,\ell+R)$, $J(n,\ell)$, $J_d(n,\ell)$ y_r plus various
logic control signals coded into two or three 8-bit words
and, to overcome transmission noise problems, duplicate
transmission is advisable. The received   data can be acted
upon or, in the event of mismatch, the controller or actuator would freeze and await the next sampling instant. At
8 bits per message and 24 messages per interval ΔX, therefore
the speed of data transmission required is

$$8\ 24\ V/\Delta X = 192V/(0.05X_p)\ bits/s$$

Now V is typically 8m/min (=0.1333m/s) and X_p = 1.5m so that
the necessary data transmission rate is only 192 0.133/0.05
1.5) = 340 bits/s and, allowing for occasional faster
machine travel and control character transmission, a data-
link capacity of, say, 700 bits/s would therefore represent
the maximum requirements for steering control. Existing
underground serial data-transmission systems using pulse-code
modulation are easily capable of this rate of transmission,
rates of several thousand baud being fairly common.
    One disadvantage of a remote computer control scheme is,
of course, the vulnerability of the data link to mechanical
damage in the underground environment. Such damage is far
more likely than in surface installations and is particularly
the case in the region along the coal-face itself. In the
permanent mine roadways the risk of damage is slight by
comparison. The problem is alleviated to a considerable

extent, however, by inducing the data pulses onto the pilot core of the machine's robust power cable. If this cable is damaged then control is unnecessary during the interval between the fault occuring and the cable being replaced, the machine itself being inevitably stationary meanwhile. In the event of data-link failure elsewhere along its length, then a standby machine-mounted controller, even of the analogue type, can be arranged to take over control for a few passes without serious deterioration of the cutting horizon since such a system is at least single-pass stable if properly tuned.

Another disadvantage of the remote control scheme is that many unmeasured machine variables, obvious locally, are not available at the surface of the mine. Closed-circuit television and adequate audio communication could assist in overcoming some of these difficulties but problems of intrinsic safety and camera robustness would require solution before television could be safely used.

The crucial advantage of remote computer control from the surface is that major software changes are fairly readily implemented as circumstances dictate and as process knowledge increases. The progressive inclusion of more sophisticated control, e.g. feedforward, integral action, optimal strategies(Section 11.6) and self tuning algorithms can be incorporated over time without disturbance to the machine hardware.

11.5.5 Bidirectional Filtering

Using stored data for steering control offers a very important advantage over the use of present-pass coal-thickness information. This advantage arises from the fact that nucleonic coal-sensors employ radiation sources of very low energy for reasons of safety and health. This in turn means that the backscattered radiation received by the associated detector is very random in nature so requiring a substantial smoothing lag X_1 in analogue systems to reduce the sensor output noise to an acceptable level. A larger lag still may be demanded by natural-gamma sensors. This lag can in turn cause a considerable deterioration in the dynamic response of the steering system because of the phase-shift it produces. With stored data control however the data may be smoothed <u>bidirectionally</u> i.e. the data may be passed through a lag $\overline{1/(1+X_1D)}$ in both forward and backward time-sequence. The steps involved are as follows:

    (i)   pass stored sensor data through filter $1/(1+X_1D)$ in forward sequence to produce $y_{1m}(n,\ell)$ and store

    (ii)   pass stored sensor data through same filter in reverse time sequence to produce $y_{2m}(n,L-\ell)$ and store

    (iii) reverse sequence of output from (ii) to produce $y_{2m}(n,\ell)$ and store

    (iv)   form final filter output $y_m(n,\ell)$ = 0.5 $\{y_1(n,\ell) + y_2(n,\ell)\}$ and output to control algorithm.

Step (i) thus produces a phase lag in the filtered output
whereas step (iii) produces an equal phase lead for any given
frequency. The final output is therefore a smoothed version
of the input but possesses zero phase-error at any frequency.
The filter is equivalent to a transfer operator H(D) given by

$$H(D) = 0.5\{\frac{1}{(1+X_1 D)} + \frac{1}{(1-X_1 D)}\} = \frac{1}{1-X_1^2 D^2} \qquad (11.35)$$

which clearly produces no imaginary terms on substituting j^ω
for D. Such filtering therefore causes no deterioration of
control system stability whilst considerably increasing its
accuracy. It is of course only possible using a digital control computer and it does increase the storage demands calculated earlier by at least 2 x 4000 bytes. Furthermore, if
X_1 is considerably less than X_p, then a smaller sampling
interval of perhaps

$$\Delta X = 0.05 \ X_1 \qquad (11.36)$$

would be necessary for a proper implementation of the filter,
{Recall Shannon's Sampling Theorem which requires digital
sampling at a frequency of at least twice the largest frequency component of the input signal and noise for the
accurate reconstruction of the original signal: in practice
a higher sampling rate still is generally needed.}
  The bidirectional filter is therefore probably best
implemented locally on the coal-cutting machine and the
filtered output then transmitted to the surface control
computer.

11.6   MINIMUM VOLUME CONTROL

  The control discussed so far has been linear but is, of
course, hard-limited in practice by the finite stroke of the
actuator raising and lowering the cutting drum. The limits
on $J(n,\ell)$ must usually be further restricted to about ± 4cm
to avoid cutting (a) floor-steps that are too large for the
a.f.c and roof-supports to negotiate on pushover and
(b) large roof-steps that prevent good contact with the roof-
bars. Setting limits

$$|J(n,\ell)| \leq J_m = \text{constant} \qquad (11.37)$$

does, however, degrade the performance of linear control very
considerably when large disturbances occur but, once a computer is available on-line, control of a much more sophisticated nature can be contemplated. We shall therefore consider manipulating $J(n,\ell)$, subject to constraint (11.37) and in
response to stored measurements of $y(n-1,\ell)$ and $W\alpha(n,\ell)$, to
minimise the volume of coal left + stone cut over successive
passes i.e. to minimise the cash loss resulting from an
impure product. We shall again assume a fixed drum shearer
(R=O) but, as discussed in Section 11.7.2 , the effect
$R\beta(n,\ell+R)$ of along-face tilt on ranging drum machines may be
compensated fairly readily.

11.6.1   Design by General Dynamic Programming

Assuming the 'rubber conveyor' equation (11.6) to hold and off-line filtering to have removed any lag in the coal thickness measurement, all along-face dynamics are eliminated and the conveyor may be regarded as M subsections of short length

$$\Delta L = L/M \tag{11.38}$$

each subsection being steerable independently of its neighbours. Argument ℓ may therefore be dropped and, for convenience of notation, $y(n,\ell)$, $w_\alpha(n+1,\ell)$ and $J(n,\ell)$ written as y_n, a_n and J_n respectively. Neglecting seam disturbance $z(n,\ell)$[†] the following transition equation may be derived from equations (11.3),(11.4), and (11.6), viz:

$$\left[y_n,a_n\right]^T = \underline{\Phi}\left[y_{n-1},a_{n-1}\right]^T + \underline{\Delta}\,J_n \tag{11.39}$$

where

$$\underline{\Phi} = \begin{pmatrix} 1 & 1 \\ 0 & 1 \end{pmatrix} \;\ldots\; (11.40) \;\text{ and }\; \underline{\Delta} = \begin{pmatrix} 1 \\ 1 \end{pmatrix} \tag{11.41}$$

From the (small-angle) geometry of Fig. 11.7 it is clear that the volume ΔV of coal left and stone cut on pass n over distance ΔL by a drum of diameter D chosen = seam thickness, is given by:

$$\Delta V(y_{n-1},y_n) = \{\text{sign}(y_n)y_n^2 - \text{sign}(y_{n-1})y_{n-1}^2\}W\Delta L/$$

$$(y_n - y_{n-1}) \tag{11.42}$$

and the total volume of the same slice over a total of N passes is:

$$V_N = \sum_{n=1}^{N} \Delta V(y_{n-1},y_n) \tag{11.43}$$

Now the n-stage decision problem of minimising V_N w.r.t $J_1,J_2,\ldots J_N$ is converted into N simpler single stage problems using the Law of General Dynamic Programming, viz

$$V_{N-(n-1)}^{*}(y_{n-1},a_{n-1}) = \min_{J_n}\{\Delta V(y_{n-1},a_{n-1},J_n) +$$

$$V_{N-n}^{*}(y_n,a_n)\} \tag{11.44}$$

where V_i^{*} denotes the minimised volume over the last i passes

[†] The effect and compensation of $z(n,\ell)$ is considered in Section 11.7.

and is dependent <u>only</u> on the state-variables y_{N-i}, a_{N-i} at the start of this final sequence.

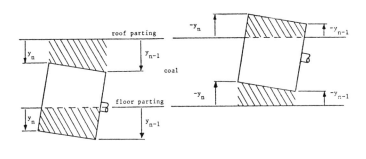

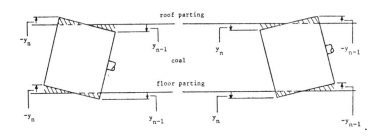

Fig. 11.7   Volumes of stone cut and coal uncut
for different drum positions.

As flowcharted in Fig. 8, starting with $V_o^* = 0$ and setting n initially to N the minimised cost V_1^* and its associated optimum control J_N^* may be computed from (11.39), (11.42) and (11.44) for a range of penultimate states y_{N-1}, a_{N-1} and stored. Thereafter, n may be incremented negatively to N-1 to allow look-up tables of V_2^* and J_{N-1}^* versus states y_{N-2}, a_{N-2}, again using (11.39), (11.42) and (11.44) and the stored table of V_1^*. The whole process may thus be repeated, for n = N-2, N-3....0 but it is found that after a number of such iterations the values of V_i^* and J_{N-i} converge for given state values and the converged tables may then be output, the latter for use in the control computer.

11.6.2   Implementation on-line

The converged optimum control look-up table takes the form shown in Fig. 11.9 and, as shown in Fig. 11.10, it is merely necessary for the on line controller to read values of y_{n-1} (from the stored filtered measurements of $y_m(n,\ell)$) and a_{n-1} from the tilt transducer on receipt of distance interrupts produced by a haulage sprocket switch at increments ΔL and from the table, select the appropriate value of

J_n^* and output this demand to the hydraulic actuator. The system is therefore a feedback controller (as before) but is now non-linear.

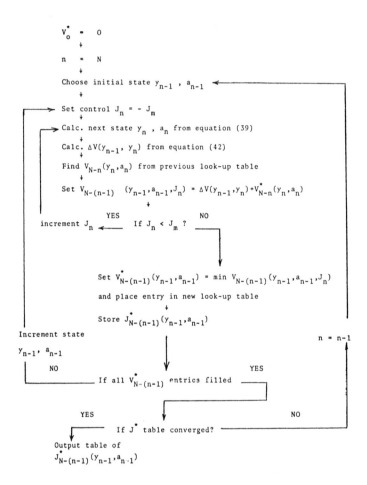

Fig. 11.8   Dynamic Programming Flow-chart

For a state range of say, ±20cm with a resolution of say, 0.5cm, the stored array would occupy a further $(40 \times 2)^2 = 6400$ bytes over and above the previously calculated storage requirements but this increment could be reduced by first fitting simple analytical functions to the switching lines in Fig. 11.9 and storing only the varying values of J^* within these boundaries.

For large initial disturbances, the performance of the minimum volume controller is enormously superior to that of the linear controller subjected to the same hard limits $\pm J_m$ as illustrated by the response to an initial disturbance

a

y \ a	-5.0	-4.6	-4.2	-3.8	-3.4	-3.0	-2.6	-2.2	-1.8	-1.4	-1.0	-0.8	-0.4	0.0	0.4	0.8	1.0	1.4	1.8	2.2	2.6	3.0	3.4	3.8	4.2	4.6	5.0
5.0		1.3	1.0	0.5	0.1	-0.3	-0.7	-1.1	-1.4																		
4.6		1.2	0.7	0.3	-0.1	-0.5	-0.9	-1.2																			
4.2		1.3	0.9	0.5	0.1	-0.3	-0.7	-1.1																			
3.8			1.1	0.7	0.3	-0.1	-0.5	-0.9	-1.3																		
3.4			1.2	0.8	0.4	0.0	-0.4	-0.8	-1.2																		
3.0				1.1	0.7	0.3	-0.1	-0.5	-0.9	-1.3	-1.4																
2.6				1.2	0.8	0.4	0.0	-0.4	-0.8	-1.2	-1.4																
2.2					1.1	0.7	0.3	-0.1	-0.5	-0.9	-1.1																
1.8					1.3	0.9	0.5	0.1	-0.3	-0.7	-0.9	-1.3															
1.4							1.2	0.8	0.4	0.0	-0.4	-0.6	-1.0	-1.4													
1.0							1.1	0.7	0.3	-0.1	-0.3	-0.7	-1.1														
0.8								1.4	1.0	0.6	0.2	0.0	-0.4	-0.8	-1.2												
0.4										1.0	0.6	0.4	0.0	-0.4	-0.8	-1.2	-1.4										
0.0										1.4	1.0	0.8	0.4	0.0	-0.4	-0.8	-1.0	-1.4									
-0.4											1.4	1.2	0.8	0.4	0.0	-0.4	-0.6	-1.0	-1.4								
-0.8													1.2	0.8	0.4	0.0	-0.2	-0.6	-1.0	-1.4							
-1.0													1.4	1.0	0.6	0.2	0.0	-0.4	-0.8	-1.2							
-1.4														1.4	1.0	0.6	0.4	0.0	-0.4	-0.8	-1.2						
-1.8															1.3	0.9	0.7	0.3	-0.1	-0.5	-0.9	-1.3					
-2.2																1.1	1.0	0.5	0.1	-0.3	-0.7	-1.1	-1.4				
-2.6																	1.3	1.1	0.7	0.3	-0.1	-0.5	-0.9	-1.3			
-3.0																		1.3	1.0	0.5	0.1	-0.3	-0.7	-1.1	-1.4		
-3.4																			1.2	0.7	0.3	-0.1	-0.5	-0.9	-1.2		
-3.8																				1.3	0.9	0.5	0.1	-0.3	-0.7	-1.1	
-4.2																				1.1	0.7	0.3	-0.1	-0.5	-0.9	-1.3	
-4.6																					1.3	0.9	0.5	0.1	-0.3	-0.7	-1.1
-5.0																				1.3	0.9	0.5	0.1	-0.3	-0.7	-1.1	-1.3

(In the central band, at left: $J^* = +J_m$; at right: $J^* = -J_m$.)

y

Fig. 11.9   Converged optimal control look-up table ($J_m = 1.5$)

$y_0 = 5$ $a_0 = -4$ in Fig. 11.11. Such control has been successfully demonstrated on $\frac{1}{4}$-scale mechanical models but awaits future trials underground.

11.7   ERROR ELIMINATION

External disturbances such as natural seam undulations, $z(n, \ell)$, have been disregarded so far, largely because they do not affect the stability of the linearly controlled process. Considering therefore the rubber conveyor equation (11.6), now elaborated to include the effect of floor-lift, $f(n, \ell)$, beneath the a.f.c. resulting from the enormous roof pressures bearing down on either side, we get:

$$h(n, \ell) = y(n-1, \ell) + z(n-1, \ell) + f(n, \ell) \tag{11.45}$$

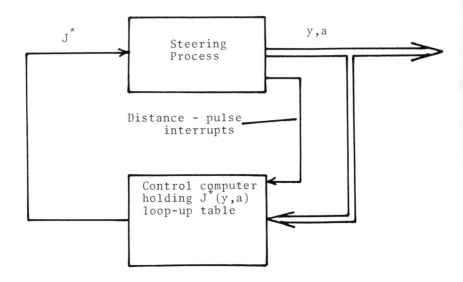

Fig. 11.10   Minimum volume control implementation

and, assuming computer control according to eqns.(11.11)and (11.25) it is readily shown that, in steady-state:

$$y_r - y(n-1,\ell) = (\Delta z - f)/k_h \qquad (11.46)$$

if

$$z(n,\ell) - z(n-1,\ell) = \Delta z = \text{constant} \qquad (11.47)$$

and $f(n,\ell) = f = \text{constant}$ (11.48)

Stability restriction $k_h < 2$ prevents error-compensation by increasing this parameter and both Δz and f might typically amount to several cm., their values, of course, being random in practice.

11.7.1   Integral Action in Face-Advance

The effect of seam gradient, $\Delta z/W$, might be compensated by applying suitable bias to the measurement of tilt, $\alpha(n,\ell)$, but this bias would need preprogramming in the computer for the full face-length to cater for gently twisting seams and would also need periodic reprogramming, manually or self-adaptively. The method might also be used in conjunction with the minimum volume controller. In current practice, an average bias for the whole face is applied because of core-store restrictions but, as these are eliminated by the use of chips of greater capacity, (or by reverting to remote control) the offset could be totally eliminated by discrete integral action of gain k_i in a control algorithm of the type:

$$J_d(n,\ell) = k_h\{y_r - y(n-1,\ell)\} - k_g W\alpha(n,\ell) + k_i \sum_{j=0}^{n}$$

$$\{y_r - y(j-1,\ell)\} \tag{11.49}$$

for the fixed-drum shearer. With $k_g = 1.0$, the resulting characteristic equation:

$$z^2 + z(k_h + k_i - 2) + 1 - k_h = 0 \tag{11.50}$$

yields stable roots provided:

$$k_i < 2(2-k_h) \text{ and } 0 < k_h < 2.0 \tag{11.51}$$

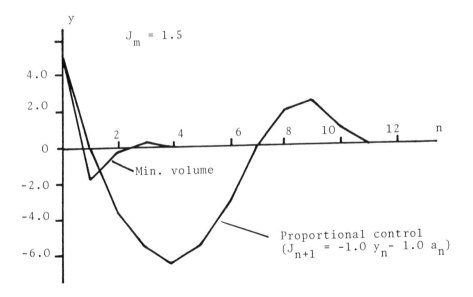

Fig. 11.11   Responses of minimum volume control and hard limited linear control

11.7.2   Roof-Height Sensing

A method currently used to eliminate the effect of floor-lift beneath the a.f.c is to employ a mechanical tracer pressed in continual contact against the previously cut roof. This transducer shown in Fig. 11.12a for the fixed-drum machine, clearly measures

$$h(n,\ell) - y(n-1,\ell) - z(n-1,\ell) = f(n-\ell) \qquad (11.52)$$

since the previous roof is unaffected by present floor-lift (which follows the pushover process).

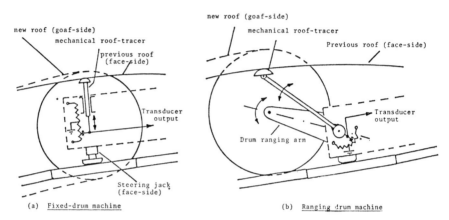

(a)   Fixed-drum machine   (b)   Ranging drum machine

* Potentiometer tracks fixed to machine bodies

Fig. 11.12   Roof height sensors for fixed and ranging drum machines

The control law now used is

$$J_d(n,\ell) = k_h\{y_r - y(n-1,\ell)\} - k_g W\alpha(n,\ell) - f(n,\ell)$$

$$(11.53)$$

and, on substitution in the process equations, this is seen to eliminate f from error equation (11.46).

The sensor, re-engineered in the form of Fig. 11.12(b) for the ranging-drum machine ($R > 0$) now measures:

$$h(n,\ell+R) - y(n-1,\ell) - z(n-1,\ell) + (R/F)\{h(n,\ell+R)$$

$$- h(n,\ell+R+F)\} = f(n,\ell) + R\,\beta(n,\ell+R) \qquad (11.54)$$

so that negative feedback of this signal now compensates the destabilising effect of $\beta(n,\ell+R)$ in the process (see Section 11.8): without the need for a vibration-prone along-face tilt-transducer. The ranging-drum machine is effectively converted into a fixed-drum machine in this way.

11.8 PICK-FORCE SENSING

Experiments have been conducted over many years to attempt to infer the height of the drum within the coal seam from measurements received from a specially strain-gauged cutting-pick but, only with the recent availability of machine-mounted computing power, has the necessary high-speed data-processing become realisable. By arranging for the instrumented pick to protrude a fixed distance beyond a nearby leading pick, a very-nearly fixed 'bite' can be ensured so that the force measured reflects the pattern of hard and soft bands of material within the composite seam strata. These bands run parallel to the seam boundaries and a thin stone band (for instance) at a depth d in the seam would produce an impulse in the pick force pattern, $F(\theta)$, at rotational angle $\theta = \gamma$ from the vertical where, if y denotes the roof-coal thickness left behind and $2r$ = drum diameter across the pick tips, then

$$y = d - r(1 - \cos\gamma) \qquad\qquad (11.55)$$

and similarly,

$$y_r = d - r(1 - \cos\gamma_r) \qquad\qquad (11.56)$$

where γ_r is the value of γ when the drum is correctly positioned at $y = y_r$. In this ideal situation, by merely comparing measurements of drum angles γ and γ_r, the error γ_e may be calculated and used to reposition the drum servo within the space of one revolution. Unfortunately, the strata shatter randomly and distinct 'marker bands' are rare so that, instead, the pick-force pattern is nowadays cross-correlated, in the θ- domain, with a prerecorded master pattern obtained immediately after launching the machine from desired initial conditions (i.e. from a state of $\gamma = \gamma_d$ for $0 < \ell < L$). Being ideally suited to repetitive signal analysis, Fast Fourier Transformation is then used to yield an estimate of the spatial delay function $\exp(-j\omega\gamma_e)$ and hence a measurement of error-angle.

Initial surface trials conducted by the N.C.B's Mining Research and Development Establishment and the University of Bath on carefully constructed mock coal-faces have produced encouraging results but only underground experience will determine the number of revolutions needed for a good estimate of γ_e and hence the inherent lag of the entire measurement system. With haulage speeds in the range 3.5 to 7m/min. and drum speeds of between 0.5 and 1.0 rev./s, the distance lag per revolution lies in the range 0.06 to 0.23m (i.e. 0.04 X_p to 0.15 X_p), the upper limit being potentially de-stabilising if, say, five revolutions are needed for noise suppression.

It is claimed that a pick-force sensing system eliminates the need for other feedbacks (α, β, f) on the grounds that the roof (or floor) coal thickness is measured almost instantaneously. Under pick force control however, even including unit gain tilt feedback, the system transfer-function G(s) is given by

$$\tilde{y}(n,s)/\tilde{h}(n,s) = G(s) = e^{Rs}\{1+(R/F)(1-e^{Fs})\}/$$
$$(1+k_h\ e^{-Xs}) \tag{11.57}$$

where X is now the data processing distance. If, for example, machine geometry is such that F = 2R, then, in the ideal case of negligible X,:

$$|G(j\omega)|_{max} = 2/(1 + k_h) \tag{11.58}$$

so that, for multipass stability:

$$k_h > 1.0 \tag{11.59}$$

but such a gain would clearly cause stability problems within the local   loop where X cannot be neglected.

If, as an alternative, proportional gain k_h is replaced by integral action, K/s,to bring about complete elimination of steady-state offset within one pass then, keeping F = 2R,

$$|G(j\omega)| \rightarrow j\omega(cosR\omega + 2j\ sin\ R\omega)/(K+j\omega) \tag{11.60}$$

and, accepting the relaxed multipass stability criterion:

$$|G(j\omega)| < 1.0\quad,\quad |\omega| < \omega_b = conveyor\ bandwidth \tag{11.61}$$

then, for multipass stability, integral gain K must be such that

$$K > \sqrt{3}\ \omega_b \tag{11.62}$$

Again this lower limit on K could create single pass stability problems since $\omega_b \gg 1/X_p$. Pick force control therefore does not eliminate the need for careful system design.

11.9   CONCLUSIONS

In this chapter, an attempt has been made to demonstrate how the use of various forms of computer control   in conjunction with either conventional or novel instrumentation can profoundly improve the vertical steering of coal-cutting machines. The use of such control should not be attempted however, without undertaking a careful dynamic analysis of the system's likely behaviour. Field trials should also be carefully planned to confirm (or contradict) analytical and simulation predictions for the experience gained to be of widespread value.

11.10   ACKNOWLEDGEMENTS

The author gratefully acknowledges that the research

underlying much of this chapter has been undertaken with
financial support from both the N.C.B and S.E.R.C over the
past 14 years. Figs. 1 to 6 were first published in the
Proc. I. Mech. E. (ref. 4) and the permission of the Council
to reproduce these diagrams is also gratefully acknowledged.

11.11 REFERENCES

1. Nicholson, H. (Ed.) ' Modelling of dynamical systems',
    Vol. 2, P. Peregrinus, I.E.E. Control Engineering Series
    13, London, 1981, 264 pp.

2. Edwards, J.B. and Owens, D.H. "Analysis and control of
    multipass processes', J. Wiley, Research Studies Press,
    Letchworth, 1982, 298 pp.

3. Cooper, L.R. 'Gamma ray backscatter gauges for measu-
    ring coal thickness on mechanised coal faces', Proc.
    IEE Conf. on Industrial Measurement and Control by
    Radiation Techniques, Guildford, 1972, IEE Conf. Pub.
    No. 84, pp. 89-93.

4. Edwards,J.B., Wolfenden, J.R. and Yazdi, A.S.M.R. Yazdi,
    'Modelling of semiflexible conveyor structures for coal
    face steering investigations', Proc. I. Mech.E., Vol.
    196, No. 32, 1982, pp. 387 to 408.

5. Edwards, J.B., 'The effect of large-scale structures on
    the stability of coal-face steering', Proc. I. Mech. E.
    Vol. 198A, No. 1, 1984, pp. 29 to 40.

6. Rosie, A.M. 'Information and communication theory',
    Electronic User Series, Blackie, London 1966, 175 pp.

Chapter 12

Computer control in the glass industry

R.A. Merryweather

12.1   INTRODUCTION

In the flat glass industry the Pilkington Float Glass Process (Pilkington (1)) has now become the predominant process. This process which produces a continuous ribbon of flat annealed glass of varying width, lends itself to an on-line automatic cut up line when compared with previous processes.

For example, the plate glass process was discontinuous after the glass was ground. It was then cut into plates, polished on one side, turned over, polished on the other side, and then put into stock. It was then examined, cut and packed by hand for despatch.

The Float Process will be described briefly before describing the cut up line controls. A modern Float Glass Plant consists of a batch house in which the raw materials for glass making are mixed together and the mixed batches are then fed to a continuous glass melting furnace. The furnace, which has approximately a capacity of 5000 tons per week, is continuously fed with the batch and melts and refines it to provide molten glass to the float bath. In the float bath the ribbon of glass is formed and cooled until it is able to be passed over the rollers without surface damage. The glass then passes through an annealing lehr and is cooled in a controlled environment down to a temperature at which it can be handled. The ribbon of glass then forms the input to the cut up line. The cut up line consists of a number of items of plant to process the ribbon of glass into the sizes required. The glass is inspected for faults, cut to size and then conveyed to its destination, where it is either sent for despatch or stock.

12.2   DESCRIPTION OF CUT UP PROCESS

The input to the process is the continuous ribbon of glass from the annealing lehr.

12.2.1 Inspection

The speeds at which the float glass ribbon is produced

today are too high for manual inspection. Automatic inspection equipment has been developed (Beattie (2)) which uses an optical scanner, Fig. 1. A number of scanners are mounted over the ribbon of glass and collimated light is transmitted through the glass and passes into the scanner. A slit defines the zone of glass which is being inspected. An image of this zone is projected onto a rotating disc which contains a number of radial slits. The speed of the disc is such as to ensure that complete inspection of the glass passing beneath the scanner takes place. The insertion of the radial slit with the ribbon line image allows the light from a small element of glass to fall on a photomultiplier. Any defects such as a stone or bubble causes a change in the light intensity and a corresponding change in the electrical output signal from the scanner.

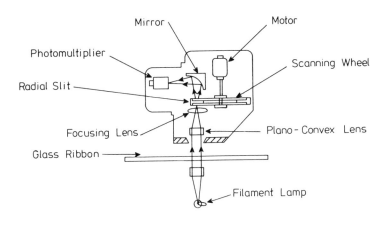

Fig. 12.1   Diagram of Scanner Head

The defect is classified by the type of signal produced and sized by the number of times it is scanned as it passes by. The electrical signals are fed to a process control computer which forms part of the inspection and cutting control system. The computer sizes the defect and if required operates one of a number of spray guns for marking the position of the defect. The fault information and tracking pulses from a line digitiser are used by the computer to operate the appropriate marker as the fault passes.

12.2.2   Cutting

The cutting of the glass involves scoring and snapping. Two types of scores are put on the glass; cross cuts and longitudinal cuts. The cross cutter is either an electric or an electro-hydraulic servo angle bar cutter (Brown and Wilson (3)). Digitisers on the glass and cutting head produce pulses which are continuously compared and an error signal is derived. The error signal is used to control either a DC servo motor or an electro-hydraulic servo valve which in turn controls a hydraulic motor connected to the cutting head. The system keeps the head in synchronism with the glass, thus producing a straight cut as shown in figure 2.

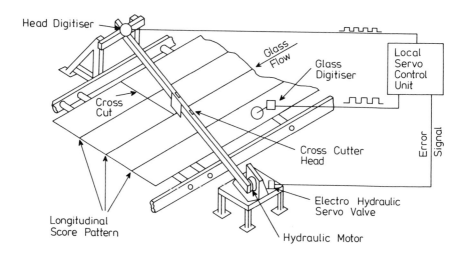

Fig. 12.2   Angle Bar Cross Cutter

The co-ordination of the cutters and the selection of which cutter to use for a given cut is the function of the automatic inspection and cutting control computer, which signals a particular cutter when a cut is required. The cutter locks onto that position and servos the head across the glass to give the required score.

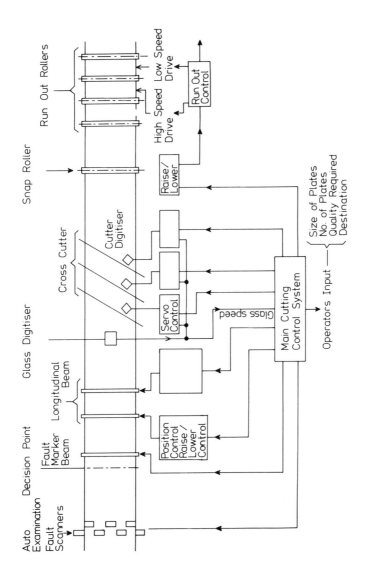

Fig. 12.3   Diagram of Automatic Examination and
Cutting

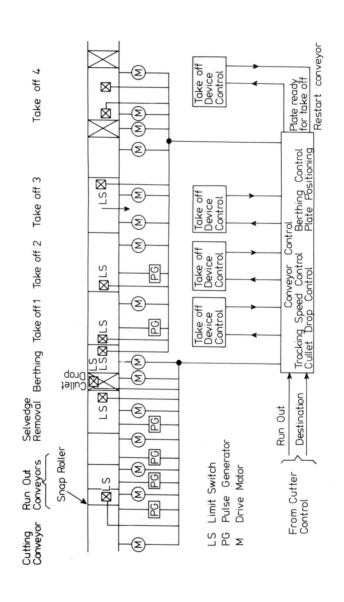

Fig. 12.4   Schematic of Control Sequence

The longitudinal scores are produced by cutting heads which are positioned across the ribbon of glass, either manually or automatically. The cutting heads are called down onto the glass ribbon by the computer using the line digitisers so that the scores are changed at the position where the cross cuts will be put on the glass. If the system is for a plant where many changes per shift are required, then automatically positioned heads are used, but the use of manually positioned heads does permit a good degree of flexibility as a number of patterns may be set up before they are required by the cutting computer. The automatic positioning of the the longitudinal cutters is controlled by a stepping motor and latch bar so the cutters can be positioned in the correct place and then clamped in position while other cutters are being moved.

The cutting operation is completed by snapping the scored glass. The method of snapping depends upon the position, number and direction of the scores. It is usual to snap out the cross cuts first and a snapping roller is used to bend the glass across the score. It is necessary to separate the free plates as soon as the snap occurs. This prevents the edges damaging one another as they travel along the conveyor. The computer raises the snap roll when a cross cut is precisely over it and at the same time a downstream conveyor is accelerated at a pre-determined rate to create a gap between plates. Longitudinal cuts are then snapped out further downstream by using a configuration of wheels set to bend the glass about an axis along its direction of motion. Fig. 3 shows a typical control system.

12.2.3 Conveyor System

Fig. 4 shows a typical conveyor control system which uses a routing and tracking control computer in conjunction with local control units to sequence the glass to its destination. As each plate or pattern of glass is snapped out from the ribbon, it is accelerated and the routing information passed to the sequencing computer so that the plate can be conveyed to its correct destination. The longitudinal cuts are snapped out at the selvedge removal position and the plate passes through to the take off devices. Should a plate be faulty, or the queuing limits in the system be exceeded, then the plate may be disposed of through the cullet drop to the cullet disposal system. Each take off unit is a self contained unit of plant with its own local control and is called into operation when a plate is ready to be packed.

12.2.4 Pack Making

Two types of automatic pack making equipment are described as typical of the devices which vary from plant to plant. In its simplest form full width plates may be produced and then removed from the line by an automatic crane. The crane picks up each plate in turn on vacuum cups

after it has been berthed on the conveyor ready for pick
off. It is then transferred to a pack being built up on a
tilting table located adjacent to the line. When a pack has
been completed then the table is raised to near vertical and
the pack of glass is transferred into stock by trucks. A
second type of device is used when the ribbon has been split
into plates and with this the plate is positioned on the
conveyor over a four sided frame which can rotate about an
axis at right angles to the conveyor. The plate is removed
by rotating the frame through 90°. The plate is then in a
vertical plane and is formed into a pack of glass on a
pallet or stillage which is indexed backwards as the pack
builds up.

12.3   THE CONTROL HIERARCHY

        The structure of the control system is shown in Fig. 5
and it can be seen that there are three levels in the
system. At the local control level units of plant are
controlled by individual servo systems, drive control panels
and programmable logic control units for the take off units.
The main level of control and co-ordination is provided by
the automatic inspection and cutting control computer,
together with the glass tracking and sequencing control
computer. These two computer systems are connected to a
performance monitoring computer which collects information
from both the automatic inspection and cutting control and
the routing and tracking computer.

12.3.1 Automatic Inspection and Cutting Control System

This computer system, Fig. 3 collects data from the
automatic inspection scanners on the defects which are
present in the glass ribbon and sizes the defects against
the criteria entered on the VDU by the operator. This
information can be used to mark the faults in the glass and
also as an input into the cutting control algorithm. The
cutting control has a number of operational modes which can
be selected by the operator depending on the products
required and the quality of ribbon being produced. A number
of cutting channels can be used and a selective cutting
algorithm which will then optimise the yield from the
ribbon. The data required by the algorithm is entered on
the VDU giving the sizes and number of plates required,
together with the permissible fault characteristics. The
computer then, when each proposed cut is at the decision
point, looks back up the ribbon at the fault information and
makes a decision of which plate to cut. This could also
include a decision to cut behind a fault in the ribbon and
cut out a small plate containing the fault to minimise lost
glass. The largest possible or highest quality plate
possible is cut from the ribbon and given the correct
destination code. This decision is then tracked down from
the decision point and the necessary actions are initiated.

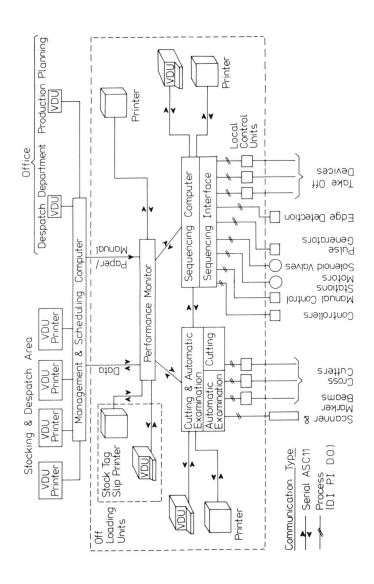

Fig. 12.5   Schematic of Cut Up Line Control Hierarchy

At the marker beam any faults to the standards set in the selected cutting channel are marked. The appropriate pattern is selected at the longitudinal cutter beam and a change made to this pattern at the correct time. A cross cutter is then called and a cut put on the glass which is then tracked to the snap roller and the plate snapped off from the continuous ribbon of glass. This plate is then accelerated away from the ribbon and passed to the routing and tracking computer, together with its destination information, identification code and control parameters.

12.3.2 Routing and Tracking

Fig. 4 shows a typical sequence control system, used for routing and tracking the glass to the required destination. The diagram has been simplified to show only representative functions, and in practice forms a very large control system. The plate is passed to the system by the automatic inspection and cutting control computer, together with its destination, identification and control information. Plates are tracked down the conveyor section to section using pulse generators and photoswitches and any operations specified in the control parameters are carried out. For example the selvedge removal device can be called into operation and snap out longitudinal scores at the edge of the plate which are then removed and disposed of into the cullet system. The control system sequences the plate through the conveyors making sure that the conditions have been satisfied before it is transferred from one section to another. If the conditions are not satisfied, then the plates are berthed up until the route is clear. The queuing of plates takes place until in the limit plates have to be disposed of and are rejected into the cullet system at a cullet drop. The glass is routed to a specified unloading station and the local unit for that pick off device signalled to remove the glass from the conveyor. The local unit then signals when it is safe to restart the conveyor. The availability of pick off units is monitored by the computer and in the event of either failure to respond or being switched off line, alarms the operator and where possible initiates recovery action. This is necessary on a main line conveyor so that the forward path is cleared for glass as soon as possible. Alternative destinations can be specified so that glass can be re-routed in the event of pick off device failure. The VDU on this system is used for operator and engineering communication. A mimic diagram can be called up which shows the disposition of plates within the system and plate counts and availability against each pick off unit. The VDU can also be used to indicate alternative destinations that should be used in the event of plate failure.

Information on the use of plates together with plant availability is signalled to the performance monitoring system.

12.3.3   Performance Monitor

The performance monitoring computer accepts data from both the automatic inspection and cutting control and the routing and tracking computer systems. The data on glass input and destination is used to form the basis of a shift log on the utilisation of glass. Pack slips are printed when a pack of glass is completed and the information is also signalled to the stock room management and scheduling system. The glass loss down each cullet drop is collected each shift and a log of loss for each product type is produced so that specific problems can be identified and corrective action taken. The availability of major items of plant is monitored and a shift log is produced for engineering control showing the down time for each major item of plant.

12.4   COMPUTER HARDWARE

The three computer systems described are based on PDP11 computers each with an identical processor, memory allocation and communication features. The computers are supplied with industrial interfacing equipment specially designed for a heavy industrial situation. The automatic inspection interface has a dual ported memory which can be loaded with fault data whilst still being accessed by the computer system. The cutting system requires interface counters which are connected to the bus and can be read and loaded by the computer. The counters are loaded with the next event required and then enabled. On countdown a signal is provided for both the computer interrupt and external plant operation so that accuracy is not dependent on program delays. All input and output functions are all equipped with LED indication so that maintenance personnel can easily identify any failure.

12.5   SOFTWARE

The software system used in each of the three computer systems is a process control package developed by Pilkington to satisfy the requirement of glass plant systems. The package forms a common basis for in plant applications with easy controlled access for engineers to maintain and update the process control scheme to meet changing requirements. It is structured around the multi level hardware of the PDP11 computer and responds directly to interrupts, timers and counters etc. The package is table driven and centred around a single control table and common data area. The table is made up of variable length records called sequences. A record consists of a number of phases which specify the actions required.

Support for process input/output, data manipulation and communication form basic subprograms. Timers, pulse counters, interrupts and program inputs and outputs can be accessed through subprograms and can be used re-entrantly by sequences. The linking required is generated on line to form a daisy chain of sequences that require service on a given interrupt. The program is written in PDP11 MACRO assembler language but knowledge of that language is not required by process control engineers to use the system.

The package is essentially a comprehensive set of dedicated software routines or subprograms which, under the control of a polled and interrupt driven Executive, can be arranged into functional event tables or sequences. It is a memory resident system running in a maximum of 32K words. The system software and associated data areas typically occupy 16K words leaving in the order of 14K words for applications software since 2K words are reserved for I/O addresses.

The modular construction allows individual systems to be tailored to the application, thus eliminating the built in redundancy which can occur within universal package systems.

Event tables or sequences can be created and modified whilst the system is running thus providing the applications and maintenance engineer with a useful tool when changes to control strategies are required. The new sequence can be constructed and tested by switching the old sequence off and turning the new one on. By doing the reverse the old sequence can rapidly be reintroduced if the new one fails. Similarly new displays can be added and existing ones modified whilst the system is stil controlling the plant.

A full range of subprograms is available ranging from control subprograms such as setting digital output bits in modules to display subprograms enabling the user to draw colour blocks or graphics on a VDU.

The system will run hardware that Pilkington as a Group use in their applications. The software drivers to run hardware not currently used can easily be interfaced to meet a particular requirement.

12.6. COMMUNICATION

The communication needs can be considered in two parts, operator communication and system communication as shown in Fig. 12.5.

12.6.1 Operator Communication

Basic operator communication is through a VDU or slow speed keyboard printer or through special purpose buttons and switches which are connected to the process inputs and outputs. The keyboard commands operate through the sequence data table and make use of high level formatting and message generating systems. This means that logs, messages and displays can be changed by the engineers without reassembly of the software. The high level support includes refreshed data options for use in mimics and dynamic display situations.

12.6.2 System Communication

The communication links used are shown in Fig. 124. The distributed control system depends on successful intercommunication through the system. The basic method of communication between computers uses a serial ASCII duplex communication protocol in an echoplex mode. This means that each byte of data is confirmed before it is used for process control. Any malfunction is easily identified by the initiating computer, either computer on the link can take control when required. Communication with the local control units and PLC's is by process input/output connection.

REFERENCES

(1) Pilkington, L.A.B., 1969, The Float Glass Process, Proc. Roy. Soc. A, 314, 1-25.

(2) Beattie, J.R., Oct. 1965, Automatic Inspection of Flat Glass for Manufacturing Faults, 20th Annual Conf. ISA, Los Angeles

(3) Brown, R.A. and Wilson, R.E., 1971, Electro-Hydraulic Servo Cross Cut, British Patent No. 1,364,876

ACKNOWLEDGEMENTS

This paper is published with the permission of the Directors, Pilkington Brothers P.L.C. and Mr. A.S. Robinson, Director of Group Research and Development.

Chapter 13

Robotics

J. Billingsley

13.1   INTRODUCTION

It is hard to define the boundary between robotics and
digitally controlled production in general - if such a boundary even exists. For many years digital controllers have
been applied to lathes and milling machines, whilst for an
equal time pick-and-place component transfer machines have
embodied the structural form of the robots of today. It
could almost be said that the robot was born when the name
was first borrowed from Karyl Capek's novel "RUR" (which
predated by many years the fiction of Greenberg and Asimov).
If a definition is absolutely necessary, a robot can be
described as "a computer with muscles", although it must live
up to its name of "robotnik", a worker.

An impetus to exploit robotics has followed on the
heels of the microprocessor applications project MAPCON. The
publicity given to the micro by this and numerous television
series has broken the ground to make computing power acceptable on the shop floor, although immense care is still
needed to avoid "technofear" when introducing robotics into
a new location. One of the greatest present barriers to the
introduction of robotics is the high capital cost. A
Unimation PUMA can cost upwards of £22 000, whilst a robot
from IBM equipped with force sensors will set the purchaser
back some £78 000. It is very difficult to justify such
figures to a Managing Director solely on the grounds of
replacing employees. It is inevitable that cheaper machines
will appear on the scene very soon. Already "toy" robots
have been produced to fill an education market, usually
requiring the addition of a personal computer and providing
only a minimum of software support. As will be seen, the
servos and mechanics of a robot cannot alone justify a price
of more than a very few thousands of pounds, and the final
price of a complete system exploitable for factory
applications is likely to fall to around £5000.

Early robots were programmed solely on a "teach and
repeat" basis. Later machines had the benefit of a language
such as VAL enabling off-line programming to be performed.
Even so, "teach mode" has figured heavily in the way these
machines have been programmed in practice. Much of the

justification for the price tag of the IBM robot is placed on its AML Pascal-like language, designed to respond to tactile sensors. As research equips robots with even more sophisticated sensor systems, so the potential for "intelligent" operation is increased. Off-line programming moves hand-in-hand with advances in CAD/CAM. Whether industry is equipped with the skills to exploit such robots is a more thorny question.

13.2 ROBOT GEOMETRY

Conventional machine tools rely for precision on lead-screws, slideways and accurately centred bearings. The spherical polar robot relies instead on accurately encoded angles and mathematical transformations - sometimes with rather dubious results. In principle, it should be possible to achieve accuracy of movement more economically in such a robot than in a conventional tool. However, this is not borne out by present machines.

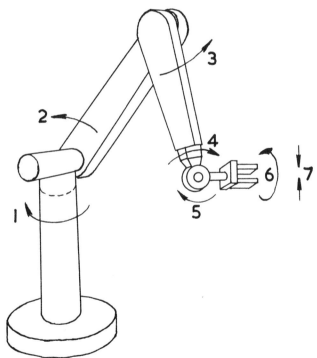

Fig.13.1 "Conventional" robot axes

The computation which relates a set of spatial coordinates to a set of joint angles involves the length of each structural element of the robot, and will be sensitive to any misalignment of axes which are assumed to be parallel, such as joints 2 and 3 (Fig.13.1). As yet, the self-calibration functions of commercially available robots are limited to relating the coarse-fine potentiometer readings against a digital encoder, and so robot accuracy is dependant on manufacturing accuracy. Precision, in contrast, may perhaps only be impaired by a variable load, and the robot will return time after time to a precisely defined location once taught. Thus teach-mode programming has a practical advantage over off-line coordinate specification for the present generation.

An improvement in structural stiffness can be gained by introducing one or more sliding members into the robot. Two hinges with vertical axes will permit free movement in the horizontal x- and y-directions, whilst a vertical sliding end unit allows precise and stiff movement in the z-direction. This geometry is already familiar in pick-and-place machines. Another configuration with two rotational movements and one slideway allows rotation in elevation and azimuth of a variable length radius - used widely in both pick-and-place machines and in some of the more heavyweight robots.

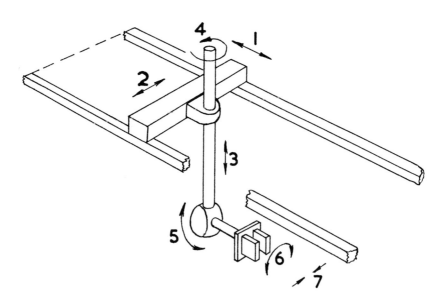

Fig.13.2   A cartesian robot

The IBM RS1 has abandoned polar movement in favour of three cartesian slideways, reminiscent of an overgrown x-y plotter (Fig.13.2). Cost reduction is not a feature of this machine! The need for geometric transformations is avoided, and attention can be paid in the software to the inclusion of force sensing from the strain gauges mounted in the end effector. Unfortunately the extended z-axis rod results in a loss of positional stiffness.

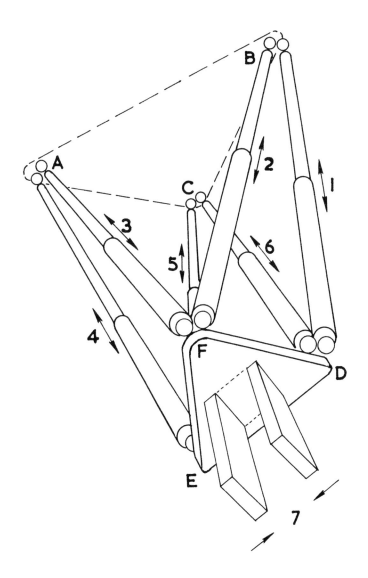

Fig.13.3 Gadfly geometry

A different approach is made in an experimental development, the 'Gadfly'. No doubt inspired by the rams used for moving the cockpit of an aircraft training simulator, this achieves all six degrees of freedom by the use of variable length linking rods (Fig.13.3). To an approximation, pairs of rods are pivoted at the vertices of a fixed triangular base. The other ends of the rods are pivoted in pairs to the vertices of a movable triangle, each pair consisting of one rod from each of two adjacent base vertices. The result is a structure which is very stiff provided that deflections are not too large. On the debit side, the limitations on movement are more severe than for the 'traditional' robot, whilst there is certainly no improvement in the complexity of computations relating axis to spatial coordinates.

13.3   ROBOT AXES AND SPATIAL COORDINATES

For now, let us concentrate on the spherical polar geometry robot as typified by the Unimation Puma. For any given configuration of the axis coordinates a1 to a6 the robot end effector will adopt a unique position x,y,z...... i.e.

$$\underline{x} = \underline{x}(\underline{a})$$

On the other hand the inverse function

$$\underline{a} = \underline{a}(\underline{x})$$

is not single-valued. The same position can be reached with the robot in a 'left-handed' or a 'right-handed' configuration. The task of controlling the robot axes to yield a demanded position is made even more difficult by the presence of 'singular points'. Here the matrix of the gradients of the coordinates

$$\nabla_{\underline{a}}\underline{x} = \begin{bmatrix} \dfrac{\partial x_1}{\partial a_1} & \dfrac{\partial x_1}{\partial a_2} & \cdots \\ \\ \dfrac{\partial x_2}{\partial a_1} & & \\ \\ \vdots & & \end{bmatrix}$$

becomes singular, so that for a small change in final position a relatively large excursion of the robot is required. This is most easily seen to occur when two of the robot axes, say the wrist axis and the yaw axis, become collinear. In 'world mode' and in 'tool mode', motion of the Puma is controlled to give linear movement, the tool-piece orientation being held constant. It is in these modes that the effect becomes most marked.

A solution to the problem of singular points, and also to problems which arise when a robot must be operated in a constricted space, is to introduce an extra redundant, robot axis. This then introduces a further problem when computing the demanded axis values; in order to yield a solution, an additional computational constraint must be applied.

13.4 AXIS CONTROL

The problem of the nonlinear relationship between coordinates and axis positions is attacked in the Puma by computing target axis angles some forty times per second. Between these points, the position is controlled by uniform interpolation performed by one microprocessor per axis.

Position feedback is taken from an incremental optical encoder. As the motor rotates, this gives two fine resolution pulse trains in quadrature, from which a signed position change may be readily deduced. This still provides no absolute position reference, for which other provision must be made. Once per revolution of the transducer a third photocell gives a single pulse. This is used in association with yet another level of transducer, a linear potentiometer. The accuracy of the potentiometer needs only to be five percent or so, sufficient to localise the position to one revolution of the optical transducer. At startup, each axis in turn is driven slowly until its reference pulse is found, at which point the absolute position is identified from the potentiometer reading.

Intelligent avoidance of the tolerance problem is made in the 'Potcal' routine. After the robot has been manually adjusted into a specified attitude, each axis is rotated through successive reference pulses whilst the potentiometers are read automatically. These values are then 'blown' into an EPROM, or can be saved as a disk file.

From demanded and actual positions, a value of position error is deduced. This is in turn translated into a velocity demand. With suitable shaping of the look-up function, a close approximation to time-optimal control can be achieved. To implement velocity control, however, the axis velocity must be measured. Early versions of the Puma used a technique common in daisy-control of early daisy-wheel printers. This involved differentiating the two photocell signals. Before amplifying and clipping, these are approximately sinusoidal in nature. The peak values of the derivatives thus indicate the velocity, but the signals require demodulation to be of use. By selecting one or other signal, or its inverse, using a switch based on the signatures of the sum and difference of the signals, an approximation to the unmodulated velocity can be derived. Use of this signal was not satisfactory, and has been superseded in later series.

Optimal control is desirable in the large, but near the target point will amplify any noise into an unacceptable and power-wasting judder. Instead, simple proportional control is used to hold the axis stationary. One or other photocell is selected, and its output used as an analogue error signal; this when subjected to phase advance, results in a stiffness of better than one position pulse for full drive. It is a matter of debate whether a robot marketed at the price of the Puma should not have motors which include tachogenerators, to minimise the risk of oscillation and to enhance performance.

13.5 TIME OPTIMAL POSITION CONTROL

Recently a novel method for time-optimal position control was developed at Portsmouth Polytechnic. This formed part of the development of a daisy-wheel printer which failed to reach production - although the method has been patented by the collaborating firm. Once again, position change is sensed by a pair of photocells. Their output logic signals are monitored by a dedicated mask-programmed microcomputer. This uses past and present values together with a number of internal logic states as an address for access into a table which represents a state-transition map. Speed control is achieved by relating the demanded speed to a delay count value, set whenever a sensor signal changes state. If the counter times out before the next sense change, then it is clear that the device must be moving too slowly; full forward drive is applied. If, however, a move is detected before timeout, then the unit is overspeed and full retardation is applied. In this way, a bang-bang time-optimal drive is achieved. Once again, however, proportional control is used for holding the final position.

13.6 FORCE AND POSITION CONTROL

As has been seen, robot position control is usually designed to be stiff. If an obstacle is encountered, full drive will be applied to overcome it, and a fuse or breaker will swiftly blow. For many tasks, however, positional stiffness is a drawback. A small misalignment between a peg and a hole can result in a large assembly force. If the peg is allowed to 'float' slightly, however, assembly is smooth. As a result, many assembly robots are equipped with a compliant 'wrist', a mechanical sprung linkage designed to permit float of the end effector. Such compliance may be constrained to result in motion about a specific centre and one such arrangement is termed 'remote centre compliance'. Here the centre may lie in front of the peg, so that the peg follows the centre meekly into the hole.

It seems inappropriate to design a robot for mechanical stiffness, only to add slackness at extra expense. Cannot the compliance be designed into the intrinsic robot, allowing specification by software of "soft compliance"? Compliance will now involve displacement of the end effector itself, not of an added mechanical link, and so the true position may be read by the computer controlling the robot. What then are the obstacles to implementing soft compliance?

The first problem becomes apparent at the servo level. To the position error of each axis must be added a force term corresponding to that axis. This must in turn be derived from a set of sensors, probably mounted in the gripper. These will produce signals which are not directly related to the servo axes, and may require a substantial transformation to be of use. Such a transformation is however no more demanding than that required for straight-line motion.

Could not the axis motors themselves be regarded as force transducers, since the torque at each axis is proportional to the corresponding motor current, Here again, all is not simple. Friction and stiction will play a part in rendering the signals invalid, and yet more transformations are needed to compensate for the robot's self weight. With adequate transducers and a suitable algorithm, however, these problems can be surmounted. The next is more daunting: What is the interface between the programmer and the system, particularly when the user does not have specialist experience. To a novice, the concepts of position control and 'teach mode' can be explained with relative ease. To enter the realms of compliance, algorithmic programming is essential. Much of the potential of robotics will only become exploitable as the users become sophisticated.

13.7   THE INTELLIGENT ROBOT

It can be argued that machine intelligence can never be achieved. Consider as an example a definition of magic as the performance of the impossible. Once an impossible action has been seen to be performed, it is no longer magic but a mere conjuring trick. Intelligence could be described as the solution of a problem for which no algorithm exists. Obtain a machine solution to the problem, and you have defined an algorithm - the need for intelligence has disappeared.

Philosophy aside, there are many applications of robots in which measurements can be made and operations performed in ways which are clever, if not intelligent, and which are sometimes beyond the reach of human operators. The Craftsman Robot project being pursued at Portsmouth Polytechnic is based on the use of a robot for the precise adjustment of energy regulators. Final testing is also performed by the robot's supervisory system, and the adjustment specification is itself adjusted online to 'craft' the product.

13.8   ROBOTICS AND CONTROL THEORY

Dynamic control of the robot's position loops will on the face of it call for no more exotic theory than was used for designing World War II gun aimers. It is on noticing the dynamic interactions between the axes that the need for greater depth can be seen. Not only can the first few axes see their inertial load change briskly as later axes flex, each component of the weight of the workpiece will be

subject to highly non-linear interactions. Research is
proceeding elsewhere into the possibility of predicting such
load changes and superimposing a corresponding feedforward
drive onto each axis.

An exciting research area comes from a recognition that
the purpose of the robot is not just to perform an action
once, but to repeat it many times with a substantially
similar load. There is then great scope for cycle-to-cycle
adaptation, both at the task level and in the way that each
manoeuvre is performed. Tales are told of a hybrid robot
combining pneumatic coarse positioning with a stepper motor
for achieving the final precision. As operations were
repeated, the coarse action approached the target point more
closely until the time-consuming stepping action was
minimised. In a similar way, drive voltage profiles to the
motors of an all-electric robot can be refined and adapted
until an optimal manoeuvre is the result. The present
generation of robots operate for much of their time in a
velocity-controlled mode, moving an order of magnitude
slower than the dedicated transfer machines used widely in
industry. For many tasks a robot will be rejected as too
slow as it deliberates on each segment of each move, whereas its drive motors are amply powerful to execute a smooth
full-drive manoeuvre if it can only be programmed. Once
again, this points to the deficiencies of the language
structure by which the performance cycle must be specified.

13.9 ROBOT SENSORS

Touch sensors have been mentioned, but a host of other
sensors can be added to a robotic system to ensure that
execution proceeds as required. Simple contacts in the
gripper can protect against an absent workpiece. Further
simple contacts can monitor the progress of the workpiece
through the manipulation process, perhaps also providing
position calibration references. A simple photosensor can
check that there is a vacant position in which to deposit
the workpiece. These all produce an output signal which is
a logic level, and can therefore readily be incorporated into
a software program written in VAL. Other sensors may be
analogue in nature, perhaps being a measured parameter
particular to the product. A secondary position measurement
system can ensure accuracy beyond the intrinsic capability
of the robot - the robot can in effect use a ruler, rather
than moving freehand.

Using a simple logic input, a robot (or a simple
mechanical actuator, for that matter) can permit analogue
measurements to be made in terms of the output required to
switch the input. A case in point is a simple grain-level
sensor, in which a weight is lowered in the manner of a
mariner's 'lead' until the tension in the suspension falls.
It is an example of 'provocative instrumentation' in which a
reading is deduced from the response to an experiment.

Considerable research effort is being devoted to the

development and exploitation of robot vision. A complete
vision system can cost many times more than the robot itself.
To perform analysis at speed requires considerable computing
power. A single television frame can yield 100,000 data
points, from which features must be extracted in a small
fraction of a second. It can be argued that the robot
operates in an ordered environment, and so should not need
to use vision for its operation. In many cases this is true,
however a misplaced component can bring the entire production
line to a halt. To recover from such a situation may not
call for a full-blown vision system, but can perhaps be
achieved with a single optical sensor. This can be scanned
about the field of view by movements of the robot itself.
Edge-following algorithms now allow features to be extracted
from the scene itself, only a relatively few points being
scanned. Operation is still too slow for continuous
operation, but can perform a rescue much more quickly than
human intervention.

13.10 ROBOTS AND FLEXIBLE MANUFACTURE

Flexibility of manufacture can be considered at several
levels. In the ultimate CAD/CAM system, a product once
designed by computer interaction would be fabricated by an
automated machine shop in which the only specialised feature
was the supervisory program. Diverse products would be made
by standard machinery, with no need for jigs or fixtures.
Such a stage is still far ahead. A level which has been
achieved is the ability to mix products of a similar nature
on a single assembly line. This has been taken beyond the
variations of colour and style long found in car manufacture,
and has been applied to the assembly and testing of electrical
instruments and gauges of mixed types.

Flexibility of a more generally accepted type is the
ability of a manufacturer to set up jigs, fixtures and
assembly and transfer machines in a 'Meccano' fashion from
general purpose components. These can be broken down as the
product mix changes, and the parts used again for the new
production. For this purpose, robots prove ideal if somewhat expensive. Each application may need a purpose
designed gripper, but the remainder of the robot remains
standard. Work has gone far to classify gripper design;
workpieces may be flat, cylindrical, irregular,
unpredictable, and may need to be free to slide or rotate
when gripped. Citing again the Craftsman Robot project, it
was necessary to grasp the workpiece in a precisely defined
location so that a small screwdriver also within the hand
could perform an adjustment. It was most expedient to use
a gripper with only a single moving finger, gripping the
workpiece against a fixed thumb. To gain clearance when
grasping the piece, the whole robot hand approached with a
slight offset, moving to close in the thumb as the finger
closed.

13.11 CONCLUSION

New robot designs are many and various. Just as an
avalanche of commercial microcomputers are providing pre-
packaged hardware from which dedicated computer systems can
be tailored, so large-scale production of low cost robots
will provide a foundation of manipulators which can be
tailored to manufacturing systems flexible and otherwise.
With the robots will come standard software packages
corresponding in market effect to the spreadsheet, ledger
and database programs of the business microcomputers. In
both areas, an added expertise is required to generate
special software to dovetail the system into a specific
application. The limit on progress is the speed with which
an industrial workforce can be built up having software
expertise while the systems are honed to be generally usable.

Robots will follow the microcomputer downmarket, and
soon £5000 will buy a powerful machine amply suited for
workshop use. Manufacturers' pressure will seek to counter
this, just as IBM are trying to drag the image of the
personal microcomputer upwards in cost. Forces of market
competition and consumer selection will have the last word.

Chapter 14

Computer control in biomedicine

D.A. Linkens

It is commonly recognised that the human body contains
a large number of control mechanisms with complex behavioural
characteristics and interconnections. It is not surprising,
therefore, that the techniques developed in the analysis of
control systems have been applied to many aspects of biomedicine. In particular, techniques of systems identification are being applied to a wide range of biomedical subsystems to elucidate the dynamic characteristics of component
parts of the human physiological system. The aim of this
chapter, however, is not to cover this apsect of systems
analysis in biomedicine, but to describe current research into the use of external automatic controllers to regulate
certain variables in the body. Thus, instead of inherent
homeostasis mechanisms, we shall consider the design and
analysis of control systems where the body is only part
(albeit the main part) within the loop. External control
systems become necessary only under conditions of illness, and
in the following sections we shall consider both the direct
control of important physiological variables such as blood
pressure and blood glucose levels, and clinical assistance
under operating theatre conditions involving such things as
levels of unconsciousness and relaxation. Although all the
applications described involve a drug administration regime
as the output of the automatic controller, it should be noted
that any other physical quantity which would affect the controlled variable could be considered e.g. electrical impulse
regime.

A series of examples is now given which illustrate the
use of systems techniques in clinical drug administration.

14.1 POST-OPERATIVE BLOOD-PRESSURE CONTROL

This example is described first because of the large
number of patients who have been treated post-operatively
using automated feedback control of blood-pressure. Over the
past few years more than 10,000 hypertensive patients have
been treated in this way by L.C. Shepherd and his co-workers
at the University of Alabama, Birmingham, U.S.A. Techniques
involving simple classical control, systems identification
and adaptive control strategies have all been applied to this
situation, and hence clearly illustrate the way in which
further knowledge about the dynamics of a physiological system and improved control can be achieved via an inter-

disciplinary research and development effort.

Before attempting closed-loop control some knowledge of systems dynamics is essential, and this was performed using PRBS excitation for the blood pressure system, Shepherd & Sayers(1). In this work blood-pressure measurement was taken as the mean arterial pressure (MAP), and its response to a number of hypotensive agents was determined. The later computer-controlled work has concentrated on the use of one of these drugs, sodium nitroprusside. Cross-correlation between the MAP response and the PRBS drug input revealed information about the impulse response of the physiological system. This indicated the presence of a time delay of about a single blood circulation time (30-40 sec) together with at least one time constant. The impulse response typically showed a one-minute period to the first minimum, 3-minutes period to second minimum, and a return to baseline within 5 minutes. Detailed modelling of these dynamic responses was performed later, but the initial information was sufficient for the design of simple classical PI feedback control.

Using typical impulse responses, simulation studies were used to select suitable parameters for a PID controller. It was found that these values required 'tuning' when closed-loop control was implemented, Shepherd et al (2). Although this was partly due to simplifications in the modelling, it was also due to patient-to-patient variability in system parameters. To give satisfactory response it was found to be necessary to include a 'decision table' in cascade with the PI controller to limit the drug input within a number of clinical and physiological constraints. In this way, the control system became non-linear in behaviour. An example of the improvement in the blood-pressure variability caused by using automatic rather than manual control is shown in Fig. 14.1

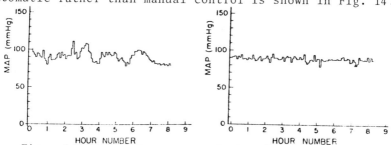

Fig. 14.1   Blood pressure during infusion of sodium
nitroprusside under (a) manual control
b) computer control (from Sheppard et al,1979)

In a range of trials, significant improvement in the quality of control was achieved with the use of this constrained PI regulator.

More detailed modelling studies have revealed further dynamic features in the blood-pressure response, including a recirculation effect and background activity containing both stochastic and sinusoidal components, Slate et al (3). The detailed model obtained as a result of these studies is shown in Fig. 14.2. The transfer function $G_d(s)$ contains two time delays and one exponential time constant, and is given by

$$G_d(s) = \frac{Ke^{-T_i s}(1 + \alpha e^{-T_c s})}{(1 + \tau s)}$$

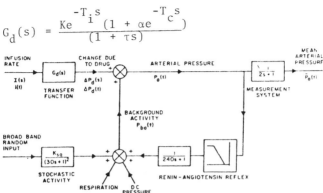

Fig. 14.2   Arterial blood pressure model for vasoactive
drug infusion (from Slate et al) 1979.

where T_i(30 seconds) represents the initial transport-lag for
the drug from the injection site, and T_c(45 seconds) represents the recirculation time. α is the fraction of a drug
recirculating, and τ is the time constant associated with
drug metabolism. Using this model for a range of drug sensi-
tivities K under the fixed controller strategy previously
mentioned showed that such a structure could be unstable, and
this has been confirmed in clinical usage. Because of the
non-robust nature of this method of control, an adaptive control structure has been investigated.

The adaptive control scheme studied by Slate (4) is
shown diagramatically in Fig. 14.3. This scheme contains a
number of control modes, and multirate sampling and filtering
of the measured signals. Thus, blood pressure is sampled
with a period of 1 second. This noisy signal is low-pass
filtered and subsequently re-sampled at a 2 second period.
This signal is used to form the closed-loop error signal
which is further sampled at a 10-second period for processing the controlled algorithms. The derivative of the error
is also required, and this is obtained via the 2-second
sampled signal by passing it through a 3-point differentiator
(which attenuates high frequency noise), followed by a low-
pass filter, with subsequent sampling at the 10 second
period. Based upon these error and derivative of error signals, the coordinator selects either a transient control mode
or a regulator mode to calculate the incremental action. The
coordinator actions can be represented by a phase-plane diagram of error versus error rate. In the transient control
mode, the increment is calculated by a relay-type controller
that includes a Smith time delay compensator. A gain schedule is included in the transient controller to produce a
fast speed of response to hypotensive pressure transients.
In the regulator mode, the infusion rate increment is calculated from the error and its derivative. Adaptation to the
patient drug gain is accomplished in an initial period after
closed-loop control has begun. A recursive least-squares

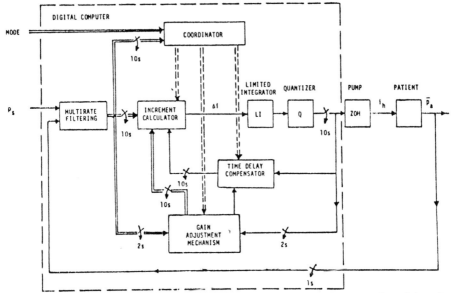

Fig. 14.3   A self-adaptive control strategy for blood-
pressure control of hypertensive patients.
(from Slate, 1980).

estimation algorithm is used to provide a measure of the drug
gain parameter from data acquired at 2 second intervals.
The estimated patient gain and the variance of this estimate
are used to adjust (at 10 second intervals) the overall gain
of the regulator, the relay output levels, and the Smith
compensator gains. These adjustments are managed by decisions made by the coordinator.
     Although the performance of this multirate adaptive
scheme was assessed only in terms of the model described
above (Slate (4))it has subsequently been implemented in
microcomputer format and evaluated in dog trials. It is currently undergoing clinical evaluation.

14.2   ANAESTHESIA CONTROL

     Three major areas of responsibility for the anaesthetist
are those of unconsciousness in the operating theatre, drug-
induced muscle paralysis during operations, and pain relief
(analgaesia) during post-operative care. Each of these areas
have been explored with respect to the use of feedback control and are reviewed in the following sections. It should
be noted that most of the work described is of very recent
origin, and is undergoing considerable development.

14.2.1   Drug-induced Unconsciousness

     This is the most commonly recognised role of the
anaesthetist, and reveals the earliest attempts to produce

automated feedback control in this discipline, under the
title of the 'servo-anaesthetiser', Bickford (5). As
pointed out in a review article by Chilcoat (6) the major
problem with this, and subsequent attempts, was the dubious
nature of the use of the EEG as a measurement for the depth
of unconsciousness. A number of alternative approaches have
been made to obtain better quantitative measurements of
unconsciousness.

In the work of Coles et al (7) a multivariable system
was proposed to control several inter-related variables in
sheep, including arterial blood pressure, as a measure of
depth of anaesthesia. Their system maintained constant
levels of end-expired CO_2 and inspired O_2, plus the reservoir-
bag volume in a closed anaesthetic breathing system.
Oscillation of the controlled variable proved to be a problem
in the blood pressure loop, a point also noticed by Smith
and Schwede (8), illustrating the problems of good feedback
control in the presence of time delays, as mentioned in the
previous section.

The measurement of unconsciousness has also been approached using 'clinical signs', such as pulse rate, arterial
blood pressure, respiratory rate, tidal volume, sweating,
movement etc. In the work by Suppan (9), one of these variables could be selected by the anaesthetist for control via
a motor- driven vapouriser administering halothane. In recent work a 'clinical scoring' approach has been used, whereby a number of clinical signs are summed together with selected weighting to give a single measure of depth of anaesthesia, Davies et al (10). This has been used clinically
with a micro-computer based system which allows for entry of
the scores via a keyboard, and provides control of a motor-
driven syringe for the administration of drugs
intravenously.

The problem of designing adequate feedback controllers
for biological systems, which often contain time delay components, is compounded by the large patient-to-patient variations in parameters for the dynamic models. This has prompted the investigation of adaptive control schemes for depth
of anaesthesia. Beneken et al (11) showed via a multicom-
partment model of the anaesthetic system that a parameter-
estimation adaptive control system could give superior performance to a conventional fixed parameter controller. This
type of approach has been followed by Tatnall and Morris (12)
on neonates. Using a twelve compartment body model, they
showed via simulation that a fixed PI controller would not
give acceptable control when allowances are made for differences in patient uptake characteristics. The self-adaptive
system is based on a simplified equation for halothane uptake in the lungs given by

$$\frac{dp_{alv}}{dt} = K_1(p_v - p_{alv}) + K_2(F_i - p_{alv}) \qquad (14.1)$$

where P_{alv}, the alveolar halothane partial pressure, is
regarded as the control variable; P_v is the mixed venous
halothane partial pressure; F_i is the inspired halothane

partial pressure; and K_1 and K_2 are patient parameters. K_1
and K_2 are identified during the first few breaths when p_v
can be assumed to be almost zero. Under these conditions
14.1 reduces to

$$\dot{p}_{alv} = -K_1 p_{alv} + K_2 (F_i - p_{alv}) \qquad (14.2)$$

and K_1 and K_2 can be estimated using the on-line measurements
of p_{alv} and F_i made with a rapid-response halothane meter.
Identification is stopped and control initiated when the p_{alv}
reaches 95% of the desired level Q_d set by the anaesthetist.
At this point the controller takes the form

$$F_i = -\frac{K_1'}{K_2'} p_v' + \frac{(K_1' + K_2')}{K_2'} p_d \qquad (14.3)$$

for which it has been shown that transient performance is
significantly affected by any errors in the estimates of K_1,
K_2 and p_v. 5 minutes after the introduction of halothane,
control is switched to a conventional PI regulator which is
used to maintain p_{alv} at the desired level. Successful clinical trials have been undertaken using this structure of
self-adaptive control, Tatnall et al (13). It should be
noted that in this work depth of unconsciousness is being
inferred solely from levels of gas concentration in the
alveoli.
    An alternative approach to the feedback methods descri-
bed above is to use open-loop control based on a known model
of drug uptake. In this case the dynamic model is used to
predict the time-course drug level in brain tissue, which is
presumed to determine the depth of anaesthesia. Purely open-
loop control of this nature would be unworkable because of
variations in patient dynamics, and hence a number of schemes
have been attempted in which the model is updated based on
infrequent measurement of certain process variables. Thus,
Mapleson et al (14) reported trials on dogs in which they
attempted to achieve an arterial halothane tension of 4mm Hg
within 5 min, and maintenance of this tension for a further
75 min. An extensive model was used, whose parameters were
updated every 10 minutes, based on measurements of cardiac
output and alveolar ventilation. A more extensive system
has been reported by Mapleson et al (15) which automatically
controls the set-point of a vaporiser. It does this based
on a computed brain tension of anaesthetic agent, obtained
from a detailed model of uptake and distribution. The model
is initially set up based on standard values and body mass,
and subsequently updated every 10 min. using measurements of
cardiac output, alveolar ventilation and arterial blood tension. The anaesthetist is included in the loop by means of
manual control of the N_2O/O_2 mixture which carries the vola-
tile agent. He specifies the desired brain level of the
volatiles in terms which include the contribution of N_2O.

14.2.2 Drug-induced Muscle Relaxation

In certain operations, such as abdominal surgery, correct levels of patient muscle relaxation are necessary. A number of drugs exist for this purpose, and the type referred to in this section are of the non-depolarising form, such as pancuronium. To attain automated muscle relaxation, a suitable measurement variable must be defined. The level of muscle relaxation can be simply quantified either in terms of an evoked electromyograph (EMG) or an evoked tension response. In the work reported here, the former method has been adopted using supramaximal stimulation at a frequency of 0.1 Hz at the ulnar nerve above the elbow. The resulting EMG is measured using surface electrodes taped to the hand. The EMG signals are amplified with a gain of 1000 at a bandwidth of 8 Hz to 10 KHz, then rectified, integrated and finally stored in a sample-hold amplifier.

Computer control of muscle relaxation using stimulation of the masseter muscle on the face of sheep has been achieved, Cass et al (16). In human trials using a simple proportional gain feedback controller, satisfactory regulation was achieved with a mean level of 74% paralysis for an 80% set-point, Brown et al (17). This offset has been successfully removed using a PI controller whose parameters were set using the Ziegler-Nichols tuning method. Using a fixed PI controller occasionally gives an oscillatory closed-loop response, as already noted in the section on blood-pressure control. This emphasises the need to identify the dose-response model for muscle paralysis.

The model required here is a combination of the drug pharmacokinetics (i.e. drug-dose to blood level concentration) and pharmacodynamics (i.e. blood level concentration to evoked EMG response). Instead of classical bolus injection methods for pharmacokinetic determination, the use of PRBS excitation has been made for model identification, Linkens et al (18). Using bit intervals of 33.3 sec or 100 sec with a sequence length of 63, successful identification has been made in dog trials. Employing an off-line technique, identification of the data has been obtained using a generalised least squares package. This revealed the presence of a pure time delay with mean value of 64 sec and two exponential time constants with mean values of 2.7 min and 20.1 min. These parameters had a range of about 4:1 in a small number of trials, illustrating the large variability in dynamics which is common in biological systems.

The feedback system described is currently being using in a range of microcomputer studies based on a Research Machines 380Z system. These include attempts to quantify the effects of other drugs, such as tranquilisers, on relaxation levels, Asbury et al (19), and the interacting effects of other anaesthesic agents such as halothane and ethrane in potentiating paralysis, Asbury et al (20). Simulation studies have shown the desirability of using Smith predictor schemes for counteraction of the pure time delay, based on a sensitivity analysis using the parameter ranges identified previously, Linkens et al (21). Adaptive control schemes are also currently being investigated using a pole-assignment form of self-tuning controller, with simulation studies showing promising results, Linkens et al (22). On-line recursive identification algorithms have been implemented and tried successfully in dog studies under either open-loop or closed-loop conditions. The aim, therefore, is to use a form of adaptive control which will give simultaneous control and identification of drug dynamics. This latter aspect is of interest since some of the newer relaxant drugs, such as Organon NC 45, do not have any known assay method at present for determination of drug pharmacokinetics via classical bolus injection methods. Thus, it can be seen that as well as automatic regulation of relaxation levels, studies of this nature can give more detailed quantification of interacting drug effects.

14.2.3 Post-operative Pain Relief

The control of pain following major surgery, such as total hip replacement, is an important clinical requirement. In conventional clinical practice the necessary feedback is provided by nursing staff who administer pain-relief drugs based on observation of the patient at about four hour intervals. Such slow sampling cannot give optimal relief of pain. In an automatic 'demand analgesia' system, feedback is provided by the patient who is equipped with a button and instructed to press it whenever he feels uncomfortable.

The use of a simple proportional gain controller in such a system employing a microcomputer programmed in a special form of 'control' Basic is described by Jacobs et al (23). In this work, pain is quantified as the rate of button-pushing by the patient. Proportional control in this case is non-optimal because it requires the patient to experience some pain before he can receive any pain-relief drug. This non-optimality cannot be removed simply in this case by introducing integral control action because of the absence of negative demands. One commercial system attempts to overcome this severe output non-linearity by introducing what amounts to a positive non-zero desired value of pain, thus allowing integral action control, White et al (24).

In work by Jacobs and his co-workers, Jacobs et al (25), Reasbeck (26), the non-linear problem is overcome, with a claimed significant improvement in performance, by using a separated stochastic control in which a non-linear state estimation is cascaded with a one-step-ahead control law. The non-linear estimator comprises a Bayes algorithm cascaded with an extended Kalman filter. The model used in this work is shown in Fig. 14.4, where perceived pain y is assumed to depend on the difference between 'comfort' due to drug administration and 'discomfort' due to surgery. The pharmacokinetic relationship between drug infusion rate u and brain tissue drug concentration is assumed to be triexponential having a transfer function of the form

$$\frac{X(s)}{U(s)} = \prod_{j=1}^{3} \frac{K_j}{1+sT_j} \qquad (14.4)$$

Little is known about the relationship between comfort and

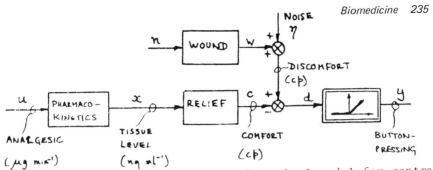

Fig. 14.4 Structure of a mathematical model for control of post-operative pain. (Jacobs et al, 1982)

tissue drug level and here it is assumed to be a simple constant of proportionality, whose estimation is itself of importance, and is included in the Kalman filter. The discomfort is modelled as the sum of an exponentially decaying stochastic term w, which represent a healing wound, plus a white noise n. The term w starts from a positive initial value and is assumed to be a Wiener process with transfer function

$$\frac{W(s)}{N(s)} = \frac{1}{1+sT_4} \qquad (14.5)$$

To define this model five state variables are required, viz.

$x_1 \equiv x$ tissue level drug concentration

x_2, x_3 two further states for eq. (14.4)

$x_4 \equiv w$ wound healing

$x_5 \equiv$ relief

The corresponding dynamic equations are linear and can be written as

$$\underline{x}(i+1) = \underline{A}x(i) + bu(i) + \zeta(i) \qquad (14.6)$$

where

$$A = \begin{pmatrix} a_{11} & a_{12} & a_{13} & 0 & 0 \\ a_{21} & a_{22} & a_{23} & 0 & 0 \\ a_{31} & a_{32} & a_{33} & 0 & 0 \\ 0 & 0 & 0 & a_4 & 0 \\ 0 & 0 & 0 & 0 & 1 \end{pmatrix}$$

$$b = [b_1 \quad b_2 \quad b_3 \quad 0 \quad 0]'$$

$$\zeta(i) = [0 \quad 0 \quad 0 \; n(i) \quad 0]'$$

(14.7)

Two non-linearities arise in the relationship between the states x and the output y. One is in the estimation specifying nett pain d,

$$d = x_4 - x_1 x_5 + \eta$$

(14.8)

The other is the severe demand non-linearity y(d) in Fig. 14.4.

Whenever d is greater than zero, the estimation of states can be done via a standard extended Kalman filter, Jazwinski (27). This filter approximates the conditional distribution $p(x|y)$ by a Normal distribution

$$p(x|y) \simeq N(\hat{x}, \Sigma)$$

(14.9)

updated according to

$$\hat{x}(i) = \tilde{x}(i) + K(i)(y(i) - \tilde{y}(i))$$

$$\tilde{x}(i) = A\tilde{x}(i-1) + bu(i-1)$$

$$\tilde{y}(i) = \tilde{x}_4(i) - (\tilde{x}_1(i)\tilde{x}_5(i) + \tilde{\sigma}_{15}(i))$$

$$\Sigma(i) = \tilde{\Sigma}(i) - K(i)c(i)\tilde{\Sigma}(i)$$

(14.10)

$$\tilde{\Sigma}(i) = A\Sigma(i-1)A^T + \text{diag}[0 \; 0 \; 0 \; v_\eta \; 0]$$

$$c(i) = [-\tilde{x}_5(i) \; 0 \; 0 \; 1 \; -\tilde{x}_1(i)]$$

$$K(i) = \tilde{\Sigma}(i)c^T(i)(c(i)\tilde{\Sigma}(i)c^T(i) + V_\eta)^{-1}$$

When d is negative, the zero value of y does not carry information to drive the Kalman filter. Instead, the information is obtained from a conditional distribution $p(z|o)$ transmitted from a Bayes' rule via a synthetic output y' which is regarded as the sum of z and a synthetic noise having variance V_η,

$$y' = z + \eta'$$

(14.11)

where

$$z \equiv w-c = x_4 - x_1 x_5$$

(14.12)

$$p(z|o) = N(m_2, v_2)$$

(14.13)

values of m_2 and v_2 are obtained via a Bayes algorithm with an assumed prior normal distribution for z given by

$$p_o(z) = N(m_o, v_o)$$

and normal white noise given by

$$p_\eta(\eta) = N(o, v_\eta)$$

For positive d there is no non-linearity and the conditional distribution for z is given by

$$p(z|y) = N(m_1, v_1)$$

where $\quad m_1 = (m_0 v_\eta + y v_0)/(v_0 + v_\eta)$ \hfill (14.14)

$$v_1 = v_0 v_\eta/(v_0 + v_\eta)$$

For negative d the likelihood function in the Bayes' rule is obtained via an ERF function and numerical computation used to obtain m_2 and v_2 in the distribution given by equation (14.13)

The values of y' and v_η' are given by

$$y' = m_2 + (m_2 - m_0) v_\eta'/v_0$$

$$v_\eta' = v_0 v_2/(v_0 - v_2)$$ \hfill (14.15)

The control law was designed to make the comfort c greater than the predictable component w of discomfort by an amount proportional to the magnitude of the unpredictable component η of discomfort. Using a one-step ahead prediction formulation this gives a control law as

$$\tilde{c}(i-1) - \tilde{w}(i+1) \equiv \tilde{z}(i+1) = K\sqrt{v_\eta (i+1)}$$ \hfill (14.16)

The required value of u(i), based on current estimates $\hat{x}(i)$ from the extended Kalman filter, is

$$u = (K\sqrt{v_\eta (i+1)} + a_4\hat{x}_4 - a_{11}(\hat{x}_1\hat{x}_5 + \sigma_{15}) -$$

$$a_{12}(\hat{x}_2\hat{x}_5 + \sigma_{25}) - a_{13}(\hat{x}_3\hat{x}_5 + \sigma_{35}))/b_1\hat{x}_5$$ \hfill (14.17)

Simulation studies have been undertaken, Reasbeck (26)., of the three systems referred to above, from which it was shown that the Kalman filter approach gave considerably fewer analgesia demands than the simple proportional or commercial controllers (23) demands against 166 or 122). This improvement is achieved, however, with a higher total drug consumption (674 µg against 332 µg or 473 µg). It is suggested that good estimates of the relief x_5 can be obtained using this method of stochastic control.

14.3 CONTROL OF BLOOD GLUCOSE LEVELS

The use of bolus subcutaneous injections of insulin in the control of blood glucose concentration levels in a diabetic patient is normal clinical practice. Better physiological response should be obtained if the glucose level is monitored regularly and insulin delivered in a regime more closely resembling the normal release mechanisms. In simple terms, the B-cell delivers insulin into the blood stream at two rates: a continuous, slow basal rate, which controls glucose output from the liver, and meal-time bursts which dispose of the digested nutrients.

With the advent of continuous blood glucose monitoring and frequent sampling profiles it has become apparent that in most insulin-dependent diabetic patients it is difficult to sustain near normal blood glucose concentrations. The so-called 'artificial pancreas' is a closed-loop system i.e. an extra-corporeal blood glucose sensor is coupled to a computer which controls the rate of infusion of insulin into a peripheral vein so as to maintain normoglycaemia, Albisser and Leibel (47). Although very successful in maintaining normoglycaemia in diabetic patients for up to a few days, it has major disadvantages for long term use. Thus, it is limited by its bulk, complexity and cost, and its use of the intravenous route for insulin administration and blood sampling. Prolonged infusions carry the risk of thrombosis and infection

The above considerations have prompted simpler portable infusion pumps without glucose sensing, and thus operate under open-loop conditions. In this approach, continuous subcutaneous insulin infusion (CSII) employs a portable electromechanical syringe pump capable of delivering insulin at two fixed rates. The lower level is continuous, while the higher rate is electrically engaged by the patient 30 minutes before each main meal, Pickup and Keen (28). A number of studies have now shown that near physiological blood glucose concentrations can be maintained by CSII for a number of days in ambulatory diabetics supervised in hospital. In terms of long-period outpatient treatment a group of 6 diabetics treated at home via CSII for 2-4 months achieved overall mean blood glucose values varying from 4.8 to 7.7 mmol/1, Pickup et al (29). There are many intermediary metabolites and hormones which have abnormal concentrations in diabetics, and may be contributory factors in the pathological processes. Treatment via CSII has been associated with a return to near-normal blood levels of lactate, pyrovate, 3-hydroxybutyrate, alanine, cholesterol, triglyceride, and free fatty acids.

In spite of the success of CSII open-loop control in certain cases, there remain 'brittle' diabetics in whom large, fast and unpredictable swings in blood glucose occur and for which open-loop control cannot help. In such cases feedback control is the only way in which near-normal blood glucose levels could be achieved. Similarly, it has been observed that CSII does not allow for classical output disturbances caused by such things as severe stress or intermittent illness. The comment has been made that CSII should only be used therefore under close medical supervision - i.e. under closed-loop control! The situation begins to approximate to the combined open-loop/closed-loop system described for drug-induced unconsciousness.

A number of control algorithms have been proposed for closed-loop control 'artificial pancreas'. The simplest one was an on-off mechanism which activated syringe pumps containing insulin and glucagon depending on threshold levels of blood glucose, Kadish (30). Kline et al (31) used a simple proportional controller driven by the deviation from normoglycaemia. In the work by Albisser three relationships for controller synthesis were used. Two of these are sig-

moidal shaped curves relating insulin and glucagon delivery
rates to the measured level of glycaemia, while the third is
a difference factor which depends on the rate of change of
blood glucose. These relationships are summarised by

$$\text{Insulin delivery} = 200(1 + \tanh(G_p-140)/25)$$

$$\text{Glucagon delivery} = 1.5(1 - \tanh(G-5C)/70) \quad (14.18)$$

$$G_p = G + (A^3 + 10A)$$

where   G   = glycaemia

          G_p = projected glycaemia

          A   = rate of change of glycaemia.

An adaptive control scheme which allows for patient
parameter variations and selectable blood glucose profiles
has been studied on dogs by Kondo et al (32). Their adaptive scheme is outlined in Fig. 14.5. The reference model
used is a second order linearised model similar to that
of Ackerman et al (33) and given by

$$\dot{x}_1 = -p_1(x_1-x_f) - p_2 x_2 + p_3 v$$
$$\dot{x}_2 = -p_4 x_2 + p_5 x_1 + u \qquad (14.19)$$

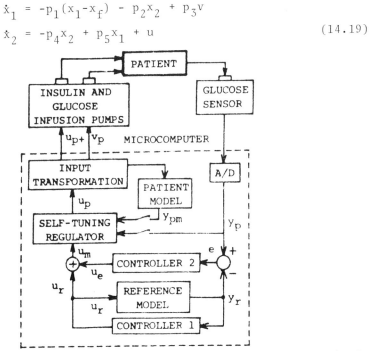

Fig. 14.5   Schematic diagram of an adaptive and optimal
blood glucose control system. (from Kondo
et al, 1982).

where x_1 is blood glucose, x_f is its fasting value, and x_2 is blood insulin level. Controller 1 is designed to minimise the cost function

$$J_r = \sum (y_r^2(k) + \rho_r u_r^2(k))$$

where proper choice of ρ_r gives the desired clinical profile. Controller 2 is designed from optimal principles to minimise the output error, y_p-y_r, which is caused by errors in initial estimates of parameters and disturbances due to meals. The self-tuning regulator is used to make the input/output relationship of the diabetic subject the same as that of the reference model. To do this requires recursive estimation of the patient parameters, together with updating of the controller law. The scheme has been successfully used in simulation studies including non-linear patient dynamics, and in dog trials.

14.4 CONTROL OF RESPIRATORY VARIABLES

The goal of the respiratory system, working together with the cardiovascular system, is to supply sufficient oxygen and to remove sufficient carbon dioxide from the tissues. To perform this task, a single variable cannot, in general, be used to describe the performance of the system. In the automatic control of artificial ventilators a number of quantities have been measured. These include partial pressure of arterial $CO_2 (P_a CO_2)$, partial pressure of alveolar $CO_2 (P_a CO_C)$, arterial $O_2 (P_a O_2)$, pH, and CO_2 production (VCO_2). The controlled variables similarly show a wide range including minute ventilation (adjusted either via the respiratory rate or the tidal volume), fraction of CO_2 in inspired gas, $(fICO_2)$, and fraction of O_2 in inspired gas (fIO_2).

Under normal physiological conditions $P_a CO_2$ is kept substantially constant, and hence the aim of some automatic control systems has been to keep this constant. $P_a CO_2$ is not, however, easy to measure, and hence end-tidal CO_2 which is obtainable non-invasively has commonly been used. In normal lungs end-tidal CO_2 approximates to $P_A CO_2$, which in turn approximates to $P_a CO_2$. An early clinical example of this approach was by Frumin (48), while microprocessor control has been demonstrated by Westonkow et al (34). An alternative approach has been to use a pH sensor and to maintain arterial pH constant by adjustment of the tidal volume, Coon et al (35). Some systems have been designed to adjust the inspired fraction of O_2 in addition to that of CO_2 e.g. Chambille et al (36).

The control of ventilatory waveform has also been considered, especially for positive pressure artificial ventilators. These force air into the lungs in a manner which is different from the normal negative pressure spontaneous breathing condition. Adverse affects caused by positive pressure ventilation are considered to be correlated with the average alveolar pressure, and can be influenced by the timing and shape of the ventilator waveform. Since alveolar pressure cannot be measured directly it is estimated from a mechanical model of the lungs. One such approach by Jain and Guha (37) used rectangular pulses, with fixed inspiratory time and pressure from the pump, and the controller designed to adjust tidal volume by varying the expiratory time.

The complexity of the system together with the multivariable nature of the measured quantities and associated control have encouraged the use of an Expert System approach to ventilator management. One such attempt is the VM programme designed by Fagan (38) using the expert system shell called EMYCIN.

14.5 ANTI-COAGULANT THERAPY

Anticoagulant drugs such as warfarin are used to combat thrombosis, and reduce blood clotting by interfering with the synthesis of prothrombin, or plasma protein whose activity controls the formation of fibrin through a chain of steps. The goal is to reduce prothrombin without causing bleeding, by designing a suitable drug therapy profile.

An early approach by Sheiner (39) planned the warfarin dosage starting from the fourth day of therapy. The initial dosage was calculated from the estimated body surface area of the patient, the second dose was half the initial dose, and no dose was given on the third day. Theofanous and Barile (40) extended the technique to cover several days of future drug applications, and presented formulas for both uniform and quasiuniform (uniform except for a single initial loading) drug schedules. Four parameters characterise the patient according to two differential equations, and the parameters, which are constrained to lie within reasonable values, are determined by nonlinear least squares data fitting. The methods were evaluated retrospectivey using data from patients receiving conventional anticoagulant therapy, and were found to perform better than some of the cardiologists.

Powers et al (41) represented the effect of warfarin on prothrombin activity by a set of three state variables (G, Q and P) which were linked by three first-order state equations. The three equations contained four parameters, but two parameters which do not strongly affect the prothrombin complex activity were assumed to be constant. By computing two state variables on the basis of the constants and assuming initial conditions, only one state variable (P) and two constants were actually estimated from the data using extended Kalman filtering. The filter gave faster identification than that using nonlinear least squares, but the microcomputer using BASIC was not suitable for calculation of optimal dosage strategies.

14.6 COMPUTER-AIDED DRUG THERAPY

In addition to on-line control in biomedicine, computers have been used as consultants giving advice on drug therapy. One example of this is in the use of digoxin for many forms of heart failure. Careful control is particularly

important in this case because of the narrow margin between
therapeutic and toxic dosages for digoxin. Early work in
this area by Jelliffe et al (42) used a one-compartment
model to describe digitalis pharmacokinetics in patients
with normal and reduced renal function. Dose regimes to
meet the required therapeutic goal (plasma concentration of
the drug) were calculated from data on past history of
dosages, renal function and body weight.

Sheiner et al (43) introduced feedback into the above
scheme using serum digoxin concentration as the modelled
variable. In this approach maximum likelihood estimation
was used to determine the pharmacokinetic model parameters.
Although claiming improved performance over physicians,
Sheiner et al (44), some studies have shown that many cases
of digitalis toxicity are not related to impaired renal
function and this would not be avoided by use of such a
kinetic model. To encapsulate the many facets of expert
clinical knowledge a digitalis management programme has been
developed by Gorry et al (45). This programme uses a formal
model of pharmacokinetics and a variety of qualitative
clinical data to construct a patient-specific model for
which the dosage regime is determined. There recommendations
are revised in a feedback loop based on the patient's clinical responses. The programme has been evaluated retrospec-
tively on clinical data in 19 patients. In the 12% of cases
which showed toxicity the patient received a higher dose
than that recommended by the programme, while it also recognised the toxicity prior to its recognition by the clinician.

The capturing of clinical expertise for systems such as
this digitalis therapy manager is currently an active area
of research and development in the field of Intelligent
Knowledge-Based Systems. Numerous expert systems shells are
being considered, most of which are implemented in LISP from
North American sources and PROLOG from European sources.

14.7 CONCLUSIONS

The applications involving automated drug administration have demonstrated that a wide range of control techniques are currently being explored in biomedicine. These
range from simple on-off control to complex adaptive control
schemes. Classical PID three-term controllers are commonly
being used, but suffer from robustness problems when the
patient dynamics are either unknown or time-varying. Biomedical systems often include pure time delays and this is
encouraging the use of controllers based on the Smith predictor principle. Parameter estimation is an integral part
of many adaptive systems, and this may become an important
component in the control scheme where knowledge of drug
dynamics is a desirable biproduct of regulation.

Measurement of a suitable variable which reflects
closely the physiological state to be controlled is commonly
a difficult matter. As a result of this, open-loop control
based on a predetermined model is sometimes mandatory. The
inadequacies of such an approach must, however, be circum-
vented using techniques such as feedforward and infrequent
feedback of sampled information. The majority of

applications use linear controller designs, since this reflects the current field of major knowledge in systems theory.
Since non-linearity is endemic in biological systems it is
clearly desirable that attention should be given to improved
design of controllers for such cases.

It is clear that the field of drug administration in
biomedicine is fruitful for systems technologists and is
stretching the available techniques for the design of adequate feedback regulators. Each control strategy will have
to be tailored to the particular application because of the
complexity of living dynamic systems. Such tailoring will
require inter-disciplinary knowledge of systems theory and
physiological behaviour. The frontiers of knowledge in both
areas should be advanced by such studies.

It is clear that in biomedical control applications the
use of computers is now mandatory. Apart from the need for
real-time computing in terms of control algorithm synchronisation, the requirements for operator interaction and patient
monitoring are particularly crucial in this area. One example
of this is in the management of intracranial pressure in
patients with severe head injury in an intensive care unit
(Mason (46)). The inclusion of alarm signalling is even more
critical than in process control, and the multiple requirements even for control of a relativey small subsystem show
the need for well designed and portable multi-tasking software. This area will require considerable attention in the
coming years.

REFERENCES

1. Sheppard, L.C., and Sayers, B.McA. 1977, Comp. & Biomed.
    Res., 10, 237-247.

2. Sheppard, L.C.,Shotts, J.F., Roberson, N.F., Wallace,
    F.D., and Kouchoukos, N.T. 1979, Proc. First Ann. Conf.
    IEEE 'Eng. in Medicine & Biology Soc.', Denver,
    Colorado, Oct 6-7, 280-284.

3. Slate, J.B., Sheppard, L.C., Rideout, V.C., and
    Blackstone, E.H., 1979, 5th IFAC Sym. Ident. & Sys. Par.
    Est., Darmstadt, F.R. Germany, Sept. 24-28, 867-874.

4. Slate, J.B., 1980, Model-based design of a controller
    for infusing sodium nitroprusside during postsurgical
    hypertension, Ph.D. thesis, University of Wisconsin.

5. Bickford, R.G., 1949, Neurophysiological applications of
    automatic anaesthetic regulator controlled by brain
    potentials. Am. J. Physiol. 159, 562.

6. Chilcoat, R.T., 1980, Trans. Inst. M.C., Vol. 2, No. 1
    38-45.

7. Coles, J.B., Brown, W.A., and Lampard, D.G., 1973,
    Med. Biol. Eng., 11, 262.

8.   Smith, J.T., and Schwede, H.O., 1972, Med. Biol. Eng.,
     10, 207.

9.   Suppan, P., 1972, Br. J. Anaesth., 44, 1263.

10. Davies, W.L., Evans, J.M., Fraser, A.C.L., and Barclay,
     M., 1982, Closed-loop control of anaesthesia. Symp. on
     'Control Systems Concepts and Approaches in Clinical
     Medicine', Sussex, 5-7 April, 87-90.

11. Beneken, J.E.W., Blom, J.A., Jorritsma, F.F., Nandorff,
     A., Bijnen, A.V. and Spierdijk, J., 1979, Biomedizi-
     nische Technik, 24, 233.

12. Tatnall, M.L., and Morris, P., 1977, Simulation of
     halothane anaesthesia in neonates, in 'Biomedical
     Computing' (Ed. W.J. Perkins), Pitmans Med. (UK).

13. Tatnall, M.L., Morris, P., and West, P.G., 1981,
     Br. J. Anaesth., 53, 1019.

14. Mapleson, W.W., Allott, P.R., and Steward, A., 1974,
     Br.J. Anaesth., 46, 805.

15. Mapleson, W.W., Chilcoat, R.T., Lunn, J.N., Blewett,
     M.C., Khatib, M.T., and Willis, B.A., 1980, Br. J.
     Anaesth., 52, 234.

16. Cass, N.M., Lampard, D.G., Brown, W.A., and Coles, J.R.
     1976, Anesth. Intens. Care, 4, 16-22.

17. Brown, B.H., Asbury, A.J., Linkens, D.A., Perks, R.
     and Anthony, M., 1980, Clin. Phys. Physiol. Meas., I,
     No. 3, 203-210.

18. Linkens, D.A., Asbury, A.J., Brown, B.H., Rimmer, S.J.
     1981, Br. J. Anaesth. 53, 666P.

19. Asbury, A.J., Henderson, P.D., Brown, B.H., Turner, D.J.
     and Linkens, D.A., 1981, Br. J. Anaesth., 53, 859-863.

20. Asbury, A.J., Linkens, D.A., and Rimmer, S.J., 1982,
     Identification of interacting dynamic effects on muscle
     paralysis using Ethrane in the presence of panturonium.
     Br. J. Anaesth., 54, 790.

21. Linkens, D.A., Asbury, A.J. Rimmer, S.J., and Menad, M.
     1982, Proc. IEE, Pt.D., 129, 136.

22. Linkens, D.A., Asbury, A.J. Rimmer, S.J., and Menad M.
     1982, Self-tuning control of muscle relaxation during
     anaesthesia. IEEE Conf. on 'Applications of Adaptive
     and Multivariable Control', Hull, 19-21 July, 96.

23. Jacobs, O.L.R., Bullingham, R.E.S., Davies, W.L.,
     Reasbeck, M.P., 1981, Feedback control of post-operative
     pain. IEE Conf. Pub. 194 'Control and its Applications'
     52-56.

24. White, W.P., Pearce, D.J., and Norman, M., 1979, B.M.J. 2, 166-167.

25. Jacobs, O.L.R., Bullingham, R.E.S., McQuay, H.J., and Reasbeck, M.P., 1982, On-line estimation in the control of post-operative pain. 6th IFAC Symp. on 'Identification and System Parameter Estimation', Washington, 7-11 June.

26. Reasbeck, M.P., 1982, Modelling and control of post-operative pain. D. Phil. Thesis, Oxford Univ.

27. Jazwinski, A.H., 1970, Stochastic Processes and Filtering Theory, Academic Press.

28. Pickup, J.C., and Keen, H., 1980, Diabetologia, 18, 1-4.

29. Pickup, J.C., White, M.C., Keen, H., Kohner, E.M., Parsons, J.A., Albert, K.G.M.M., 1979, Lancet II, 870-873.

30. Kadish, A.H., 1964, The regulation and control of blood sugar level. Physiology and cybernetic simulation in 'Technicon International Symposium', New York, 82-85.

31. Kline, N.S., Shimano, E., Stearns, H., McWilliams, L., Kohn, M., and Blair, J.H., 1968, Med. Res. Eng. Second Quarter, 14-19.

32. Kondo, K., Sano, A., Kikuchi, M., Sakurai, Y., 1982, Adaptive and optimal blood glucose control system designed via state space approach. Inst. M.C. Symp. on 'Control Systems Concepts and Approaches in Clinical Medicine', Sussex, 5-7 April, 103-106.

33. Ackerman, E., Rosevear, J.W., and McGuckin, W.F., 1964, Phys. in Med. & Biol., 9, 203-213.

34. Westenkow, D.R., Bowman, R.J., Ohlson, K.B., and Raemer D.B., 1980, Med. Instrum., 14, 311.

35. Coon, R.L., Zuperku, E.J. and Kampine, J.P., 1978, Anesthiology, 49, 201.

36. Chambille, B., Guehard, H., Londe, M. and Bargeton, D., 1975, J. Appl. Physiol., 39, 837.

37. Jain, V. and Guha, S.K., 1972, IEEE Trans. Biomed. Eng. BME-19, 47.

38. Fagan, L.M., Kunz, J.C., Feigenbaum, E.A., and Osborn, J., 1979, IJCAII, 6, 260.

39. Sheiner, L.B., 1969, Comp. Biomed, Res., 2, 507.

40. Theofanous, T.G. and Barile, R.G., 1973, J. Pharm. Sci., 62, 261.

41. Powers, W.F., Abbrecht, P.H. and Covell, D.G. 1980, IEEE Trans. Biomed. Eng., BME-27, 520.

42. Jelliffe, R.W., Buell, J., Kalaba, R., Sridhar, R. and Rockwell, R.A., 1970, Math. Biosci., 9, 179.

43. Sheiner, L.B., Rosenberg, B. and Melman, K.L., 1972, Comp. Biomed. Res., 5, 441.

44. Sheiner, L.B., Halkin, H., Peck, C., Rosenberg, B., and Melman, K.L., 1975, Ann. Intern. Med., 82, 619.

45. Gorry, G.A., Silverman, H., and Pauker, S.G., 1978, Am. J. Med., 64, 452.

46. Mason, J.,1984, Encyclopedia of Systems and Control, Pergamon Press, in press.

47. Albisser, A.M. and Leibel, B.S., 1977, Clin. Endocrin & Met., 6, 457.

48. Frumin, M.J., 1956, Anaesthesiology, 18, 290.

Chapter 15

Expert systems for process control

R. W. Sutton

15.1   INTRODUCTION

Expert systems are emerging as a practical application of two decades of research in artificial intelligence. The current interest in such systems has been stimulated by firstly the Japanese Fifth Generation Computer Project and secondly by the recently established Alvey programme on Information Technology in the U.K.

Both these programmes include substantial allocation of resources for further research to extend the power of expert systems and to make them significantly more "intelligent" than they are at present.

It is clearly impossible to cover all aspects of current expert system technology in a single chapter so the approach adopted will be to present an engineer's view of such systems and the uses to which they might be put in the field of process control. This view is based on the general principles of PROSPECTOR, an expert system developed at SRI (Reference 1) for mineral prospecting. An overview of current expert systems is contained in Reference 2.

15.2   WHAT IS AN EXPERT SYSTEM?

An expert system may be defined as:-
"A system which embodies in a computer the knowledge of an expert and which is organised in such a way that it can act as an intelligent consultant and when necessary explain its line of reasoning."

15.3   WHAT IS EXPERT KNOWLEDGE?

Expert knowledge may be said to consist of:-
(a) Facts
(b) Judgement
(c) Rules of Thumb
(d) Educated guesswork

In general, such knowledge can be expressed in the form of IF Situation THEN Action type rules. Furthermore both the situation and action parts of a rule may have associated with them uncertainty.

15.4 HOW DOES AN EXPERT SYSTEM DIFFER FROM A CONVENTIONAL COMPUTER PROGRAM?

The essential difference between an expert system and a conventional program lies in the separation of the expert knowledge from the main body of the program, rather than its embedding in the body of the program code.

15.5 WHAT ADVANTAGES DOES THIS GIVE?

This separation of the knowledge from the main body of program code means that:-

(a) It is not necessary to have all the knowledge about the problem domain available ab initio. A system can be built initially with only a small number of rules.

(b) Rules can be added, modified or deleted as more knowledge becomes available.

(c) The rules for a new problem domain can be substituted for the current set of rules.

All this can be done without the need to change the program which interprets the rules.

15.6 INFERENCE NETWORK OF ASSERTIONS

Expert knowledge may be represented by a network of connections or relations between evidence and hypotheses.

Although assertions are statements that should be true or false, in a given situation there is usually uncertainty as to whether they are in fact true or false.

Initially the state of each assertion is simply unknown. As evidence is gathered some assertions may be definitely established, whereas others may become only more or less likely. In general, a probability value is associated with each assertion.

The "connections" in the inference network determine how a change in the probability of one assertion will affect those of other assertions.

15.7 KNOWLEDGE REPRESENTATION

The rules in an expert system may be represented in the Bachus-Naur form:-

```
<rule>::=  (IF<antecedent>THEN<rule-strength><rule-strength>
<consequent>)
<antecedent>::= <statement>
<consequent>::= <descriptive-statement>
<statement>::= <logical-statement>|<descriptive-statement>
<logical-statement>::=  (AND [<statement>]+)|
                        (OR [<statement>]+)|
                        (NOT <statement>)
```

It is seen that a rule links an antecedent to a consequent. Both the antecedent and the consequent are propositional statements - assertions about the world that may or may not be true.

To accommodate uncertainty every statement has associated with it a probability value which measures the degree to which the statement is currently believed to be true.

15.8 EXTERNAL REPRESENTATION

The user enters the problem rules into the knowledge base in the form shown below.

```
space      NAME
text       description/*some English text*/
inference  prior number
           rules antecedents ANOTHERNAME tl value fl another
           value

space      ANOTHERNAME
text       description/*some other English text*/
inference  prior anothernumber
```

15.9 LOGICAL RELATIONS

With logical relations the truth (or falsity) of a hypothesis is completely defined by the truth (or falsity) of the assertions that define it. Such relations are composed of the primitive operations of conjunction (AND), disjunction (OR), and negation (NOT).

In general, it is not known whether assertions are true but the probability that they are so can usually be estimated. The fuzzy-set formulae of Zadeh (ref 3) may be used to compute the probability of a hypothesis from the probabilities of its component assertions.

The probability of a hypothesis that is defined as the logical conjunction of several pieces of evidence equals the minimum value of the probabilities corresponding to the evidence. Similarly, a hypothesis defined as the disjunction of its pieces of evidence is assigned a probability value equal to the maximum value of the probabilities corresponding to the evidence.

15.10 PLAUSIBLE RELATIONS

With plausible relations each assertion contributes "votes" for or against the truth of the hypothesis. Bayes Rule may be used for the plausible reasoning scheme and relates three quantities involving an evidence assertion E and a hypothesis assertion H:

prior odds on hypothesis $O(H)$
posterior odds on hypothesis $O(H/E)$
measure of sufficiency LS

Bayes Rule gives:

$$O(H/E) = LS*O(H)$$

where

$$LS = \frac{P(E/H)}{P(E/\overline{H})}$$

is the likelihood ratio.

A large value of LS means that the observation of E is
encouraging for H. As LS approaches infinity E is
sufficient to establish H in a strict logical sense. A
complementary set of equations describes the case where E is
known to be absent. In this case

$$O(H/\overline{E}) = LN*O(H)$$

where

$$LN = \frac{P(\overline{E}/H)}{P(E/\overline{H})}$$

is called the measure of necessity

If LN approaches zero E is logically necessary for H.
If LN is large the absence of E is encouraging for H.
In general, it may not be possible to state that E is
either definitely present or definitely absent. In this
case a linear interpolation is used so that in general

$$O(H/E) = LP*O(H)$$

where

LP = 1 + LS [prob (E) -prior prob (E)] / [1 -prior prob (E)]

= 1 + LN [prior prob (E) - prob (E)] / [prior prob (E)]

15.11 POTENTIAL APPLICATIONS IN PROCESS CONTROL

Three possible areas of application for expert systems
in the field of process control are:-
(a) Fault diagnosis
(b) Plant operation
(c) Design
Fault diagnosis in complex plant is of considerable
interest because it is frequently the case that skilled
maintenance staff will have rules of thumb about the likely
cause of malfunction based upon past experience of a
particular plant or of others like it. Such knowledge is a
valuable adjunct to information which may be available from
alarm panels, etc. particularly where multiple alarm
indications are given.
There are a number of complex processes, for example,
in the steel industry such as blast furnaces and oxygen
steelmaking plant which do not lend themselves to simple
mathematical models for control systems design. Such
processes can, however, be operated by human beings whose
judgemental capability enables them to achieve good
performance. Expert Systems techniques lend themselves to

the capture of this "expertise" in sets of rules which might be used either to enable less skilled operators to run the processes or might form the basis of an automatic system which interrogates the knowledge base as required.

The design of both plant and plant control systems frequently requires expert knowledge over and above analytical techniques. Again this knowledge can be coded into rules for aiding the user in the design process.

The principal difficulty with expert systems applications lies in the extraction of the rules of the problem from the expert; experts frequently are reluctant to give up their knowledge or are unable to express it adequately for embodiment in a computer system.

Additionally, the ascribing of numerical values to the inference rules is alien to the way in which experts normally work, that is, in terms of broad non-numeric opinions such as "I am almost certain that".

Both these difficulties can and have been overcome in a number of existing systems. The time and cost involved in generating a useful expert system is not trivial but the potential rewards can be considerable. Perhaps the best example is the R1 system developed at Carnegie-Mellon University (Reference 4), which configures VAX computer systems and which is now in daily use by DEC.

REFERENCES

1. Duda, R.O., et al 1979, Model design in the PROSPECTOR consultant system for mineral exploration. In D. Michie, ed., Expert systems in the microelectronic age. Edinburgh University Press pp 153-167.

2. Hayes-Roth, F., et al 1983, Building expert systems. Addison-Wesley Publishing Company Inc.

3. Zadeh, L.A., 1979, Possibility theory and soft data analysis, Rept. UCB/ERL M79/66, Electronics Research Laboratory, University of California at Berkeley.

4. McDermott, J., 1980b, R1:An expert in the computer systems domain. In AAAI 1, pp. 269-271.

Index